Hamilton Williams

Britain's Naval Power

A short history of the growth of the British navy from the earliest times to Trafalgar

Hamilton Williams

Britain's Naval Power
A short history of the growth of the British navy from the earliest times to Trafalgar

ISBN/EAN: 9783744742856

Printed in Europe, USA, Canada, Australia, Japan

Cover: Foto ©ninafisch / pixelio.de

More available books at **www.hansebooks.com**

NELSON.

BRITAIN'S NAVAL POWER

A SHORT HISTORY

OF THE

GROWTH OF THE BRITISH NAVY

FROM THE EARLIEST TIMES TO TRAFALGAR

BY

HAMILTON WILLIAMS, M.A.

INSTRUCTOR IN ENGLISH LITERATURE TO NAVAL CADETS IN H.M.S. BRITANNIA

London
MACMILLAN AND CO.
AND NEW YORK
1894

TO

HIS ROYAL HIGHNESS

𝔓rince 𝔊eorge

DUKE OF YORK, K.G., K.T.

CAPTAIN R.N.

THIS SIMPLE NAVAL HISTORY

IS

BY PERMISSION

RESPECTFULLY DEDICATED

PREFACE

THIS short history of the British Navy is the outcome of a serious demand for such a book to supply a want recognised and admitted by all branches of H. M. Navy, and also, it is believed, by those ashore who wish their boys to know something of the story of British Naval renown.

The information has chiefly been gathered from the Naval Histories of Campbell, Southey, and Yonge, the two volumes of Sir Harris Nicolas, Mr. Froude's *Seamen of the Sixteenth Century*, a Pamphlet on the Armada by Mr. W. H. K. Wright, F.R.H.S., and the well-known work by Captain Mahan, U.S.N.

It is a matter of regret that the first Volume published by the Navy Records Society, dealing with the defeat of the Spanish Armada, was not issued until this work was in the press. Otherwise several statements now made on that subject would have undergone considerable modification, and one or two misapprehensions which had previously obtained general credence would have been corrected.

No special fitness for the task can be claimed by the compiler, save a very keen interest in the subject : his pen is an inexperienced one : there are numbers of naval officers more capable for the work than himself; but the lot fell to him, and in offering this book to the public, he can only allow himself to hope that its errors may not prove of so glaring a nature as wholly to destroy its usefulness.

L'ENVOI

At the instance of my old friend Mr. Aldous, so well known for his services on H.M.S. *Britannia*, I warmly recommend the work of his colleague, Mr. Hamilton Williams, to readers of every class. To the rising generation especially it should be valuable. There is not, so far as I know, any other short Naval History in existence; certainly there is none on which the same pains and study of authorities have been bestowed.

In the admirable little book which is now put forth it is shown by what efforts our naval inheritance has been won. We see the patriotism and the sacrifices made by our forefathers. We admire the heroism and the sufferings of our sailors. The story of the past cannot fail to inspire the present generation with the resolve to maintain a Navy worthy of our splendid traditions.

Normanhurst Court, Battle,
13th November 1894.

CONTENTS

CHAPTER I

Alfred the Great forms a navy—Constructs ships on his own lines—Defeats Danes at sea—Edgar improves and enlarges the navy—Guards the coasts—Ethelred's neglect and hesitation—Norman Conquest—No English fleet to meet it—Loss of the *Blanche Nef* . . . . Page 1

CHAPTER II

Richard I. collects a large fleet for the Crusades—First English fleet in foreign waters—Attacks Limasol—Sails in the *Trench-the-mer*—Fights a huge Turkish dromon—John excommunicated—French fleet at Damme—Salisbury destroys it—Eustace the Monk and Hubert de Burgh—The Cinque Ports—Sir R. Tiptoft's fight in the Channel 9

CHAPTER III

Edward III. claims the crown of France—A French fleet ravages the English coasts—Battle of Sluys—Edward lands at La Hogue—Battle of "L'Espagnols sur mer"—Neglect of navy—Winchelsea burned—Battle of La Rochelle—Capture of an English fleet off Brittany by Spaniards—No notice is taken of it . . . 19

CHAPTER IV

Channel and mouth of the Thames held by pirates—Depredations of French and Spaniards on the English coasts—Charles VI. prepares a huge fleet for invasion of England—Panic in London—Fleet driven back by bad weather—Earl of Arundel defeats a combined fleet in the Channel—Henry IV.—Attacks and reprisals by private vessels and squadrons—Henry hands over the defence of the coast to merchants—The plan utterly fails—Henry is nearly taken by pirates—Henry V. restores the navy—Crosses over to France with a splendid fleet—Duke of Bedford fights the French fleet at Harfleur—Earl of Huntingdon defeats the French in the Channel

Page 31

CHAPTER V

Henry VI.—Decline of our naval power—The fleet divided between the rival Roses—Henry VII. restores the navy—Builds the *Great Harry*—Columbus—Cabot—Henry VIII. makes war on France—Sir Edward Howard attacks the French fleet off Brest—*Regent* and *Cordelier*—France again prepares to invade—French fleet anchors in St. Helen's Roads—Loss of the *Mary Rose*—Dispersal of the French fleet—Edward VI.—Mary—Navy rots at its anchors—Elizabeth—The privateers—Pioneers and rovers—Philip of Spain prepares to invade England—Drake harries the Spanish coasts—He "singes the King of Spain's beard"—The Armada sails—It meets foul weather—Puts in to Coruña—The Queen's navy—Comparison of forces—Armada sails again—The fight in the Channel—At Calais—Flight—Storm—Destruction—Elizabeth's meanness—Sir Richard Grenvile in the *Revenge*—Death of Elizabeth . 41

CHAPTER VI

James I.—Charles I.—Buckingham's fiascos—The Dutch—Cromwell's Navigation Act—Saluting the flag—Van Tromp insults Dover—Blake attacks him—De Ruyter attacked by Ayscough—Battle off the Kentish Knock—Blake beaten by Van Tromp—Battle of Portland—Battle off Essex coast—Battle off Dutch coast—Death of Van Tromp—Cromwell makes war on Spain—Capture of a plate fleet—Blake at Santa Cruz—Death of Blake—Charles II.—Quarrels between English and Dutch East India Companies—War breaks out—Opdam defeated off Lowestoft by Duke of York—The Four Days' Fight off the North Foreland—The St. James' Fight—The Dutch in the Thames—Peace of Breda—Secret treaty of Dover—Battle of Solebay—French fleet plays the traitor—Further fighting—Treaty of London 62

CONTENTS

CHAPTER VII

William of Orange—Battles of Bantry Bay, of Beachy Head, of La Hogue—Attacks on St. Malo, Dieppe, and Calais—Peace of Ryswick—Spanish Succession—Anne—Rooke's Victory at Vigo—Benbow and Du Casse—Wade and Kirby are shot—Great storm—Capture of Gibraltar—Battle of Malaga—Shovel in the Mediterranean—Loss of the *Association*, *Eagle*, and *Romney*—Forbin and Duguai Trouin take the *Cumberland* and others—Treaty of Utrecht   .   .   .   .   .   .   Page 80

CHAPTER VIII

George I.—The "Fifteen"—A Spanish fleet seizes Palermo—Admiral Byng's victory off Cape Passaro—George II.—Jenkins's ear—Admiral Vernon at Porto Bello—Failure at Cartagena and Santiago—Anson takes the great galleon—Matthews and Lestock off Toulon—Loss of the *Victory*—The "Forty-Five"—*Lion* and *Elizabeth*—Anson off Finisterre—Hawke off Brest—Peace of Aix-la-Chapelle—Braddock's defeat and death—The Seven Years' War—French attack Minorca—Byng sent to relieve it—Byng fights and abandons it—Execution of Byng—Attacks on French coast—French prepare to invade—Rodney at Havre—Boscawen and De la Clue off Lagos—Hawke and Conflans in Quiberon Bay—Elliot and Thurot off Isle of Man—George III.—Belleisle taken—Spain makes war—*Hermione* taken—The Havana taken by Pocock—Manila taken—The *Santisima Trinidad* taken   .   .   98

CHAPTER IX

The tea-tax—Sir Peter Parker at Norfolk, Virginia—Attack on Charleston repulsed—Lord Howe in the *Eagle*—Bushnell's torpedo—Douglas' squadron on Lake Champlain—French declare war—Howe and D'Estaing at Rhode Island—Barrington and D'Estaing—Keppel and D'Orvilliers off Brest—Spain joins France—Byron and D'Estaing—France and Spain prepare to invade—Huge fleet off Plymouth—Rodney and De Langara off St. Vincent—Gibraltar relieved—Rodney and De Guichen in the West Indies—Great hurricane—Nelson at San Juan—Second relief of Gibraltar by Admiral Darby—Parker and Zoutman off the Dogger Bank—De Grasse and Hood at Fort Royal—De Grasse and Graves off the Chesapeake—De Grasse and Rodney off Martinique—Lord Howe prepares to relieve

Gibraltar again—Loss of the *Royal George*—The great attack on Gibraltar—Sir Edward Hughes and M. de Suffren in the East Indies—Treaty of Versailles . . . . Page 125

CHAPTER X

Mutiny of the *Bounty*—War with the French Republic—Hood at Toulon—Nelson in Corsica—"The Glorious First of June"—Martinique and St. Lucia taken—Dutch declare war—Cornwallis escapes from the French fleet—Bridport off Lorient—Hotham in the Gulf of Genoa—*Ça Ira* and *Censeur*—Hotham off Hyères—Attempt on Ireland—Spain joins France—Battle of St. Vincent—The Mutinies—Attacks on Cadiz—Nelson at Santa Cruz—Battle of Camperdown 156

CHAPTER XI

General Humbert lands in Ireland—His surrender—Warren's victory off the west coast of Ireland—Nelson sent to the Mediterranean—French expedition to Egypt—*Vanguard* dismasted—Pursuit of French fleet—Battle of the Nile—Admiral Bruix's cruise from Brest—Operations on the Italian seaboard—Defence of Acre—Surrender of Dutch fleet to Lord Duncan—Capture of the *Thetis* and *Santa Brigida*—Siege of Malta—Capture of *Généreux* and *Guillaume Tell*—Surrender of Malta—Loss of the *Queen Charlotte* by fire—The *Freya* incident—"Armed Neutrality of the North"—Battle of Copenhagen—Nelson's home command—Attack on Boulogne—Ganteaume's attempt to relieve the army in Egypt—Linois and Saumarez at Algeciras—Treaty of Amiens 190

CHAPTER XII

Preparations for invasion—War again declared—French ports unceasingly watched—Buonaparte declares himself Emperor—Nelson off Toulon—Admiral Latouche Treville—Spain prepares for war—Capture of Spanish treasure-ships—*Mercedes* blows up—Nelson's weary watch—Buonaparte's plans of invasion—The flotillas—The French fleets—Missiessy is the first to move—Villeneuve slips out of Toulon—Nelson pursues him blindly—Combined fleet escapes to West Indies—Nelson follows—He chases them back to Europe—They encounter Sir R. Calder—Calder tried by court-martial—Combined fleet retires to Cadiz—Nelson is sent there—Battle of Trafalgar . 225

LIST OF ILLUSTRATIONS

	PAGE
NELSON . . . . *Frontispiece*	
NORMAN SHIPS—WILLIAM SAILING TO ENGLAND .	4
CONTINUATION OF THE RECORD OF THE NORMAN INVASION, SHOWING THE SAIL, STEERING OAR, AND MOORINGS .	7
SEA-FIGHT—EARLY 14TH CENTURY MS. ROY 10 E 10	13
EXPEDITION OF THE KNIGHTS OF FRANCE AND ENGLAND UNDER THE DUKE OF BOURBON TO AFRICA IN 1390 .	34
HENRY VIII. EMBARKING AT DOVER	43
SIR FRANCIS DRAKE	47
THE ARMADA IN THE CHANNEL	52
THE ARMADA OFF CALAIS	54
MAP OF THE COURSE OF THE ARMADA .	58
PETT'S " SOVEREIGN OF THE SEAS "	63
ADMIRAL BLAKE	69
THE " ROYAL CHARLES " BEING TOWED OFF TO HOLLAND .	74
THE BATTLE OF SOLEBAY	76
THE STERN OF THE " ROYAL CHARLES " . . .	78
DESTROYING THE SHIPS AFTER THE BATTLE OF LA HOGUE .	85
ADMIRAL LORD RODNEY	139
PLAN—BATTLE OF ST. VINCENT . .	176
PLAN—BATTLE OF THE NILE . .	198
PLAN—BATTLE OF COPENHAGEN	215
PLAN—BATTLE OF TRAFALGAR	242

ERRATA

Page 44, 12 lines from foot, *for* twelve *read* two.
,, 44, 11 lines from foot, *for* 1525 *read* 1514.
,, 56, Marginal note and corresponding line, *for* Monday, 29th, **read** Sunday, 28th.
,, 171, Marginal note, *for* September *read* July.

CHAPTER I

Alfred the Great forms a navy—Constructs ships on his own lines—Defeats Danes at sea—Edgar improves and enlarges the navy—Guards the coasts—Ethelred's neglect and hesitation—Norman Conquest—No English fleet to meet it—Loss of the *Blanche Nef*.

"ON the British Navy, under the good providence of God, the wealth, safety, and strength of the kingdom chiefly depend." So runs the preamble to the Articles of War, and few Englishmen would wish to dispute the fact. But while we glory in the tale of the Armada and of a long line of brilliant victories, culminating in the supreme day of Trafalgar, we are apt to forget the means whereby these victories were assured to us. It is well that our people should study not only the triumphs of our Fleet, but its reverses also; that they should make themselves acquainted with every step in that long and often bitter struggle through which the British Navy won its way from insignificance to the mastery of the seas.

To meet invasion successfully the enemy must never be permitted to place his foot on our shore. Our insular position and our absence of frontier benefit us only so long as we encounter our assailants on the passage between their coast and ours. It is not surprising that this fact should not have been immediately recognised. Certainly the original Britons did not know it (though Southey asserts that they had large and powerful vessels built of strong oak), for their defence began as the Roman landed. Nor, in the three hundred years during which Britain was a Roman province, do our conquerors appear to have taught us this, with all their naval knowledge, for, after their departure, no effort seems to have been made afloat to drive off the forces of the Angles, the Saxons, or the Jutes.

It was reserved for Alfred the Great, under pressure of the Pagans of the North, to discover what is now regarded as a self-evident proposition, that *the first and only real line of defence for an island consists in an efficient navy.* Sea-fights had taken place before his time between the invading Danes and our forefathers, in some of which the latter were successful; but to Alfred was given the inspiration that the true defence was never to let the foe land. To effect this object he began to build the first British fleet. It was not a slavish copy of the ships of the enemy, nor even a reproduction of the best British models, but built on lines of his own, adapted to the necessity of the case, "full-nigh twice as long as the others; some had sixty oars, some had more; they were both swifter and steadier and also higher than the others; shapen neither like the Frisian nor the Danish, but so as it seemed to him that they would be most efficient." With this fleet, small in numbers, we may suppose, compared with that of the enemy, but possessing superior fighting powers, Alfred on several occasions encountered and defeated the Danish pirates, capturing many of their ships, and thus teaching his people the value of the

Alfred builds a navy.

command of the sea, and bequeathing the knowledge to his successors to be enlarged and utilised with a wider experience.

The legacy of a commanding navy was improved by those who followed him. Alfred died in 901, and sixty years afterwards we find Edgar, called the Peaceful, protecting the coasts of his kingdom with three powerful fleets, one on the north, another on the east, and a third on the west coast, numbering altogether between four and five thousand sail. This was the monarch who is said to have been rowed up the Dee by eight dependent kings: by Kenneth King of the Scots, Malcolm King of Cumberland, M'Orric King of Anglesey and the Isles, Dyfnwal, Gwffith, and Howel, three Welsh kings, Jago King of Galloway, and Jukil King of Westmoreland. It is of Edgar that the ancient chronicler observes that: "No fleet was so daring, nor army so strong, that 'mid the English nation took from him aught the while that the noble king ruled on his throne." Each year he made the circuit of his coasts, and put his fleets through something in the nature of naval manœuvres to keep up their efficiency.

Edgar protects the coasts.

But as now the efficiency of a force depends in great measure on the efficiency of the government which controls it, so in those days did the strength of the navy wax or wane with the character of the King. Close on the heels of his father Edgar came the wretched sovereign whom all succeeding generations have known by the fatal name of the Unready or Ill-advised. Ethelred was indeed a terrible example of a wavering mind. First, he bought off his Danish foes with £16,000; then, he would attack them both by land and water, but when the ships were ready

Norman Ships—William sailing to England. (*Bayeux Tapestry.*)

he had not the courage to move. Again he bought them off, this time with £24,000; and then, as if enraged at the price of his own weakness, he massacred all the Danes in his dominions. Once more a bribe of £36,000 gave him momentary peace, and again he prepared a mighty fleet after the fashion of his wise father, and proposed to regain command of the sea. But the disordered mind of the King had infected his officers. Part of his fleet deserted, part was miserably wrecked and scattered in a storm; the remainder followed the lead of the King and his Court, laid the ships up, and abandoned the enterprise.

Ethelred's weakness.

Possibly, had Edmund Ironside, the worthy son of an unworthy sire, lived to occupy the throne for more than a few months, his defence of his kingdom might have been as magnificent afloat as it was on shore. But, whether by treachery or by natural cause, the year of his accession was also that of his death, and the Danish invasion became the Danish occupation.

This invasion, like that of the Angles and Saxons preceding it, had been the work of many years, and was made up of the sum of many expeditions, the tide of victory ebbing and flowing so often that nearly two centuries had passed before the final result was attained. It was to be followed after the lapse of but fifty years by an invasion, the sudden and overwhelming character of which completely distinguishes it from any that had gone before, and invests it with a terrible and unique dignity. This was the Norman Conquest. As to the number of the ships which carried over William's invading force accounts differ widely:—400 large

The Norman invasion.

ships with 1000 transports is the estimate of one writer, 3000 ships carrying sails the estimate of another. Enough for us to know that it was a mighty force, and that, encumbered as it was with men-at-arms, with mailed knights, and with horses, it offered a splendid opportunity of attack to a well-appointed fleet, had there been such waiting to receive it in mid-channel. Where, then, was the fleet of England? The answer is significant. Such a fleet, described as the largest ever seen in England, had been assembled at Sandwich in anticipation of the attack, in co-operation with an army of equally large proportions. Harold, we know, had hurried north with the army to meet the Giant of Norway and the traitor Tostig; but the fleet, on which the safety of England depended, had dispersed, the only reason alleged being that their provisions were exhausted. So, unchecked by any effort of our first line of defence, the invasion broke in one huge wave upon our unprotected shore and swept all before it.

Thus on four occasions England fell into the hands of the invader—Roman, Saxon, Dane, and Norman—because our coast was unprotected. It should be noted that the attack of the Dane was absolutely checked while the navy of Edgar was maintained in efficiency, and that the Norman was only successful in that the defence began after his foot was firmly planted on our shores. Even the Conqueror himself, though victorious at Senlac, was shortly after obliged, through want of a naval force, to resort to the plan of the unlucky Ethelred, and to bribe away a fleet of Northmen which threatened our eastern coast. But the peace thus obtained was

Continuation of the record of the Norman Invasion (*from the Bayeux Tapestry*) showing the Sail, Steering Oar, and Moorings.

employed by the Duke in forming a navy so strong that we hear of no more such attacks from the Danes, who, as the Saxon chronicler expressly asserts, "durst not maintain a fight with King William."

Beyond the piteous story of the loss of the *Blanche Nef* in the Ras de Catteville in 1120, when the heir to the throne and the flower of the young nobility of England and Normandy were lost on a November night in the midst of song and revelry, the reigns of Rufus and Henry I., the wild anarchy of Stephen, and even the stern rule of Henry II. offer no naval events of sufficient importance to be chronicled here ; and so we pass on to the reign of Richard of the Lionheart, the first English monarch to carry an English fleet into foreign waters.

CHAPTER II

Richard I. collects a large fleet for the Crusades—First English fleet in foreign waters—Attacks Limasol—Sails in the *Trench-the-mer*—Fights a huge Turkish dromon—John excommunicated—French fleet at Damme—Salisbury destroys it—Eustace the Monk and Hubert de Burgh—The Cinque Ports—Sir R. Tiptoft's fight in the Channel.

THE rescue of the Holy Sepulchre from the hands of the infidel, and the establishment of a Christian monarch upon the throne of the House of David, was a subject which had enflamed the knightly heart of Europe for many years before Richard came to the throne of England. He had already taken the cross ere he wore the crown; but his accession to royal power afforded him ampler means of pursuing his object, and he lost no time in availing himself of them.

Having come to the throne in 1189, in April 1190 he collected at Dartmouth an enormous fleet, which was to join him at Marseilles. The winds were adverse, however, through nearly all that summer. It was not till September that he took command of his fleet, not at Marseilles, but at Messina; nor was it till the following April that he sailed with it for the coast of Syria. All writers unite in describing it as magnificent, though their quaint terms do not much help us to an adequate idea of its

Richard I. collects a fleet, 1190.

appearance. Thirteen "dromons" or "very large busses," 150 smaller "busses," and 53 well-armed galleys, with several galliasses and other light vessels formed his fleet; the 13 large "busses" being described as having a "threefold expansion of sails," which seems to point to their being three-masted vessels. They sailed in eight separate lines, each line a trumpet-call distant from the next, and Richard himself in the eighth line commanded and regulated the whole. It was not all fine weather sailing, however. Several of his ships were lost in a gale off the coast of Cyprus; the vessel containing his bride, Berengaria of Navarre, and his sister, was driven into Limasol, and there ill-treated by Isaac of Cyprus. The fiery Richard on his arrival at once proceeded to his vengeance. He took Limasol, defeated Isaac, threw him into prison, loaded him with silver chains, and exacted a heavy recompense in money and land. Once more, on 5th June, he sailed in his favourite galley, *Trench-the-mer* (the wave-cutter), and shaped his course for Acre. The fleet had already made the land when, in the neighbourhood of Baruth (Beyrout), they sighted an enormous ship, described by one of the annalists of the time as only second in size to Noah's ark. She was "stoutly built," with three tall masts, and "her sides were painted, in some places green and in others yellow, so elegantly that nothing could exceed her beauty." She carried 1500 men, Greek fire in abundance, and "200 most deadly serpents for the destruction of the Christians." For some time there was a doubt as to her nationality as she showed no colours; but having at length induced her to declare herself, Richard at once commenced the attack

Richard I. takes Limasol, 1191.

with his usual impetuosity. She was not, however, a foe to yield without a struggle; and indeed, for a long time it seemed as if the victory might be hers. So lofty were her sides that the King's ships found it well-nigh impossible to shoot on to her decks, while they themselves were overwhelmed by the storm of arrows, stones, spears, and Greek fire showered on them from so great a height. Boarding was tried and failed, and the English began to show a disposition to draw off. Then the King in a paroxysm of fury swore that if the great ship escaped, every one of his men should be crucified or put to the torture. Urged in this strange fashion to fresh exertions, the crew of the *Trench-the-mer* leaped overboard and succeeded in fouling the enemy's rudder, so that she could not steer. A second attempt to board carried the Englishmen on to the dromon's deck; but the weight of numbers was too overpowering, and they were driven back with heavy loss. One last resource remained. The great ship was helpless, her rudder useless either for advance, retreat, or manœuvre. The English galleys formed in line, and at a given signal, at full sweep of their powerful oars, hurled their iron beaks together upon the huge dromon. She gave a shuddering lurch, and, with her side smashed in in a dozen places, sank at once, carrying all but fifty-five of her crew with her. We are specially told that the 200 serpents were drowned; and that the King generously rewarded his men with all that they could save from the ship, which does not appear, on the face of it, to have been much. With Richard's doings in Palestine, with his imprisonment, his ransom, and his death at Chaluz, we are not con-

Richard I. fights a Turkish dromon.

cerned. Nor does the reign of his brother John offer much of naval interest. We may except the attack made by the Earl of Salisbury on the French fleet, which, to the number of 1700, was assembled in or near the port of Damme, for the invasion of England and the removal of her excommunicated King. The attack was a surprise; the French ships were denuded of their crews, and over 400 vessels were either taken or destroyed; but the affair scarcely rises to the dignity of a naval engagement.

<small>Battle of Damme, 1213.</small>

But hardly had John died and left his throne to his little son Henry III. when an event occurred which illustrates at once the value of the first line of defence. It will be remembered that after the signing of Magna Charta, the barons of England, rendered desperate by the vengeance of the incensed monarch, turned to France and offered the crown of England to Prince Louis, who at once came over and joined the barons in London. But the sudden death of the vindictive John and the accession of the infant Henry, transformed Prince Louis from friend to foe; and at the Battle of Lincoln he learned painfully that he was looked upon as an intruder. His friends in France, however, were not inclined to let him tamely abandon so great a prize as the English crown. Robert de Courtenay sailed to his relief with a large army and a fleet of over 80 large vessels, under the command of the famous or rather infamous rover Eustace the Monk, a name of dread along all the southern coast of England. But in the Governor of Dover Castle, Hubert de Burgh, England possessed a man fully capable of encountering so redoubtable a foe. At first his summons to arms was not responded to with the enthusiasm which he had a right to expect. "We are not sea-soldiers, nor pirates, nor fishermen," replied those to whom he addressed himself, "Go thou and die!" But presently inspired by his determination bolder counsels prevailed, and with 16 large and well-armed ships, and 20 smaller ones, he moved out to meet the enemy. These were sighted somewhere off the North Foreland, and De Burgh, apparently anxious to gain the weather gage, held his luff as if making for Calais. "I know,"

Battle of Sandwich, 1217.

SEA-FIGHT—EARLY 14TH CENTURY MS. ROY 10 E 10.

said the Monk, gazing hard at the English fleet in the distance, "those wretches think to attack Calais like thieves; but it is no use, the place is well defended." He was soon undeceived. Presently the English ships put their helms up and bore down together upon the rear of the enemy's line; then, eager as ever for close quarters, they grappled ship to ship, and a fierce fight commenced. Clouds of arrows flew from the English decks; stones, after the fashion of the times, were hurled from the tops; and our men, being to windward, made use of a strange weapon, quicklime, which they threw into their enemies' faces, then boarding while they had them at a disadvantage, they cut the halyards, and the great sail with its heavy yard fell upon the French "like a net upon ensnared birds." Many of their ships were sunk by the rams of the galleys; many of the French knights jumped overboard and sank rather than be taken; while the courage of the dreaded Eustace seems to have failed him in the hour of defeat, and he was discovered miserably hiding in the hold of his ship. His prayers for mercy, his offers of money, his promises of service were alike unavailing. His head was then and there struck off, and afterwards displayed on shore as a terror to all future sea-rovers. Of the entire French fleet but fifteen escaped, and the gallant De Burgh, taking his prizes in tow, returned to Dover "ploughing the waves in victorious triumph." This fight is to be noticed as the first of the long series of naval engagements between the English and French, a series which ended only with Trafalgar,—and as proving conclusively the inestimable value of a strong and well-appointed fleet patrolling the narrow sea and making it impossible for an enemy to set foot in England until its resistance has first been crushed.

It is sad to think that the man to whose courage and determination this victory was mainly due, the gallant Hubert de Burgh, suffered at the hands of his royal master much the same unworthy treatment which was the lot of that other champion, Simon de Montfort; and that in the gusts of unreasoning passion which so often swept through Henry's weak mind, the liberty and life of the Governor of Dover were again and again trembling in the balance on some paltry and well-nigh impossible charge, while his real and splendid services were utterly forgotten.

The whole of Henry's long and wearisome reign illustrates the dangerous uncertainty of his character. One day he is seen heaping fantastic favours upon his friend of the hour; the next ordering him to prison or to death; now making an extraordinary display of military effort, followed almost instantly by utter prostration and inaction. Twice he made such preparation for the invasion of France as had never before been seen in England: twice he landed an enormous force on the shores of Brittany; but no victory can be named to record his triumphs, and in each instance the army tamely returned, having accomplished nothing.

This, perhaps, is as fitting a time as any to draw attention for a moment to those harbours on the southern coast of England known as the Cinque Ports. Originally only five in number, as their name implies, they were added to as the exigencies of the time demanded, until, in the reign of Henry III., they consisted of Hastings, Winchelsea, Rye, Romney, Hythe, Dover, and Sandwich. To them was especially assigned the protection of the coast from foreign attack, that part on which they stood being naturally open to an invading host. They could be called upon to supply vessels to the number of 57, with crews amounting to 1197, at any moment for the king's service; and in recognition of these services they were granted certain exceptional privileges, some of which, such as the right of the barons to sit at the king's right hand at the coronation banquet, may appear to us now useless and frivolous. But as time went on we see the Cinque Ports, instead of being bulwarks of defence for the coast and champions of the freedom of the sea, de-

The Cinque Ports.

generating into simple dens of pirates. Their lords, abusing the power placed in their hands for purposes of protection, used it with ruthless brutality to enrich themselves, by preying upon every peaceful trading vessel which came into their hands, until the anxious merchants learned to dread nothing more than proximity to those to whom, above all, they should have looked for defence. Not only were the Cinque Ports thus unenviably distinguished, but the whole Channel seems to have swarmed with pirates, English, French, Spanish, Flemish, Scotch, Irish, Genoese, all on the look-out for the unprotected trader, no matter from what port or of what nationality, whether from a country at peace or a country at war. The State papers of the thirteenth century teem with complaints addressed to the King from merchants whose ships had been taken or pillaged, sometimes at sea, sometimes actually in an English port, now by a Flemish pirate, now by a rover of Bristol, now by Robert de Battayle or some other baron of the Cinque Ports. Now it is a German merchant who complains that his ship the *Cruxenbergh* has been attacked in the port of Orwell by two ships full of armed men, who kill one of his crew, wound others, and carry off the ship; now it is the *Paternoster* of Yarmouth which is met off the Foreland by Peter Bert of Sandwich, by Gervays Alard of Winchelsea, and by Robert Cleves of Greenwich, who take her rich lading of wine out of her and leave her at length despoiled of her cargo, but thankful to be allowed liberty and life. In short, as the highroad swarmed with highwaymen so did the high sea with pirates; each stretch of coast produced a fresh set of marauders ever on the watch for the passing victim: each port harboured a nest of villains keen for robbery and even for bloodshed so long as it was not their own.

It was this unrestrained licence, this utter disregard of all semblance of law or of humanity, this raising of every man's hand against his neighbour, which brought about in the year 1293 one of the most extraordinary combats at sea which have ever taken place in our history. Two of the crew of an English ship landed on the coast of Normandy for water; one was slain by the natives, the other fled to his ship, which instantly put to sea. A crowd of Norman ships set sail in pursuit. They failed to overtake her, but coming upon six peaceful English vessels they fell upon them, took two, and hung their entire crews in the rigging. The remaining four fled, reached the Cinque Ports, and so roused the indignation of their fellows by their tale of outrage that a fleet of ships poured out intent on vengeance. The Normans were discovered at the mouth of the Seine, and in the bloody battle which ensued six were taken, the remainder terribly defeated. Attack followed attack, reprisal reprisal, numbers were slaughtered on both sides, but the vengeance of neither was sated.

At last it was determined that the quarrel should be brought to a final conclusion by a great conflict in mid-channel. Details were arranged with a grim precision which in itself presaged the horror of the coming fight. The scene of combat was marked out by anchoring a large and empty ship at the spot agreed upon. The English induced the Irish and Dutch to join them; the Normans retorted by obtaining the help of French, Flemish, and Genoese.

Sir Robert Tiptoft's victory, 1293.

On April 14th, in cold, snowy weather, the hostile fleets met, 60 English ships under Sir Robert Tiptoft against more than 200 Normans. A terrible slaughter ensued; and, if the story of the chroniclers is to be believed, nearly the whole of the Norman fleet fell captive into our hands. And it must be remembered that no war was going on at this time; that these were not the respective navies of England and France struggling for the honour of their country. They were merely a medley of traders, of sea-rovers, of pirates, of adventurers, divided almost by hazard into two opposing parties, and fighting to satisfy the vengeful spirit which a thousand wrongs and outrages on either side had roused to fury, and which nothing but blood could allay. Possibly this is another example of that "Merrie England" which so many persons in the present day ignorantly sigh for.

CHAPTER III

Edward III. claims the crown of France—A French fleet ravages the English coasts—Battle of Sluys—Edward lands at La Hogue—Battle of "L'Espagnols sur Mer"—Neglect of navy—Winchelsea burned—Battle of La Rochelle—Capture of an English fleet off Brittany by Spaniards—No notice is taken of it.

THE reign of the ill-fated Edward II. is unmarked by any great naval occurrence; but when his warlike son ascended the throne and began to assert his claim to the crown of France, the Navy of England came at once into prominence. Then began that career which, though checked more than once by neglect or mismanagement, still continued to grow in importance, until at length after centuries of effort it reached its height in the possession of the supremacy of the sea. But ere it attained to that lofty position it had many a struggle to win its way through, and many a fall from which it found it hard to rise.

The claim of Edward III. to the crown of France was met by Philip of Valois with energy and determination; and it might seem as if, instead of repelling invasion of his own land, he was retorting on Edward by carrying the war at once into England. An enormous fleet, containing, if Froissart is to be believed, at one time as many as 40,000 soldiers, was fitted out by him, and at once commenced a

Edward III. claims the French crown.

series of ravages which seem to us hardly credible. Four times in the years 1338 and 1339 did they threaten Southampton, once sacking it while the people were at mass, and setting it on fire. Twice in one week they attacked Plymouth, burning all the ships in the harbour and many houses. Dover, Sandwich, Winchelsea, Hastings, and Rye in turn suffered a similar fate; and after a fight which almost reminds us of that of Sir Richard Grenvile in the *Revenge*, the two finest ships in the English navy, the *Christopher* and the *Edward*, were taken with some others and carried off in triumph to swell the ranks of the conquerors. No wonder that the young King desired his Commons to advise him as to the measures necessary for the safe guarding of the coast. But they professed themselves ignorant on the matter, and left the responsibility to lie heavy upon him.

Philip attacks the English coast, 1338, 1339.

In the early summer of 1340 Edward while at Ipswich was informed that Philip's fleet lay in immense numbers at Sluys, the most important port on the Flemish coast. He proposed at once to proceed thither and ascertain its strength; but he met with as little encouragement as did Hubert de Burgh when advocating a similar expedition. Again courage and persistency availed, and with 200 ships, shortly to be reinforced by an additional 50, Edward sailed to the encounter, an English King in command of an English fleet for the defence of the English coast.

Battle of Sluys, 1340.

On Friday June 23rd the French fleet was clearly seen lying in the harbour of Sluys; but baffling tides prevented Edward from attacking until the next day, during which interval the French dropped down nearer to the mouth of the river. They are described as drawn up in four divisions, the ships of each division lashed together by cables and iron chains, while to each mast a small boat was hoisted filled with stones to be hurled upon the heads of the enemy. In their first division they seem to have placed their largest and strongest vessels; and the indignation of the English was roused to fury when they recognised among them the *Christopher* and the *Edward*, with two other English ships, now flaunting the colours of France. The whole amounted to 190 vessels, carrying no less than 35,000 men, and commanded by Sir Hugh Kiriet and two other renowned admirals.

Placing his largest ships in the van, crowded with archers and sheltering smaller vessels filled with men-at-arms, Edward signalled his fleet at 11 A.M. to advance, making sail on the starboard tack in order that he might engage the enemy to windward and with the sun in their faces. For a moment the French thought that he was standing off; but presently the whole English line bore down before the wind upon the French van, determined at all hazards to retake the pride of their hearts, the "beautiful *Christopher*," and wipe out the disgrace of her capture and that of her fellows. Sir Robert Morley, the Earls of Huntingdon and Nottingham, and Sir Walter Manny were the first in the fight, followed by a host of the noblest names in the English Peerage. Then ensued a terrific combat. They grappled each ship as they reached her, fast as hooks and irons would hold; the archers poured in incessant streams of arrows and quarrels from the high poops and forecastles; nobles, knights, and men-at-arms swarmed in thousands up the sides of the French ships, leaped on to their decks, and fought in that narrow space with swords, lances, hatchets, maces and glaives, till each deck was piled with corpses and each scupper ran with blood; while on the heads of the crowd below the men in the tops rained down showers of huge stones. This is no fancy picture. On the deck of one ship alone 400 corpses were counted, while the entire crew of one English galley were crushed to death with stones. Neither is it to be supposed that so terrific an attack was the work of an intense but momentary access of fury. They fought on one side with dogged insular persistency, on the other with brilliant bravery for "all that day and the night after," as is testified by Edward's own letter to his son. But at last victory began to declare itself. The *Christopher* was retaken, and amidst yells of triumph the English colours were once more hoisted at her mast-head. The *Edward* followed; the *Katherine* and the *Rose*, two other French prizes, surrendered; by degrees the whole French van fell into our hands, and then panic seized upon the second and third lines, and they made frantic efforts to escape. But all round them were the English ships, and in despair their men lowered their boats, leaped into them in thousands and were drowned. The fourth line, however, was more fortunate, and gained the open sea, even repelling an attack made on it by some of our vessels; but a few days later the greater part of this also was overtaken and captured. The loss of the French is stated by Edward himself at 30,000, while that of the English, impossible though it may appear, was comparatively small. So unsatisfactory were the methods of the chroniclers of these days that we know not what part Edward played in the action, nor even what ship had the honour of bearing his flag; but one tells us that he was grievously wounded in the thigh, which, as he makes no mention of it himself in any of his letters, it is extremely difficult to believe. Thus, for the second time since the Norman Conquest was the naval renown of England asserted to the world; and so crushing was the defeat that among all Philip's courtiers not one was found bold enough to break the dire news to him, a task at length undertaken by the least likely of all his train, the Court fool.

This victory of Sluys, the overture to a combat which was to last, to the misery of both countries, for more than one hundred years, was followed by a truce made, as truces were in those days, only to be broken at the very first opportunity, which was soon found in the dispute for the Dukedom of Brittany. Again a truce was arranged, only to be instantly and flagrantly violated by Philip; and then Edward determined to enforce the lesson of Sluys on shore. In July 1346 an enormous fleet, estimated at any number from 1000 to 1600, bore him from the Wight to La Hogue, and safely landed him there with his gallant young son and with that army which in the following month gained unending renown at Cressy. With his movements in France it is not our province to deal, nor are the doings of the fleet of sufficient importance to be related here. Calais, the siege of which was the corollary to Cressy, after holding out for more than twelve months, fell on September 3rd, 1347, and for a time hostilities ceased.

Edward III. lands in France.

Cressy, 1346.

But now another enemy was beginning to attract the attention of English merchants. A Spanish squadron, in its passage from Flemish ports through the Channel and down the coast of France, pounced upon all English vessels which came in sight, slew all their crews, and made prizes of the ships and cargoes in defiance of the truce which included Spain as well as France. Once more Edward realised and accepted his position as the champion of his people. He called his fleet together for the punishment of the marauders, and on August 28th, 1350, he went on board his favourite ship, the cog *Thomas*, at Winchelsea, while the Prince of Wales together with his brother John of Gaunt, then only ten years old, and the flower of the English nobility found quarters in various ships of the fleet. The royal household were assigned to a vessel appropriately called *La Salle du Roi*, under the command of Sir Robert de Namur. Once on board, nothing remained for the King and his fleet, which numbered some 50 ships, but to await the arrival of the enemy, who were known to be then at Sluys loading rich and valuable cargoes ere their return to their own shores. Already had Edward, like Nelson previous to Trafalgar, explained to all his captains and officers his plan of attack, and men were kept constantly aloft to signal the first sight of the expected foe. For three days they waited impatiently without result,—days whose weariness was relieved on board the *Thomas* by music and song,—but at four o'clock in the afternoon of Sunday August 29th the look-out hailed the deck with the news that the enemy in great force was in sight. Instantly the trumpets were commanded to sound for action. With a fair wind, confident in their size and superiority, and contemptuous of danger, the Spanish fleet came on to the attack. Nor were the English one whit less eager for the encounter. Leading his fleet into the middle of the enemy the King in the *Thomas* collided with one of the leading Spaniards with such violence as to carry away her mast, thereby drowning all those who were preparing in the top to hurl their volleys of stones upon the Englishmen below; but at the same time the force of the shock was so great that the King's ship could barely be kept afloat. Swinging clear of this adversary the cog found herself almost immediately foul of another, to which she was at once made fast with hooks and grapnels, and the English, led by their King, swarmed over her lofty sides to take her by boarding, or perish on her deck, for the royal ship was fast sinking. Stimulated by this knowledge, and fighting with their national persistency, they soon gained their object. The unhappy Spaniards were hurled into the sea, and their ship became the prize of the gallant Edward, whose banner was at once hoisted at her mast-head, while the *Thomas* sank alongside. Meanwhile a similar fate had fallen to the lot of the Prince of Wales and his young brother. They, too, had grappled a Spaniard far larger than themselves, for the Spanish ships are said to have been to those of the English "as castles to cottages," and had suffered so much in the encounter that their vessel was filling fast. Moreover, their efforts to board had been steadily repulsed, and they were in dire distress and danger when the ship commanded by the Earl of Lancaster drove in upon the other side of the Spaniard, and, instantly

Battle of "L'Espagnols sur Mer," 1350.

making fast, boarded with loud cries of "Derby to the rescue!" The wheel of fortune turned; the Spaniards gave way, their ship was taken, and all were cruelly hove overboard by the followers of the triumphant Prince, whose ship, like that of his father, foundered at the moment of victory. The fight now raged on all sides with intense fury. The English ships were probably superior in mere number to those of the Spaniards, which are said to have amounted to forty; but in size, in height, and in the strength of their crews they were as far superior to us as in that later struggle in the same waters which more than two centuries afterwards ended in an equally disastrous defeat.

While the ships of both fleets were thus locked in furious fight, and before victory had begun to declare itself for either side, the crew of the *Salle du Roi* found themselves closely lashed to the steep side of an enemy, whose people made strenuous and incessant efforts to reduce her to surrender. Overmatched though they were, the English fought doggedly on, now striving to carry their huge foe by boarding, now straining every nerve to drive the enemy from their own decks. Suddenly the Spaniard, thinking to win by stratagem that which he could not gain by hard fighting, hoisted his huge square sail to the mast-head, and went off, dead before the strong breeze, dragging his unwilling foe with him. In the gathering gloom of the evening the pitiful plight of the English was unnoticed, and as, in the din and confusion of the battle, they swept past the King's own ship, their cries of "Rescue *La Salle du Roi!*" were unheard, or, if heard, unheeded. Capture, and the certain death consequent upon capture, stared them in the face. Farther and farther they rushed from all hope of help, while their untiring foes, in overpowering number, kept up an unceasing hail of missiles from their superior height. Suddenly a figure sprang in the twilight from the poop of the *Salle du Roi*, clambered quickly up the Spaniard's side, rushed forward, and before any could divine his purpose cleft with one sweep of his sword the main halyards of the enemy, bringing the great sail with its ponderous yard crashing down on deck; then with lightning strokes he cut through the stays on each side of the mast, and regained his own ship unhurt. Taken unawares confusion fell upon the Spaniards, which speedily became panic as Sir Robert de Namur with all his men poured in upon them. Their anticipated prize became their captor, and they awoke from their dream of triumph to find themselves in the jaws of death. We learn from Froissart that the hero of this gallant deed was one Hannekin, a body servant of Sir Robert. Of the 40 Spaniards more than one-half were taken prisoners; and shortly after nightfall Edward and his victorious fleet entered the ports of Rye and Winchelsea with their prizes, the seamen to celebrate their victory, the King to hasten to reassure and cheer the Queen, who, from the hills commanding the shore, had watched with deep anxiety the progress of the fight.

In a country whose very existence as a Great Power depends on her supremacy at sea, and whose greatness is built up of incidents such as this, it is inexplicable that this battle should have been by tacit consent omitted from most popular histories, and only grudgingly alluded to in others. In itself it is worthy to rank among the greatest of our naval combats. As a heroic spectacle in which the King and his gallant young sons stand forward as the champions and protectors of their people, sharing equally their dangers and their triumphs, it is unequalled. No wonder that an enthusiastic and admiring people gave to their victorious ruler the title of "King of the Sea."

To every medal, however, there is necessarily a reverse: on one side is the monarch's head crowned with laurel; on the other the royal arms typifying the means by which that wreath was won. Our medal in this instance shows Edward crowned with a naval crown, but, alas, the reverse is sadly mutilated and disfigured. It is an almost incredible fact that in less than ten years after the battle of L'Espagnols sur Mer, the navy of England was rotting with neglect, and that while Edward was carrying all before him in France, the English coast was left utterly defenceless against the attacks of the French fleet. Thus when in 1360 a landing was feared in the neighbourhood of the Cinque Ports, orders were given not for the ships to be manned and made ready for the encounter, but to be hauled far up on shore out of reach of the enemy. As a natural result we read that Winchelsea was attacked while the people were at mass, that the town was burned, and that neither age, sex, nor rank was spared in the massacre that ensued. The Peace of Bretigny this same year put an end, for a time, to the terrors of the inhabitants of our southern shores; but when again war broke out in 1369, we find with shame that no steps had been taken in those nine years of peace to restore the navy, and that the burning of Portsmouth was the first blow struck by the enemy. So deplorable was

Decline of the navy.

the condition of the navy that the Commons, who a few years before had pronounced themselves unfit to advise on such matters, now forcibly drew the King's attention to the ruin which threatened them through this cause, and prayed him to take immediate steps to avert it.

But the King was now getting old, and was, moreover, under the spell of evil counsellors, and the naval renown of England was destined to fall yet lower and lower. In 1372, the young Earl of Pembroke, Lieutenant of Aquitaine, was sent in command of a fleet to relieve La Rochelle, then besieged by the French. On arriving there he found a strong Spanish fleet under the Admiral of Castile drawn up to oppose his entrance. The Spanish ships were as usual much larger, stronger, and better equipped than ours, and were also much more numerous. But though the material of our navy had been shamefully neglected, the spirit that conquered at Sluys and off Winchelsea was yet unsubdued. All that day our men fought against woeful odds till darkness fell and found them exhausted but unyielding. Night gave them temporary rest, but not the aid which they had hoped for from La Rochelle. Dawn saw them again struggling with their powerful foe, but all to no purpose. Pierced through and through with huge iron bars hurled at them from the high decks of their adversaries, battered with leaden bolts, and racked with cannon shot (which Froissart distinctly mentions as being here used), they were at length utterly and completely defeated, and every ship of the English fleet was taken by the enemy, with the exception of one which sank with considerable treasure

Battle of La Rochelle. English defeated, 1372.

on board. The Earl of Pembroke was made prisoner, and many a gallant knight of England and of Poitou was slain. Again the Commons were roused to complaint, but the once glorious Edward returned them but an evasive answer. Worse was to follow. In 1375, at a time when we were at peace with Spain, a fleet of 39 sail were attacked by the Spaniards in a harbour of Brittany, were either captured or destroyed to the value of £120,000, and of this outrage no notice was taken, nor was any redress exacted by him whom twenty-five years before his adoring people had hailed as "King of the Sea."

CHAPTER IV

Channel and mouth of the Thames held by pirates—Depredations of French and Spaniards on the English coasts—Charles VI. prepares a huge fleet for invasion of England—Panic in London—Fleet driven back by bad weather—Earl of Arundel defeats a combined fleet in the Channel—Henry IV.—Attacks and reprisals by private vessels and squadrons—Henry hands over the defence of the coast to merchants—The plan utterly fails—Henry is nearly taken by pirates—Henry V. restores the navy—Crosses over to France with a splendid fleet—Duke of Bedford fights the French fleet at Harfleur—Earl of Huntingdon defeats the French in the Channel.

TRULY the realm of England had fallen upon evil times, and if evil in the lifetime of Edward III., how much more so when he was succeeded by his infant grandson. "Woe to the land that is governed by a child," runs the old adage, and the truth of this was recognised alike by England and by her foes. The state of the navy was nothing less than deplorable. French, Spaniards, and Flemings flaunted it in the Channel, made prizes of English vessels, harried the English coasts, robbed, burned, and slew without hindrance. Again and again did the Commons of England deplore the decay of the navy, and petition the King to take immediate measures for its restoration. They represented that ships of Normandy held the mouth of the Thames and captured every trader that tried to pass; that in addition to the loss of their trade and their ships large sums of

Richard II. 1377.

The Commons complain.

money had to be spent each year in the ransom of their friends; that there was no security either at sea or in port, and they implored the King to appoint some competent admiral to ensure the safety of the sea. But all to no purpose. The Court was occupied with other and selfish aims. There were individual displays of the old spirit, but they were useless. In vain did Sir Hugh Calveley sally forth from Calais to burn Boulogne; in vain did Sir John Clarke fall, bravely fighting, on the coast of Brittany; in vain did the gallant sailors of Dartmouth and Portsmouth, "hired by none, bought by none," fall upon the French in the Seine and inflict a severe check upon them; in vain did the warlike Bishop of Norwich offer to furnish 6000 men and 20 ships for an attack on the common foe. We were no longer masters of the narrow sea. A French fleet, under the celebrated John de Vienne, burnt Rye; a strong French force landed in the Isle of Wight; Winchelsea was twice taken and burned; Hastings shared the same fate. The Prior of Lewes, fighting boldly for his people, was made prisoner at Rottingdean. If Froissart is to be believed, Yarmouth, Dartmouth, and Plymouth were given to the flames; Scarborough was attacked; Spanish galleys sailed up the Thames and burned Gravesend; and an English fleet was entirely defeated by the Spaniards in the Channel. But the climax was reached when, in 1385, Charles VI. of France assembled an enormous fleet at Sluys for the avowed invasion of England. Then the national courage was utterly paralysed. The people of London began to hide, "like timid hares and mice," and universal panic reigned. The Court took no measures of any kind

Charles VI. prepares to invade, 1385.

for encountering the enemy at sea, and the first line of defence was entirely abandoned. Most mercifully for the country collapse fell upon the invading force. Procrastination led to delay, delay to postponement; and when at length the fleet sailed, contrary winds drove it back to its starting point, whence it dispersed to its various ports, never again to be reassembled.

Once, and once only, towards the end of the war did the spirit of England flash forth in a blaze worthy of the brilliant deeds of the past reign. A combined fleet of French, Flemings, and Spaniards, alike freighted for profit and fitted for pillage, was passing up the Channel when they were attacked by the Earl of Arundel, who was waiting for the purpose of intercepting them. The enemy, being richly laden, seem to have been anxious to avoid the fight, and held on their course; but Arundel pounced upon them "as sparrow-hawks pounce on small birds," and though gallantly resisted by the Flemish admiral, Sir John de Bucq, whose ship was armed with three cannon throwing heavy stones, he succeeded in utterly defeating them off Sluys, and capturing 80 out of a fleet of 100 sail. This was in 1387, and during the next year a truce relieved our coasts for a time from the strain of incessant apprehension from which they had suffered for so many years. *Arundel defeats a combined fleet, 1387.*

But no sooner had the ill-fated son of the Black Prince made unwilling way for his cousin, Henry IV., than naval affairs assumed a new and a more acute phase. A truce reigned, it is true, between France and England, which Charles VI., though regarding Henry as an usurper, would not break, and which Henry, well knowing his precarious hold upon the *Henry IV., 1399.*

throne, dared not disregard. Yet between the maritime populations of the two countries there was no such check on either side, and the mutual hatred was intense. But the tide had turned, the spirit of

THE KNIGHTS OF UNDER THE DUKE OF BOURBON.
EXPEDITION OF FRANCE AND ENGLAND TO AFRICA IN 1390.

England was beginning to rise. There was now no talk of cowering behind walls and sheltering in fortifications. The bolder spirits of the English coast began in their turn to make descents upon the

French shore, descents requited with the most cruel barbarity.

On one side the Sire du Chatel, Sir Charles de Savoisy, and Pedro Niño the Spaniard; on the other Lord Berkeley, the celebrated Harry Pay of Poole, and John Hauley of Dartmouth, harried, burned, and destroyed. Did the English make a descent upon the coast of France, the Sire du Chatel pursued them with vengeful haste, caught them revelling in their spoil off the Race of St. Matthew, fought them until all their missiles were exhausted, threw all their fighting men into the sea, and took possession of their entire fleet; then, retaliating upon their countrymen in like manner, made straight across the Channel and sacked and burned Plymouth. This was in August 1403, and ere November was over the town of St. Matthew was a heap of ashes, its people slain, a large force of Bretons armed in its defence defeated, and the whole coast given up to fire and sword. *Attacks and reprisals.*

Next year the French attacked the Wight, and we wreaked our vengeance on Brittany. Portland tempted them to land, but the courage of the islanders was such that none went back. Du Chatel thought to find Dartmouth an easy prey for his three hundred ships, but was himself slain, with many of his companions. On our side the gallant young Thomas of Lancaster, though beaten off at Sluys, took La Hogue, Harfleur, and several other towns; while Lord Berkeley and the rover, Harry Pay, pounced down upon every hostile vessel that they met in the Channel. The place of the Sire du Chatel was ably filled by Sir Charles de Savoisy and Pedro Niño. Combining their forces in 1405 these two in savage retaliation swept along the coast of Cornwall, made a fruitless attempt on Plymouth, attacked Portland, and learning that they were not far from the home of Harry Pay, determined to make an example of the place which had given birth to so terrible a scourge of their coasts. This they did; not, however, without encountering such a resistance from the archers of Poole as to make many of them appear "fledged with arrows."

So utterly, however, was the idea of a strong national guard of the English coasts lost sight of, so entirely was the supreme importance of the first line of defence forgotten, or, as it may be, so difficult did Henry find it to procure funds for the formation of a navy, that in the year 1406 he actually entrusted the custody of the coast to the merchants and ship-owners. The arrangement was doomed from its inception to failure, and speedily proved itself incapable of affording any adequate protection. Indeed, as a proof, if such were needed, of the boldness and insolence of the foes by which our shores were infested, it is stated by one writer that the King himself, merely sailing from the Isle of Sheppey to the coast of Essex, narrowly escaped capture by "certain pirates of France," who slipped in among his convoy unawares and carried off four vessels, with all the King's "chamber stuff and apparel."

Henry IV. entrusts the defence of coast to merchants, 1406.

Henry V. restores the navy, 1413.

With the accession of Henry of Monmouth, young, popular, full of military ardour, ambition, and determination, we should naturally look for a great improvement in the state of the navy; and this expectation is fully realised. As the author of *The Libel of English Policie*, exhorting all England to keep the narrow sea, tells us, he built far larger ships than ever had been in the English navy before; and he not only built them, but he superintended their building himself, in order to be satisfied that his commands were carried out. From ancient pictures and descriptions we can form some idea of these vessels, with their lofty poops and forecastles, their sides painted bright red or black, and literally covered with heraldic designs in gold and colours; some with collars and garters of gold, "a fleur-de-lis within each collar, a leopard within each garter"; or the *Nicholas of the Tower*, with her black sides covered with the ostrich plumes of the Prince of Wales, the stems and scrolls of gold, her great sail carrying a white swan in the centre, a "streamer" representing St. Nicholas flying from her mast-head, while four smaller flags representing St. Edward, St. George, the Royal Arms, and the Plume of Wales flew from other places aloft.

Once more, urged by the personal energy of the young King, the nation reared a strong first line of defence against the depredations of her hereditary foes. In 1414 Henry V. renewed the claim of England to the throne of France. In 1415 he sailed from Southampton in the *Trinity Royal*, with 1400 ships, 6000 men-at-arms, and 24,000 archers to back his claim by force of arms, landed near Harfleur, took it after a siege of thirty-six days, and a month afterwards added the name of Agincourt to the roll of famous victories in the history of his country. But the French, unprepared at first, were now roused, and Harfleur was strictly invested both by land and sea, while a French fleet hovered round the English coast, and even attempted to blockade

Henry V. lands in France, takes Harfleur, wins Agincourt, 1415.

Portsmouth. But in these enterprises they met with small success, receiving at least as much harm as they inflicted.

In 1416 the Duke of Bedford sailed with a strong fleet to the relief of Harfleur, and found the French drawn up at the mouth of the Seine awaiting his attack. On August 15th the English fleet, which had been at anchor outside, weighed and stood in while the French advanced to meet them. The engagement differed little in detail from many a previous action. The ships grappled as was the custom; the enemy being so superior in height of deck that their men were beyond the thrust of the English lances. It was a hand-to-hand fight for five or six hours, but ended at length in the total defeat of the French. Three great "caracks," including one called from her size the *Mother of All*, and a host of smaller vessels were taken, while the *Black Hulk of Flanders* foundered during the fight. Great numbers of the enemy were slain. The English ships, lying for many days after the battle becalmed and motionless, were surrounded by the bodies of the dead, while harassed night and day by the French galleys, which rushed out from their vantage ground higher up the river and made every effort to destroy the victorious fleet by fire.

> They fought full sore afore the water of Sayn,
> With Carrikes many, well stuffed and arrayed;
> And many other shippes great of Hispayne,
> Barges, Balyngers, and Galleys unaffrayed,
> Which proudly came upon our ships unprayed;
> And by the even their sails avaled were set,
> The enemies slain in battle and sore bet.
>
> And many dryent were that day in the sea,
> That as our fleet rode there then still alway,

Unto the feast next of her Nativity,
The bodies flote among our ships each day ;
Full piteous was and foul to see them aye,
That thousands were—twenty—as they then told,
That taken were in that same battle bold.

In which meanwhile, while as our ships there lay,
It was so calm withouten any wind,
We might not sail ne fro thence pass away.
Wherefore their Galleys each day there gan us find,
With oars many about us did they wind,
With wild fire oft assayled us day and night,
To brenne our ships in that they could or might.

So writes Hardyng, himself engaged the year previous at the siege of Harfleur, and consequently carrying with him some authority as an annalist.

But Henry's ambition was not sated by the victories of Agincourt and the Seine ; the crown of France was ever before his eyes, and he braced himself for a fresh effort to gain it. This time his aim was directed at Normandy, and he prepared to lead the expedition in person. The French learning his intention sent a powerful fleet, comprising among its immense numbers nine Genoese caracks, the largest, it is said, that were ever seen on these coasts, to scour the Channel, and to intercept the King in his passage. But the Council remonstrated so strongly with the King on the risk he ran in personally engaging the enemy at sea, that he was reluctantly compelled to abandon the idea, and to place in his stead the Earl of Huntingdon. On July 25th, 1417 (but in what part of the Channel we do not know), the French fleet was encountered, and the Earl of Huntingdon proved himself no unworthy substitute for his royal master. He bore down upon the enemy

Earl of Huntingdon's victory in the Channel, 1417.

Treaty of Troyes, 1420.

in so fierce and reckless a manner that the lofty forecastles of many of the ships were actually carried clean away, and the men who manned them hurled with them into the sea. He locked ship to ship and fought in desperate fashion for nearly the whole day, until four of the nine great caracks were his, with many smaller ones, while the rest, flying in wild confusion, barely made their escape. Four days after this Henry crossed the Channel unmolested, and landed close to Harfleur. When he returned to English shores, the Treaty of Troyes had been signed, the Princess Katherine was his wife, and the highest object of his ambition, the crown of France, was almost in his grasp. But ere two years had passed he was dead, leaving the realisation of his highest hopes and ambitions to his little son.

CHAPTER V

Henry VI.—Decline of our naval power—The fleet divided between the rival Roses—Henry VII. restores the navy—Builds the *Great Harry*—Columbus—Cabot—Henry VIII. makes war on France—Sir Edward Howard attacks the French fleet off Brest—*Regent* and *Cordelier*—France again prepares to invade—French fleet anchors in St. Helen's roads—Loss of the *Mary Rose*—Dispersal of the French fleet—Edward VI.—Mary—Navy rots at its anchors—Elizabeth—The privateers—Pioneers and rovers—Philip of Spain prepares to invade England—Drake harries the Spanish coasts—He "singes the King of Spain's beard"—The Armada sails—It meets foul weather—Puts in to Coruña—The Queen's navy—Comparison of forces—Armada sails again—The fight in the Channel—At Calais—Flight—Storm—Destruction—Elizabeth's meanness—Sir Richard Grenvile in the *Revenge*—Death of Elizabeth.

WITH the coronation of the boy Henry VI. at Paris, as King of France, in 1431, the summit of English ambition, after an intermittent struggle of nearly a century, was reached. But as in the world of nature the attainment of the summit after arduous climbing is followed, after an interval of long or short duration, by a more or less hurried descent, so it was with our sovereignty of France. The crown, which had cost us one hundred years to attain, was utterly lost in twenty; and but a short time further elapses ere we read once more the old and shameful story of Sandwich sacked by the French.

Henry VI., 1422.

With the civil wars of the Roses all question of naval supremacy was lost sight of. The naval forces of England were turned against each other, and under the able command of Warwick, the Kingmaker, the naval partisans of the White Rose held the Lancastrians in check. Once firmly established on the throne, Edward IV. retorted on the French by scouring the coast from Brittany to the Isle de Rhé with a fleet of 500 sail; while, on the other hand, the neglect of his successor to guard the coast of England resulted in the landing at Milford of Henry of Richmond, and the fall of Richard III. at Bosworth.

Possibly it was this very neglect and its lesson which stimulated Henry VII. to a policy exactly the reverse, for, so well equipped and so constantly ready did he keep his squadrons that the necessity for them never appeared. Not content with the ships which had formed the navy of past years, most of which seems to have been hired when occasion demanded, he built the *Great Harry*, the first of that name. This is sometimes regarded as the first real vessel of the royal navy, in that she was built primarily for fighting purposes, though probably engaged during peace time in commerce; while previously the reverse had been the rule, ships being built for trade but used in time of war for fighting.

Henry VII. builds the Great Harry, 1485.

But already there were other signs of the new era which was shortly to open for England. While Bartholomew Columbus was plying Henry with his strange theories and fantastic charts, his brother Christopher was discovering the New World, and firing the imaginations of the adventurers of every country in Europe. Five years later, John Cabot of Bristol, in a ship equipped at Henry's expense, landed in the Island of Baccalaos, now known as Newfoundland, and thus became the pioneer of that host of adventurers, discoverers, and ocean-rovers whose gallant deeds raised England to the position of mistress of the sea.

HENRY VIII. EMBARKING AT DOVER.

With the advent to the throne of Henry VIII., young, eager, ambitious, wealthy beyond belief, and allied by marriage with Spain, war with France was almost certain; nor was it long before it broke out. In 1512 a royal fleet put to sea under Sir Edward Howard to pillage the coast of

Henry VIII., 1509.

Brittany; and the admiral knowing that the French fleet was in the neighbourhood of Brest, determined to attack and destroy it. He had no difficulty in finding the enemy, and though they were much inferior to us in number, trusting apparently to the tremendous size and weight of their flag-ship, the *Cordelier*, they made no effort to avoid the action, but at once commenced a fierce fight. But the *Cordelier*, then carrying 900 men, though said to be fitted for 1200, irrespective of sailors, fell on board the *Regent*, probably the finest ship in our service, with a crew of 700, and, making fast, each ship tried to carry the other by boarding. In the midst of the struggle one of the two ships caught fire; the efforts of the crew to put out the flames while defending themselves against the enemy were ineffectual; the conflagration seized the other ship; and at last, with a terrific explosion, both ships blew up, and every soul on board was lost. So stunned were both fleets by a calamity of so appalling an extent that they mutually drew off and abandoned the conflict. After dragging heavily on without material benefit to either side for some twelve years, the war was finally brought to a close in 1525.

But a few years later, as Mr. Froude points out, the situation was materially altered. Henry was no longer *Defensor fidei*, but excommunicate. France and Spain were friends, while both were hostile to England. Ireland was in rebellion: Scotland had joined the Catholic League; and Henry was hard put to it to find a navy powerful enough to stem the threatened tide of invasion. In 1544 the Port of Havre alone contained 300 ships ready to cross the narrow sea, seize the Wight, and destroy the

English fleet, which, manned by 12,000 men, was keeping guard over Portsmouth, their watchword "God save the King," their countersign "Long to reign over us." Next year the storm burst. The French fleet anchored in St. Helen's roads, but again the hand of Providence was stretched out over us. In spite of the repeated attempts of the French galleys, in spite of the woeful loss of the *Mary Rose*, which capsized and sank with 400 men, the expedition was a failure; a deadly sickness attacked the French, and they dispersed, having accomplished nothing. *Loss of the Mary Rose, 1545.*

The six troubled years of Edward VI., the five far more deplorable ones of Mary, add nothing to the renown of our naval force. Indeed, during the latter period, the ships collected with such trouble by Henry VIII. simply rotted at their anchors; though, if proof were wanted that the spirit of England was yet alive, it may be found in the fact that Philip II., coming with a gallant fleet and all the pomp and circumstance of a Spanish Court to claim his bride, was treated to a broadside by the English admiral for not lowering his colours when in English waters.

But with the accession of Elizabeth, the dawn of our naval supremacy was about to break in stormy but brilliant splendour—a dawn preceded, as ever, by that darkest hour so well known to those who keep their watch on deck. Dark indeed it was. A weak woman—her right to the throne more than doubtful—her Protestantism well known—Scotland with a young queen whose claim to the English throne was far stronger than that of Elizabeth—Spain covertly hostile—France loudly exulting in the recovery of *Elizabeth, 1558.*

Calais—the first line of defence of the nation neglected, reduced, and rotten—these seemed hardly the elements out of which to form a glorious reign. Yet Elizabeth was equal to the task before her. The war with France was brought to an end. The Courts of England and Spain were ostensibly at peace; the people of England and Spain were openly at war. It was the battle of Protestantism against Popery. The Spanish navy was the finest in the world : the English navy can hardly be said to have existed; but its place was filled by a countless host of privateers which, under commission from the Prince of Conde, swept up and down the Channel and made prize of every ship which flew the flag of Spain. It was a paying game. One Francis Clarke, who fitted out three frigates (and the frigate of that time was little more than an open boat), carried eighteen prizes into Newhaven in six weeks, and realised a profit of £50,000. Horrible cruelties were committed on both sides, and the cold and measured tortures of the Holy Office found their answer in the furious barbarity of the English rovers.

In these circumstances a new race of seamen was springing up. Frobisher dared the cold and storms of Labrador; Davis left a lasting testimony to his courage in the strait that bears his name; Sir Humphrey Gilbert perished in the same inhospitable seas, foundering with all hands in the *Squirrel* of 10 tons; Hawkins pushed his trade to the West Indies, only to find himself foiled by the hatred of the Holy Office; Drake served his apprenticeship under him, and brought back from S. Juan de Ulloa a freight of vengeance which a lifetime did not suffice to exhaust.

Philip of Spain looked upon himself as the chosen instrument of the Almighty for the restoration of

Sir Francis Drake.

heretic England to the Catholic fold. Patiently and silently he matured his plans, irritated but unchecked by the incessant outrages of the " Beggars of the Sea." But a time came when his purpose could no longer be concealed; and it was an open secret that the vast host of ships fitting out in Spanish ports was intended for the conquest of England. Meanwhile Drake had fulfilled the vow which he had made at Panama. He had burst into the Pacific, had harried, burned, and pillaged the rich towns of the Spanish colonies, had taken the great *Cacafuego* with her hold packed with silver ingots, with gold bars, and with precious stones; and had returned triumphant, after circumnavigating the globe, eager to prosecute the struggle which was at once so congenial and so remunerative. Again he sailed, not now as a private adventurer, but as a knight and an admiral of the English navy, the hero of the nation. And now the worst fears of the Spaniards as to the dread and mysterious man who had risen up against them were more than realised. Drake, Draco, the Dragon, the bodily presence of heresy, the incarnate Evil One was upon them. In 1586 he attacked Vigo; then flying across to the West Indies he laid San Domingo and Cartagena under a heavy ransom. In 1587 with four ships of the royal navy and twenty-four others he swept like a destroying angel down the coast of Spain and Portugal, entered Cadiz in spite of its galleys and forts, drove the former under the guns of the latter, burned or destroyed 150 splendid ships magnificently equipped for war, placed the plunder on board his own vessels, and then, steering to the north, plunged into the harbour at Lisbon, and repeated there the havoc of Cadiz in almost equal measure. Failing in his attempt to make the Spanish admiral come out and fight him at sea, he left for England, carrying off an East Indian carack of vast wealth on his voyage home. This, in his grim humour, he called "singeing the King of Spain's beard."

But great as the blow was, it never for an instant shook the purpose of Philip. The preparations for the Armada went on unceasingly, the more so since, to his other reasons for the invasion, there was now added vengeance for the murder of Mary of Scotland. Harassed, delayed, obstructed it might be, but abandoned—never. It was a tremendous scheme, and might well cause the keenest anxiety in England. The Duke of Parma, with 30,000 troops, was to await in the Netherlands, near Dover Strait, the arrival of the Armada; the Armada, with 30,000 men, was to sail to the mouth of the Thames and cover the crossing of Parma. Each separately was formidable; together they would be irresistible.

On May 30th, 1588, the Armada, the Most Happy, the Invincible, as it was styled, left the Tagus —65 great galleons of the largest size, and others, amounting in all to 132 ships; 30,611 men, 2088 miserable galley-slaves, 600 priests and attendants, 3165 guns. At their head was the Duke of Medina Sidonia, who had most reluctantly and with strong prescience of ill taken the place of Santa Cruz, lately dead, and in whose utter and confessed incapacity lay the germ of total failure. But there were splendid sailors with him: Martinez de Recalde, vice-admiral, Pedro de Valdez, Miguel de Oquendo, Hugo de Monçada, and a host of others. Surely with these he could not fail. So thought Philip, and apparently with reason. From the very commence-

The Armada sails May 30th, 1588.

ment things went wrong. Foul weather came on at once; it was a thrash to windward, for which the huge galleons were quite unsuited. Three weeks elapsed ere they reached the Groyne, as we then called Coruña, and, when they assembled there, already there was a pitiful tale to tell. All were more or less battered; two galleys had been seized by the galley-slaves, who murdered all else on board and escaped; one great galleon had foundered with all hands; the men were eager to desert, and the greatest precautions had to be taken, while the ships were refitting, to prevent them. In the meantime, in England the sailing of the Armada had been the signal for a splendid display of patriotic devotion. The Queen's navy, thanks to the skill and care of Sir John Hawkins, was in splendid order; but in number it was simply contemptible. Of the 38 ships of which alone it consisted, 15 were mere open boats, only 13 were over 500 tons, one only, the *Triumph*, reached 1000; and it, with three companions, the *Bear*, the *Elizabeth Jonas*, and the *Victory*, was looked on by the old sea-dogs of the day with deep distrust as new-fangled and unseaworthy. But these four ships were Sir John Hawkins' own design, and grandly repaid the skill and patience which had been expended on them. To supplement this meagre force the city of London supplied thirty ships well-equipped and armed, double the number which Elizabeth had demanded; and every port along the coast strained its resources to the uttermost to supply the deficiency of vessels, while wealthy individuals fitted out others from their private means. Thus at length an armed naval force was produced comprising every class of vessel, the genuine warship, the privateer, the armed merchantman, the coaster, and even the open pinnace; a scratch fleet indeed, but manned with crews whose courage was dauntless, whose skill was unrivalled, and whose hatred of the Spaniard was intense. The fleet thus formed outnumbered the Armada by as many as 65, reaching the imposing number of 197; but the tonnage of all these together only amounted to half that of the enemy, their crews bore the same proportion, while their guns were but one-fourth as numerous; in other words the Spaniards had 15,000 men and 2328 guns more than we had. But the spirit of the nation was roused, the Beggars of the Sea were about to match themselves against the Supreme Mistress of the Ocean.

But suddenly there came the tidings that the Armada had put into the Groyne, battered and strained, and Elizabeth, with that terrible unreasoning parsimony which formed so large a part of her character, at once ordered the fleet to be laid up. Well was it for her and for the country that her chosen admiral-in-chief, Lord Howard of Effingham, who flew his flag on board the *Ark Royal*, of 800 tons, saw more plainly than she the unutterable folly of such an order, and bravely dared to disobey it. On July 12th the Invincible Armada was once more under way, but ill fate dogged it still; the weather was still wild, and at the mouth of the Channel, the "Sleeve," as it was then generally called, the *Santa Ana*, of 800 tons, foundered with 390 souls and 50,000 ducats on board. Still it held on, and on July 19th the pirate Fleming burst upon the historic group, who were playing bowls on Plymouth Hoe, with the news that the Armada was in sight.

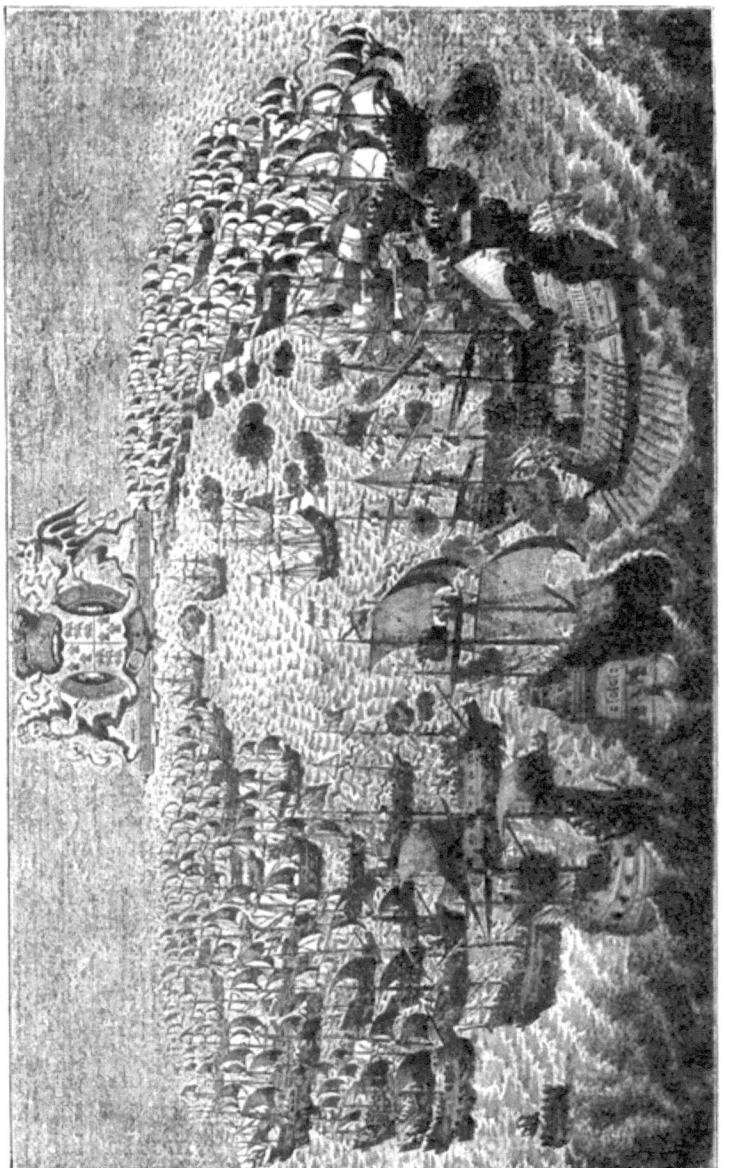

THE ARMADA IN THE CHANNEL.

THE FIRST ENCOUNTERS

Promptly and resolutely, without hurry, without panic, the English fleet warped out of the Catwater and stood off to meet the enemy, that enemy which in one huge crescent measuring seven miles from point to point made the very sea as it were to groan under its burden.

On Sunday July 21st the great fight began— the Spaniards wallowing heavily up Channel before a fresh westerly breeze, the English flashing across their rear, sailing two feet to their one, plying them with shot and arrows, inflicting grievous wounds between wind and water as the clumsy hulls rolled so far to leeward as to make it impossible to point the guns at their smaller but more active enemies; while these never allowed the great galleons to close, but sped away on the other tack ere the lumbering giants could be induced even to look up into the wind. It was this frightful unhandiness which caused their first great disaster in the fight. The *Capitana*, of 1200 tons, carrying the flag of Pedro de Valdez, fouled another vessel, lost her bowsprit and her foremast, dropped helplessly astern of her comrades, and fell next morning into the hands of Drake himself. After a show of resistance which vanished at the bare mention of that dreaded name, she surrendered with all her crew and 55,000 ducats. Drake at once despatched her to Dartmouth.

Sunday, 21st July 1588.

So far, so good; but even at the end of the first day's fight the miserable parsimony of Elizabeth threatened to negative the gallantry of her subjects. The meagre supply of powder was already giving out! Part of this pressing need was supplied next day by the Spaniards themselves. On board the flag-ship of Oquendo, the master gunner, driven to a state of

THE ARMADA OFF CALAIS.

wild fury by the insults of his captain, made a frantic attempt to blow up the ship and all on board. A partial explosion took place, the upper deck was riven in all directions, numbers were killed and wounded, and the author of the disaster jumped overboard and was drowned. Oquendo himself was absent on board another galleon, and his flag-ship, hopelessly damaged, was abandoned by her officers and men, and fell, with all her wounded still on board, into the hands of Sir Thomas Howard, by whom she was towed into Weymouth. In spite of the explosion she was found to contain a vast store of powder, which was at once distributed among the English fleet. But even with this unexpected aid the battle of the 23rd was much hampered by the want of ammunition, and on the 24th it ceased altogether as if by mutual consent. Both fleets had now passed Portland, and on the 25th, with magazines replenished for the next twenty-four hours, Howard forced the fighting, no longer avoiding the enemy, but attacking them at close quarters; indeed, so fierce was his attack that at one time the *Ark Royal*, with damaged rudder, hardly escaped from the press of her gigantic foes. As at the first, the Spanish guns could hardly be brought to bear at all, while the English shot made frightful slaughter among the closely-packed Spaniards. Let Medina Sidonia tell his own tale in his own desponding way: "The enemy pursue me—they fire upon me from morning until night—but they will not close and grapple—they are swift and we are slow." He, too, was suffering from want of ammunition, and he entreats Parma to send him some. At the close of this, the hottest fight of all, Howard bore up for Dover to fill his empty magazines, while the Armada struggled into Calais Roads to gain the rest which they so greatly needed.

But Howard had no mind that they should rest. Turning eight of his least serviceable vessels into fire-ships, he sent them, with a strong tide in their favour, on the moonless night of Monday the 29th, right into the huddled mass of the already dispirited and shattered enemy. The panic which he anticipated took place. They cut their cables, they hoisted sail, they crashed into each other, they ran aground in the darkness ; and in the midst of the panic, the confusion of cries, the crash of falling spars, the flapping of thrashing canvas, Drake was upon them,—Drake the Evil One, at the sound of whose very name the true Catholic shuddered and crossed himself. Then it was no more a fight; it was a slaughter. One huge unwieldy galleon, the *San Lorenzo*, took the ground off Calais, and her 400 men were put to the sword; the great *San Felipe* went ashore at Nieuport, and her crew, more fortunate, escaped to Parma ; the *San Mateo* grounded off Sluys, and her entire company swelled the list of victims. Only the shameful lack of powder in our fleet saved the whole Armada from capture or destruction, and at nightfall Howard drew off with barely a cartridge left. But the next morning he and Drake were once more at work, and indeed it hardly needed their presence to make the Spaniards' plight more pitiful. Battered, crippled, leaking, with decimated crews, with exhausted magazines, with failing provisions, and with the wind rising to a gale, they were barely holding their own off the low shores of Holland, upon which the furious breakers were clearly seen rolling, and on which the

Monday, 29th of July, attack with fire-ships.

north-west wind was surely driving their wallowing hulls. "We are lost!" cried Medina Sidonia. But in their extremity the wind veered to the south-west, and enabled them to clear the treacherous shore. For a moment they thought of turning back and tempting the fortune of war once more, but the gale grew stronger and stronger, and they turned their heads to the north. For two days Howard and Drake, with 90 vessels, pursued them, and then, mindful of the growing storm and their own safety, turned back and barely reached the shelter of the Thames.

Meanwhile the Armada, Invincible no longer, fled northward. The gale grew fiercer; every day brought some fresh disaster; the battered galleys foundered in the furious North Sea; the ships scattered in all directions, and rushed blindly onward through the gale and mist and rain. Some were cast away upon the coast of Norway; one drove ashore upon the Faroe Isles, another on the Orkneys; those who turned to the westward fared almost worse. One, seeking help and safety in the Isle of Mull, was burned by the savage natives, with all her crew on board; those who reached Catholic Ireland, hoping there to find the sympathy they so sorely needed, were terribly undeceived. Wherever they landed they were at once set upon and slain. Even the shelter of the harbours was denied them, and they were driven again to sea to meet a frightful death on the storm-racked coast of the south-west. In one bay alone, we are told, lay 1100 bodies, "and the like was in other places, though not to the like number." Between Rossan Point and Valentia Bay 8000 Spaniards are thought to have perished. Medina Sidonia himself, fortunate in the

The Armada flies to the north.

presence with his flying ships of Pedro Calderon, the pilot, avoided the coasts of Scotland and Ireland,

Map of the Course of the Armada.

and at length arrived at Coruña, to which port there crept sadly in the slow lapse of days 52 miserable, shattered, sea-worn hulks, the pitiful remnant of that gallant fleet which four months before had sailed from Lisbon with such high confidence and swelling pride. And long after, as if risen from the dead, when all hope of their safety had been abandoned, the galleons of Recalde and Oquendo appeared in the offing, and made their slow way each to its nearest port, with no sound, however, of rejoicing, for the staunch old seaman Recalde, and the gallant high-spirited young Oquendo lay dying, borne down by exposure, exhaustion, and defeat.

In England the national triumph was marred by the miserable meanness of the Queen. Unable to rest her gaze solely and thankfully on the splendid services of her fleet and the single-hearted devotion of its chiefs, she haggled shamefully over every penny expended in that great and terrible struggle, and even brought a charge of peculation against Howard in the very crisis of the danger, because he had used some of the Spanish ducats to provide necessaries for the sick. Hawkins, whose accounts were considered equally unsatisfactory, was practically ruined: the men, starved during the fighting, were left unpaid for many a long day; and no rewards had been bestowed upon any single individual, when Elizabeth, in royal state, surrounded by the trophies snatched from the Armada, made public thanksgiving in St. Paul's for the greatest deliverance ever vouchsafed to our nation.

Elizabeth's meanness.

Once again had the country owed its safety to its first line of defence; once more it had been abundantly proved that the only method of meeting invasion is never to permit the foe to reach our shore. The Armada was hopelessly shattered; 80

vessels, 20,000 men, had perished, but none the less was Philip's purpose fixed, and the invasion in his mind was but postponed. But now the English carried the war unsparingly into the enemy's country. Drake and Norris attacked Coruña, Lisbon, and Vigo; Cumberland took Fayal in the Azores; Sir Thomas Howard in 1591 led an expedition to the same islands to surprise the Spanish treasure fleet, but, surprised himself by the arrival of a Spanish force of 53 great ships, barely *Grenvile in the* escaped capture, leaving Drake's old ship the *Revenge, 1591.* *Revenge*, now commanded by Sir Richard Grenvile, surrounded by her huge foes. All that day and through the night she fought. The *San Felipe*, of 80 guns and 1500 tons, sank alongside; yet another galleon essayed to board and was sunk by the English crew; a third shared the same fate; a fourth was driven on shore; till at last, all her pikes broken, her powder spent, her masts gone, her men killed or wounded, and her admiral dying, she surrendered,—only to founder next day with her Spanish crew on board.

In 1596 Howard, Essex, and Raleigh, after the example of Drake, entered Cadiz harbour, took the city and destroyed 50 or 60 large new galleons lying under the guns of the forts. Again the Azores were attacked. Fayal fell a second time; Cumberland pillaged Puerto Rico; and in 1602 Sir Richard Levison and Sir William Monson fell upon Cezimbra, near to Lisbon, destroyed the galleys lying there, and made prize of a galleon containing a quarter of a million of money. But the strife was nearly over. Philip died in 1598, Elizabeth in 1603; and with the accession of the timorous James came peace between England and Spain,—the latter fallen from her high estate as mistress of the sea; the former having won for herself a name as an ocean power, which was to grow in glory until she took the place from which she had already driven her great adversary.

CHAPTER VI

James I.—Charles I.—Buckingham's fiascos—The Dutch—Cromwell's Navigation Act—Saluting the flag—Van Tromp insults Dover—Blake attacks him—De Ruyter attacked by Ayscough—Battle off the Kentish Knock—Blake beaten by Van Tromp—Battle of Portland—Battle off Essex coast—Battle off Dutch coast—Death of Van Tromp—Cromwell makes war on Spain—Capture of a plate fleet—Blake at Santa Cruz—Death of Blake—Charles II.—Quarrels between English and Dutch East Indian Companies—War breaks out—Opdam defeated off Lowestoft by Duke of York—The Four Days' Fight off the North Foreland—The St. James' Fight—The Dutch in the Thames—Peace of Breda—Secret treaty of Dover—Battle of Solebay—French fleet plays the traitor—Further fighting—Treaty of London.

THE reigns of James I. and of his ill-fated son are marked by no deeds worthy of record on the part of the navy; rather indeed the contrary, for, under the baneful influence of Buckingham, the various attempts to relieve Rochelle resulted in an exhibition of folly and incompetence on which we have no need to dwell.

But under the iron rule of Cromwell the navy of England was destined to gain fresh laurels and to assert its superiority over a new and even more sturdy foe. For many years the Dutch had been steadily growing as a great commercial power, and between them and England there was considerable jealousy. The respective trading companies in the East Indies had already come to blows; the demand

Pett's "Sovereign of the Seas."

that Dutch ships should lower their flags in English waters was most irritating to them, and Cromwell's Navigation Act, which hampered their trade with England, was especially galling. It wanted but a spark to start a conflagration. In May 1652 at Dover, a Dutch man-of-war refusing to lower her flag was fired upon and taken. The Dutch admiral, Van Tromp, then at sea with 42 ships, at once sailed by Dover, flaunting the flag of the Republic. Admiral Blake, though having but 23 ships under his command, rushed out furiously, fought him for five hours, took two of his ships, and drove him off. War was at once declared. Each side made great preparations. In August, Admiral De Ruyter, with 40 ships, sailing into Plymouth was attacked by Sir George Ayscough with 38, who gained the weather-gage, pounded him till nightfall, and forced him to retreat. Next month the same De Ruyter with 70 ships fought Blake with an equal number off the Kentish Knock, and in a battle which lasted well into the night, lost many ships, either sunk or taken, though the Dutch dispute the loss of any.

But these actions were but the prelude to far sterner encounters. In November Van Tromp, once more in command and with a fleet of over 100 vessels, caught Admiral Blake not far from Dover with only 37 ships, he having divided his fleet into squadrons for the protection of the coast. Undismayed by the overwhelming numbers of the enemy, Blake determined to fight, his flag flying on board the *Triumph* of 60 guns. A heroic action ensued. Overmatched and outnumbered the English ships fought without hope of victory, without thought of surrender. The *Triumph*, with two others, was long engaged with twenty of the enemy; the *Garland* and *Bonaventure* were overpowered and taken; the *Brederode*, Van Tromp's flag-ship of 90 guns, fell foul of the *Triumph* and boarded her. Three times the Dutchmen swarmed over her decks: three times they were driven back by the exhausted English; and at last Blake drew off his ships under cover of night, after having blown up one of his opponents.

Triumphant in his victory, Van Tromp is said to have hoisted a broom at his mast-head as a sign that he swept the seas, a challenge responded to later by Blake, who chose for his emblem a whiplash in token of his determination to beat his adversary.[1] The whiplash in the form of a pendant remains as the distinguishing mark of a man-of-war; the broom, hoisted by our coast sailors at the mast-head of a boat, indicates a coming change of ownership.

Early next year Blake was again at sea with 80 sail, and in the middle of the Channel on February 18th he came upon Van Tromp with a fleet of almost equal numbers, and with a huge convoy of merchantmen. At first it went ill with us, for Blake, in the *Triumph*, with a few others, was far ahead of his fleet, and for some time bore the brunt of the battle; but as our ships came up the fight raged on more equal terms. It was a fight of giants. Blake himself was severely wounded in the thigh, his captain and secretary were killed, his ship utterly disabled, the *Fairfax* was "wretchedly torn," the *Speaker* towed out of action a wreck, the

Battle of Portland, Dutch defeated, 18th February 1653.

---

[1] It is but fair to state that the Dutch authorities repudiate this story of Van Tromp as inconsistent with his character.

Prosperous boarded and taken first by one side and then by the other, the *Sampson* captured. On the other side one Dutch ship foundered with all hands: one when boarded was found not to have a single soul alive; and when night fell the Dutch loss amounted to six ships, either taken or sunk. The second day dawned. Again they fought with undiminished fury; again night closed upon the unending strife, leaving five more warships and 16 merchantmen in our hands. Once more the sun arose and looked upon the fight; but both sides were now thoroughly exhausted, and Van Tromp drew off his battered fleet and diminished convoy into the shallow waters of his own coast, whither Blake dared not follow him.

But the sturdy Dutchman was not yet beaten. In May he was again afloat with a magnificent fleet of 98 ships of the line, with which he actually had the audacity to batter Dover Castle. Monk, hearing of this, sailed from Yarmouth with Admirals Deane, Lawson, and Penn, and hurried to the spot with 95 vessels. The rival fleets met off the coast of Essex, and on June 2nd another terrific fight took place. At the first broadside Deane fell, cut in two by the new Dutch missile, the chain-shot. Lawson cut off De Ruyter's squadron, and would have destroyed it had not Van Tromp himself come to its aid; a Dutch ship blew up, and night found the Dutch much disheartened, yet the fight was renewed at eight next morning, and carried on with unflinching courage. But at 2 P.M. the arrival of Blake with 18 fresh ships turned the tide. Van Tromp in the *Brederode* made a despairing effort to take Penn's flag-ship, the *James* of 66 guns.

At the very moment that our boarders, having repelled her attack, were in the act of charging upon her deck, the almost exhausted magazine of the Dutch flag-ship exploded, killing numbers both of Dutch and English, but leaving Van Tromp unhurt. In spite of his heroic efforts he was at last forced to draw off his crippled fleet and retire, having lost eight or nine of his ships, sunk or burned, and leaving 11 others as prizes in our hands. Negotiations for peace ensued, but Cromwell's attitude was unbending, and the Dutch, though much shaken, prepared resolutely for another encounter. Once more, and for the last time, the gallant Van Tromp put to sea with a fleet of 90 splendid ships, to the mingled surprise and admiration of the English. Blake's wound incapacitated him for service; but Monk, Penn, and Lawson were ready for the enemy. The fleets, of about equal number, engaged off the Dutch coast on Sunday July 31st. As it was the last, so it was the fiercest fight of all. Monk gave the bloodthirsty order "No quarter!" "No captures!" The enemy had the wind of us; their fire-ships plunged in among our fleet. The *Oak* and the *Hunter* caught fire and were destroyed; the *Triumph* burst into flames, which drove most of her men overboard, but which were at length mastered. Van Tromp's hopes began to rise, but at noon he fell dead, shot through the heart, and with him fell the courage of his people. Consternation spread through his fleet; one by one the ships turned and fled, pursued by the English till they reached the shelter of the Texel. How terribly Monk's cruel order was carried out is seen by the fact that six of their ships were sunk, that 26 were burned

Dutch defeated, Van Tromp killed, 31st July 1653.

that 5000 men were killed, but that no single prize was brought back as visible proof of victory. But the Dutch were beaten; their resistance was over. Peace was signed, and the English flag was humbly saluted wherever it was met.

Peace, 4th April 1654.

Proud of the prowess of his navy, and ambitious of asserting his power still further, Cromwell now secretly prepared to make war upon Spain, while basely concealing his intention by assurances of friendship and goodwill. A West Indian expedition under Admiral Penn failed in its principal object, the capture of Hispaniola, but added Jamaica to the list of British possessions; while Captain Stayner, cruising with some frigates off Cadiz, intercepted a treasure fleet of eight ships, sank two, drove two ashore, and took two others, the rich lading of which was subsequently carried in triumph from Portsmouth to London in a procession of thirty-eight waggons. Some idea may be formed of the paltry size of the frigates of those days from the fact that the Spaniards mistook the English force for fishing boats! But now Blake, a name almost as dread as that of his great predecessor Drake, having, at Cromwell's order, destroyed the bristling batteries and numerous fleet of the piratical Dey of Tunis, and reduced his fellow corsairs of Tripoli and Algiers to submission, sailed in 1657 for Santa Cruz, in the Island of Tenerife, to intercept the great treasure fleet which, consisting of 20 vessels, was bearing the wealth of the New World to Spain. On opening the harbour his delight was great to see the coveted prize lying at anchor. They themselves were heavily armed: the position was commanded on every side by frowning fortifications; but Spanish

Cromwell makes war on Spain, 1656.

Blake at Santa Cruz, 1657.

galleons were child's play to the men who had beaten the Dutch, and Blake had taught them to despise castles and batteries. Without hesitation he made his attack. In four hours the forts were silenced; in two more the galleons, with all their incalculable

ADMIRAL BLAKE.

wealth, were destroyed. The loss to Spain was enormous; the gain to England was but negative. This was Blake's last fight; his health was fast failing, and, as his ship entered Plymouth Sound, before she could drop her anchor, the great Admiral of the Commonwealth was dead.

Blake dies, 1657.

One year later and Cromwell himself followed his trusty servant to the grave. Then, after a short but troubled period, the Monarchy was once more restored, and Charles II. filled his unhappy father's throne, mainly assisted thereto by that same Monk, now general, now admiral, whose order of "No quarter!" "No captures!" had made our last victory over the Dutch so shamefully notorious. Nor had these last ever forgotten it. They did but nurse their vengeance till their shorn locks had grown again; and now when the flighty Charles replaced the stern Protector, and when their arch-enemy Blake was in his coffin, they began once more to seek a cause of quarrel against us. Such a cause was easily found. The rival East India companies were ever quarrelling. Charles took up the cause of our company. New York, then a Dutch settlement known as New Amsterdam, was seized, and in 1665 the Dutch for a second time declared war. Each side at once armed and sent to sea a most powerful fleet. The English were commanded by James, Duke of York, afterwards James II., by Prince Rupert, the famous cavalry soldier, and by the Earl of Sandwich. The Dutch sailed under the flags of Admiral Opdam, of Cornelius Van Tromp, and of Admiral Evertzen. There was no delay: the rival shores lay near to each other; and on June 3rd 114 English ships encountered off Lowestoft 103 Dutch vessels, each fleet well supplied with fire-ships. The fight began at 3 A.M. and raged till noon with but little advantage on either side; but at 1 P.M. Opdam's ship blew up with the loss of every soul save five, and sent a thrill of horror through the Dutch fleet. Here four Dutch ships falling foul of each other were wholly destroyed by a fire-ship; there three more, similarly entangled, shared the same fate; in another quarter the *Orange* of 75 guns was a roaring mass of flame; and ere nightfall the Dutch fled in wild confusion with the loss of 30 vessels. Crushing as was the defeat, the Duke of York was severely blamed for not taking more advantage of the disorganisation of the enemy; while, on the other hand, the Dutch Government ordered three of their captains to be shot, two to be ignominiously dismissed, and one to stand publicly on a scaffold with a halter round his neck, in proof of their deep displeasure.

The blow was a heavy one, but the war was by no means over. The Dutch fleet was repaired; De Ruyter took Opdam's place; the French promised their aid; and at the end of May the enemy was once more at sea with 91 fine vessels. Monk (now Duke of Albemarle) and Prince Rupert were in the Downs with an equal force; but, on the very day that De Ruyter weighed anchor, Prince Rupert sailed with about 30 ships to guard the Channel from the French, and Monk with 60 was left to face the full force of the enemy. He did not shrink from the encounter, though fully aware of his inferiority. He attacked the Dutch half-way between the shores of Essex and Holland, and plunged furiously into a struggle which was destined to continue for four days, and in which, though beaten, the English won the unstinted admiration of their foes. Overmatched as they were, matters went hard with our fleet from the very first. The wind did not permit them to fight their lower-deck guns; Monk lost his foretopmast in the gale; the *Essex*

<small>The four da fight off the North Foreland, June 1 1666.</small>

and *Swiftsure* were taken; the *Henry* nearly shared the same fate, but though entirely disabled and in flames, grappled by three blazing fire-ships, her captain's leg broken by a falling spar, and many of her crew driven overboard, the gallant remnant rescued her and towed her out of action. Through the whole of the next day the unequal fight went on, not without serious loss to the Dutch, for Evertzen had already fallen, another admiral was now killed, and De Ruyter himself hard pressed; yet, when the third day dawned, Monk, with only 16 ships capable of action, was forced to retreat, fighting every inch of the way. And now Prince Rupert with the white squadron hove in sight, and Monk dared once more to hope for victory; but at this juncture the finest ship of all his fleet, the *Royal Prince*, ran on the Galloper shoal and was forced to surrender with all her men. The fourth day found the English, undismayed, still striving to undo their previous reverses; but the Dutch were too strong for them, and at length Monk reluctantly drew off his shattered fleet, having lost 20 ships and destroyed 10 of the enemy. But these, though victorious, could not conceal their admiration for their adversaries. "If the English," said De Witte, the chief Minister of Holland, "were beaten, their defeat did them more honour than all their former victories. All the Dutch had discovered was that Englishmen might be killed and English ships burned, but that English courage was invincible."

With admirable energy the English fleet was refitted, and on July 25th, 80 British and 88 Dutch ships met once again off the North Foreland. The battle was of the same fierce and determined character as the preceding one; but the result was different. Prince Rupert and Monk amply avenged the defeat of the previous month, and with the loss of but one ship, they destroyed or took 20 sail of the enemy. Four admirals fell, one was taken prisoner, 7000 men filled the roll of killed and wounded, and De Ruyter himself, unhurt and in despair, cursed his fate that there was not found a bullet to put an end to his existence also. Following up their victory the English attacked the coast of Holland, burnt 160 great merchantmen lying, richly laden, in harbour, and returned home having inflicted a loss of more than a million of money upon the Hollanders. This was apparently the final blow. The Dutch sued for peace: the negotiations dragged slowly on; and Charles, over-confident, laid up his fleet. But the indomitable foe was on the alert. No sooner was the King's folly known, than De Ruyter put to sea, sailed unchallenged up the Thames, destroyed Sheerness, burnt four large men-of-war, carried off the *Royal Charles*, and spread terror and dismay throughout London. His further advance was stopped by sinking ships to block the channel. The English fleet, hastily assembled under Sir Edward Spragge, drove him from our shores, and the Peace of Breda on July 21st put an end to the second Dutch war.

"Sir Robert Holmes—his Bonefire."

The Dutch fleet in the Thames, 166

Peace of Breda, 1667.

Not only was there now peace with our gallant foes, but, recognising for a moment that France was far more our enemy than Holland, and that the interests of the latter country were in many points identical with our own, we made, under the name of the Triple Alliance, a compact with that nation, and Sweden, the object of which was

The "Royal Charles" being towed off to Holland.

to force Louis to abandon his policy of aggression in the Netherlands. But Charles was a Stuart; incapable of straightforward dealing in politics; openly Protestant, secretly Romanist. Louis was his cousin; a great Catholic monarch, eager to advance the cause of Romanism. Charles was wildly extravagant and needy; Louis was wealthy and ready to use his wealth to gain his purposes. While the nation was rejoicing in the Triple Alliance, Charles had signed the secret Treaty of Dover, by which the two monarchs, among other matters, agreed to make war upon the Dutch and to divide Holland between them.

A large sum of money and a powerful fleet voted by Parliament for use against France were now to serve for the destruction of our new allies. An unprovoked attack upon a rich fleet of Dutch merchantmen returning from Smyrna was followed by a formal declaration of war on the part of Charles and Louis against Holland on March 28th 1672. *Third Dutch war, 1672.* Surprised and indignant though they were, the Dutch were well prepared; and De Ruyter at once sailed with a splendid force of 90 ships of the line and 40 fire-ships, to seek the false foe with whom they had believed themselves to be in firm alliance. Our fleet, under the Duke of York and Lord Sandwich, to the number of 65, with a French force of 36 under the Comte d'Estrées, was lying off the coast of Suffolk in Southwold Bay, then called Solebay. Lord Sandwich considered the position ill-chosen, but his warnings were disregarded, the Duke even taunting him with being afraid of the enemy. Suddenly, between seven and eight in the morning of May 28th, the Dutch fleet fell upon them, led *Battle of Solebay, 28th May 1672.*

THE BATTLE OF SOLEBAY.

by De Ruyter, and accompanied by Cornelius De Witte, brother of the chief Minister of Holland, who, clothed in his robes of magisterial office, surrounded by halberdiers, on a platform covered with a gorgeous carpet, sat in a splendid chair of ivory on the upper deck of the *Seven United Provinces*, and was thought by this fantastic display to add dignity and encouragement to the fleet. Lord Sandwich's apprehension was well founded. Many of our ships were obliged to cut their cables to get under way in time. The Dutch poured in upon us; the Duke was forced to quit his ship after two hours' fight; the *Royal James* of 100 guns, flying the flag of Lord Sandwich, was surrounded by the enemy, and after sinking one line-of-battle ship and three fireships, after losing all her officers save the Earl, and two-thirds of her men, was grappled by another fire-ship and burst into flames. Many of her surviving men escaped in boats; but Lord Sandwich, bearing in mind the taunt of the Duke, refused to leave his ship and perished with her. All day long the fight, "the hardest fought battle," according to De Ruyter, "that he ever saw," raged with inexpressible obstinacy; but it was between English and Dutch alone. Well was Charles repaid for his treachery to his ancient enemies by the falseness of his new made friends. The French fleet, acting under secret orders, stood off and made no effort to assist us. Nevertheless, as night drew on, De Ruyter sailed away, having burned four of our ships, and leaving one of his finest vessels in our hands as the only prize. Both sides claimed the victory, a pretty sure indication of a drawn battle; but it must be noted that the odds were three to two against us.

The Test Act of the next year removed the

THE STERN OF THE "ROYAL CHARLES."

Duke of York, an avowed Romanist, from the

command of the navy. Prince Rupert took his place; Sir Edward Spragge that of the gallant Sandwich. Three more battles were fought off the Dutch coast, which we vainly attempted to invade; on the 28th May (the anniversary of Solebay fight), on the 4th of June, and on the 11th of August. All three were of the same ferocious character; in all three each side claimed to be the victor; in all three the French persistently held aloof, and the only French officer who, for very shame, took his ship into action was, on his return to France, thrown into prison. In the first of these fights so fierce was the melée that Cornelius Van Tromp was four times forced to shift his flag—from the *Golden Lion* to the *Prince on Horseback*, from her to the *Amsterdam*, and from the *Amsterdam* to the *Comet;* while in the last, Sir Edward Spragge, driven from the *Royal Prince* to the *St. George*, was obliged to abandon her also; but, in rowing to the *Royal Charles*, his boat was sunk by a shot and he himself was drowned. This, however, was the end. The Dutch were anxious for peace; we were no less desirous of it. On February 9th, 1674, the treaty was signed in London. Our supremacy at sea was acknowledged, and Dutch fleets were ordered humbly to lower their flags even to a single British ship.

Three more drawn battles, Spragge killed, 1673.

Peace of London, 1674.

CHAPTER VII

William of Orange—Battles of Bantry Bay, of Beachy Head, of La Hogue—Attacks on St. Malo, Dieppe, and Calais—Peace of Ryswick—Spanish Succession—Anne—Rooke's victory at Vigo—Benbow and Du Casse—Wade and Kirby are shot—Great storm—Capture of Gibraltar—Battle of Malaga—Shovel in the Mediterranean—Loss of the *Association*, *Eagle*, and *Romney*—Forbin and Duguai Trouin take the *Cumberland* and others — Treaty of Utrecht.

William of Orange, 1689.

THE remainder of the reign of Charles II. and the short and mischievous reign of his brother James add little to the history of the navy; but with the flight of James and the bloodless invasion of William of Orange, there was a general and complete change in affairs. James II. and Louis XIV. were cousins, Catholics and friends; William and Louis were political and religious enemies. Now, therefore, our false friend of the last Dutch war was our fierce foe, while our sturdy rival for the supremacy of the sea was transformed into our equally sturdy ally. Our weakest spot, as ever, was Romanist Ireland. There accordingly the first efforts of Louis were directed, and there, off Bantry Bay, the first shot was fired, Admiral Herbert with an inferior force attacking a French fleet which had landed troops for the support of James. The action was of little or no importance. Yet Herbert was raised to the peerage, under the title

Battle of Bantry Bay, 1689.

of Lord Torrington, and rewards were showered broadcast upon his fleet; for William's hold upon the throne was far from secure, and it must be borne in mind that James II. was himself a naval officer, had commanded in Solebay fight, and had many adherents in the naval service.

During the winter of 1689 all three countries were busily preparing for the coming contest; and in the spring of 1690, Lord Torrington, the hero of the hour, put to sea with a combined English and Dutch fleet of 56 ships of the line. But the French were on their mettle: their dockyards were far better organised than ours; and they retorted on us with a fleet of 84 splendid ships, many of them far superior to ours, under the command of the Comte de Tourville. The odds were heavily against us; but the Queen's orders to Torrington were to fight at all hazards, and when the rival fleets met off Beachy Head on June 30th, the English admiral had no option in the matter. The issue of the fight, almost certain from the commencement, was rendered still more so by adverse circumstance. The wind was light, almost calm; many of the English ships did not get into action at all; Lord Torrington's flag-ship never fired a shot. The Dutch fleet of only 22 vessels bore the brunt of the attack, and suffered accordingly. Six Dutch ships, with two admirals, were lost; one English ship, the *Anne* of 74 guns, was burned by us to prevent her capture; and in the end our fleet retreated towards the Thames. Lord Torrington was no longer a hero. Rightly or wrongly blame was freely cast upon him. He was tried, defended himself with great composure, and was acquitted; but William withdrew

Battle of Beachy Head, 30th June 1690.

his commission the same day, and never afterwards employed him. His place was now taken by Admiral Russel; but no great fleet action was the immediate consequence of the change, and the year 1691 passed with little to mark it.

Louis in the meanwhile was making large preparations. Once more England was to be threatened with invasion; once more a host of transports was assembled to carry 20,000 men across the Channel; once more a hostile fleet was to co-operate with the invading force. The Comte d'Estrées was to cover the passage; the Comte de Tourville to settle scores with the English fleet ere it could effect a junction with the Dutch. But it was too late; the junction had already taken place.

It was an anxious time for Mary. Her husband was away in Holland; her fleet, on which alone the safety of England depended, was commanded by men who could not but have sympathetic leanings towards James, and many of whom were asserted to be wavering in their allegiance to William. She took a bold step. She was a woman; she knew a woman's power over the hearts of men; and she put it to the test. She addressed a letter to Russel, telling him that she had been informed that some in the fleet were not to be relied upon; that she had been urged to dismiss many, but that she refused to believe the report; that she reposed entire confidence in all, and that she would not remove one. The answer of the fleet was drawn up on board the flag-ship. It was enthusiastic and loyal. The first line of defence would do its duty. This was on the 15th of May, and in four days more the fleet gave a still more emphatic answer in the victory of La Hogue. Russel's

Mary writes to Admiral Russel.

fleet was the more powerful: it consisted of 99 ships of the line, of which 36 were Dutch. His own flag flew on board the *Britannia* of 100 guns, noticeable as the first ship of that name in the British navy: he had with him five other English admirals, including Sir Cloudesley Shovel and George Rooke. The Comte de Tourville had but 63 ships in all, and nearly 20 of these were detached on separate duty when he was sighted by the allies off Cape La Hogue on the morning of May 19th. In spite of the immense disproportion, the French admiral did not hesitate. As in the case of Torrington at Beachy Head, he had positive orders from his sovereign to fight, and he obeyed them to the letter. At 11.30 A.M. he laid his ship, the *Soleil Royal* of 106 guns, alongside the *Britannia*, and the two three-deckers pounded each other for an hour and a half, until the Frenchman, terribly battered by the far quicker fire of the English ship, towed off and managed in the calm and fog that ensued to escape for a time. Hindered by fogs and calms, unable to stem the fierce tide of the French coast, both fleets found it necessary again and again to anchor lest the ebb should sweep them off to the westward. The Dutch force hardly got into action at all: many of the Blue squadron never fired a shot; and Admiral Russel's division of 31 ships was the one on which the full force of the action fell. On the 22nd the *Soleil Royal* with two others ran ashore near Cherbourg, and all three were burned by Sir Ralph Delaval; 13 others, warped close in for safety at La Hogue, were destroyed by Vice-Admiral George Rooke under a heavy fire. Had it not been for the thick weather and baffling airs many more

Battle of La Hogue, 19th May 1692.

might have been taken or burned; but though Russel was acknowledged by the Admiralty to have done all that he possibly could in the face of such difficulties, there were many who blamed **him** for **not** having done more.

After La Hogue there was no more talk **of** invasion for some time. The first line of defence had nobly redeemed its pledge. The French now devoted their energies to cutting up our trade, which they did to a most serious extent; while, on our side, Commodore Benbow was ordered to rout out a swarm of privateers, who had their nest at St. Malo, and to destroy the hive. **This** he did with the aid of a prodigious fire-ship, **which he** sent in on the night of November 19th, and which, though she struck on a rock before reaching her proper destination, almost more than fulfilled the intentions of her designer. She was about 300 tons burden, contained 100 barrels of powder, covered with all sorts of combustibles of the fiercest kind, over which were heaped huge carcasses filled with bullets, chain-shot, short iron bars, the bottoms of glass bottles, etc. Her explosion was like the shock of an earthquake : 300 houses were unroofed; all glass and china within a radius of three leagues was broken; her capstan, weighing two cwt., was hurled over the walls, and wrecked a house **on** which it fell; and the seaward wall of the town was almost entirely demolished.

<small>Benbow's fire-ship at St. Malo, 1693.</small>

This was followed next year by a series of **attacks** upon the French coast. That on Brest failed, **with** such serious loss to ourselves as almost to amount to a disaster; but Dieppe was burned, and Havre **and** Calais were bombarded, a method of

Destroying the Ships after the Battle of La Hogue.

warfare which, repeated in 1696, effectually put a stop to a second scheme of invasion planned by Louis, and so sickened him of the war that in 1697 he signed the Treaty of Ryswick, and for a brief period peace reigned once more.

<small>Peace of Ryswick, 1697.</small>

The peace thus made was little more than a truce. Precautions had already been taken, in the event of the death of Charles II. of Spain, to prevent the whole of the vast possessions of the Spanish crown from falling into the power of Louis XIV. Twice he had been obliged to sign agreements, under the name of "Partition Treaties," framed with that object. But when, in 1700, Charles of Spain died and left his dominions to Louis' grandson Philip, the French King at once threw over the treaty and took possession. This in itself was enough to rouse the indignation and apprehension of the English; but when, a year later, swollen with pride at his vast increase of strength, he had the hardihood, on the death of James II., to proclaim his son as King of England, the anger of the nation boiled over and a renewal of the war was inevitable.

<small>Louis proclaims James III.</small>

But ere the war was proclaimed William of Orange died, and his throne was occupied by his sister-in-law Anne. This was in March 1702, and in May a Grand Alliance having been made by England, Austria, and Holland, the declaration of war was issued. The Duke of Marlborough ashore, and Sir George Rooke afloat, held the chief commands. The first efforts of the latter were directed against Cadiz, mindful possibly of Drake and his splendid exploits there. But now the defences of the Spanish port were found too strong; and Rooke was anxiously seeking for some exploit in which to

<small>Anne, 1702. War of the Spanish succession.</small>

employ his fine fleet of 50 ships, when intelligence reached him that 15 Spanish galleons laden with treasure and guarded by 18 French line-of-battle ships, were then lying in the harbour of Vigo. He at once made for that port which, after much delay from bad weather, he reached on the 11th October. The galleons and the French fleet were still there; but the difficulties of attack were immense. The narrow entrance to the port, three-quarters of a mile wide, was protected by 70 guns; at its inner end was a strong boom supported at each extremity by a line-of-battle ship; within, broadside on to the entrance, were five more ships of the line. Rooke's biggest ships drew too much water. He shifted his flag to a smaller one; his three junior admirals did the same. Troops were landed to take the town in the rear, and the ships of light draught, 25 in all, advanced. Vice-Admiral Hopson in the *Torbay* charged the boom under a cloud of canvas. It broke under the strain, the ships rushed in, but a hail of shot poured on to them from the ships and batteries on all sides. The *Torbay* was almost destroyed by a fire-ship which blew up alongside: the *Barfleur* was pierced through and through by the batteries; and many of our ships in the hottest of the fight often dared not return the fire of the forts lest their shot should injure the English soldiers ashore. Yet, at the end of the day 15 French line-of-battle ships and two frigates with all the galleons were either burned, sunk, or taken, and specie to the value of over £2,000,000 was ours, while much more was lying at the bottom of the harbour. This was a heavy blow to the French and Spaniards, and was

Rooke's victory at Vigo, 1702.

looked upon by us as a most auspicious opening to the war.

But the lustre which this action shed over the British navy hardly sufficed to remove the gloom caused by an incident almost without parallel in our service, but which, from that very reason, it is impossible to pass over unnoticed. In the West Indies, with orders to co-operate with the Spaniards against us, was the French admiral Du Casse with a squadron of four ships of the line and one frigate. Our force in those waters consisted of two ships of the line, one ship of 54 guns, and four large frigates, commanded by Vice-Admiral Benbow, who will be remembered as distinguishing himself in the previous war. Hearing that Du Casse and his squadron were cruising off Carthagena, Benbow immediately sailed to try and bring him to action. His force was superior in number of guns, and should have been able to inflict a disastrous defeat upon the Frenchman, but he was unaware of the deadly spirit of disloyalty which pervaded the minds of his officers; disloyalty, not to the sovereign under whose flag they sailed, but to their own admiral. It is suggested that Benbow was curt, imperious, harsh. Probably he was, for these were hard, rough times, especially afloat; but nothing can excuse the conduct of those who, bound at all times to obey him, were doubly bound in the presence of the enemy. The English squadron consisted of the flag-ship *Breda*, 70, Captain Fog; the *Defiance*, 64, Captain Kirby; the *Greenwich*, 54, Captain Wade; the *Ruby*, 48, Captain Walton; the *Pendennis*, 48, Captain Hudson; the *Windsor*, 48, Captain Constable; and the *Falmouth*, 48,

Benbow and Du Casse, 1702.

Captain Vincent. Each of these captains appears to have treacherously agreed to avoid an action with the enemy, in order that they might together vent their spite upon their brave but brusque commander. Even the captain of Benbow's own ship had given his consent to the plot, although his subsequent conduct went far to make amends for his crime, for such, in time of war, it was.

On August 19th, 1702, the enemy was sighted; but it was late, and night fell ere we came up with him. For a short time the *Defiance* and *Windsor* opened fire upon the French frigate, but on receiving his fire in return they both luffed up out of range. On the 20th at daybreak Benbow found himself very near the enemy, but totally unsupported save by the *Ruby*, whose captain, to his honour, had already repented him of his shameful pledge; the others were intentionally kept far astern. There was little wind, and the flag-ship and the frigate chased the enemy all that day and through the following night, until, on the 21st, Du Casse, seeing the rest so far off, turned upon the pair and furiously attacked them. The *Ruby* was very severely handled, but, aided and protected by the *Breda*, she boldly stood up to her powerful antagonists; yet, while these two were barely holding their own, the *Defiance* and *Windsor*, who had come up level with the rear ship of the enemy, never fired a shot. On the 22nd, owing to a shift of wind, Du Casse, who was, of course, unaware of the state of affairs in the English squadron, made good his retreat; but on the 23rd Benbow once more got within range, and exchanged broadsides with all the enemy's ships; indeed, he even recovered a small prize which the French had taken some time before. At this stage

Captain Vincent of the *Falmouth* appears to have been seized with remorse for his treachery, and to have come to the aid of his chief. But the *Ruby* was now so disabled that she was ordered to make the best of her way to Port Royal; and the brave Benbow continued the chase with the assistance of the *Falmouth*, the rest of his rebellious squadron still holding aloof. Daybreak on the 24th found him lying in a cot on the quarter-deck, his right leg horribly shattered by a chain-shot, a terrible wound in his face, another serious wound in his arm, hammering away at a 70-gun ship. Three times he had boarded her in person; her mizen-mast and rigging were gone, her mainyard shot away, her sides riven in all directions; but the rest of the enemy were bearing down on him with a strong breeze. Then, to the wounded admiral's shame and anger, the *Windsor*, the *Pendennis*, and the *Greenwich* came up, passed to leeward of the helpless Frenchman, and each pouring a broadside into her, bore away to the south; while the *Defiance*, who would have done the same, no sooner found by her fire that there was still some fight left in her than she put her helm hard up and fled dead before the wind. But now the other French ships bore down to the rescue, and pouring their broadsides into the *Breda*, took their disabled comrade in tow, leaving the flag-ship so shattered as to be unable to pursue. Yet sick at heart, and mortally wounded as he was, Benbow's magnificent courage and persistence never failed him. He ordered his ship to be re-fitted, the signal for pursuit to be hoisted, and messages to be sent to his cowardly captains to return instantly to their duty. It was to no effect.

Captain Kirby of the *Defiance* even had the shameless effrontery to come on board the *Breda*, to stand over the wounded form of his gallant admiral, and to tell him "that he had better desist, that the French were very strong, and that from what was past he might guess that he could make nothing of it." The other conspirators agreed, as Kirby said, that there was nothing to be done, and Benbow returned to Jamaica determined at least to do his one remaining and imperative duty ere he died. He called a court-martial for the trial of his treacherous subordinates. Only one conclusion was possible. All were found guilty; but the guilt of all was not equally grave. Fog and Vincent were suspended, but forgiven in consideration of their good conduct in the fight. Constable was cashiered and imprisoned during Her Majesty's pleasure. Hudson died a few days before the trial. Wade (who was proved to have been drunk the whole time) and Kirby, the instigator of the entire plot, were sentenced to be shot; they were sent home, and the warrant was carried out on board the *Bristol* at Plymouth. Shortly after justice had thus been done, the gallant Benbow died of his wounds, but not before he had received a letter from Du Casse himself which must have cheered his spirit by its honest and outspoken sympathy. It ran thus: —" Sir, I had little hopes on Monday last but to have supped in your cabin; but it pleased God to order it otherwise. I am thankful for it. As for those cowardly captains who deserted you, hang them up, for by God they deserve it.—Yours, DU CASSE."

The year 1703 is marked by no naval action of sufficient moment to be chronicled here, but it was

Great storm. Eddystone Lighthouse swept away. Admiral Beaumont lost, 1703.

closed by a storm of frightful fury, attended by the gravest disaster to the service and the country at large. It began shortly before midnight on November 26th. The tide rushed up the Thames with such violence as to flood Westminster Hall, and choke London Bridge with wrecks. The lighthouse on the dread Eddystone, the pride of Plymouth, built but five years before, was so completely destroyed that a piece of chain jammed between two rocks was the sole vestige that remained. Rear-Admiral Beaumont was lost on the Goodwins, with five ships, three of them with all hands, while of the admiral's crew of 269 but one man was saved. In all, 13 men-of-war and 1500 seamen perished. Sir Cloudesley Shovel, lying in the Downs, barely escaped the fate of Admiral Beaumont by cutting away his mainmast; while his second in command, Admiral Fairborne, was driven by the fury of the gale into the Baltic, and was for months returned as lost at sea.

The following year, however, was to add fresh laurels to our crown. Sir George Rooke still held the chief command in the Mediterranean, and, finding himself unable to bring the Toulon fleet to action, he concocted with Sir Cloudesley Shovel the audacious idea of making an unexpected attack on Gibraltar. The great Spanish rock had always been regarded as impregnable. This reputation proved its ruin; for when, on July 21st, the British and Dutch fleet, 60 ships in all, sailed into the bay, the garrison had been so reduced in order to fill up vacancies in the Spanish army in the field, that there were barely men enough for the daily change of guards. Rooke, however, was fully prepared to find it swarming with troops, and had made his

Sir G. Rooke takes Gibraltar, 1704.

arrangements accordingly. He landed a force of 1800 men to cut off the rock from the mainland, and then summoned the place to surrender. Don Diego de Salinas boldly refused. The attack began on July 23rd with so furious a cannonade that in five hours 15,000 shot had been fired into the place. Under such a storm the Spaniards were unable to hold their position on the South Molehead, and when this was observed, a landing party was at once sent in to take possession of that point. But the Spanish defence was not yet exhausted. The first who landed, pushing eagerly forward, rushed into the battery only to be instantly blown to pieces by the explosion of a mine beneath them. But others quickly followed, and when a strong redoubt between the mole and the town had fallen into our hands the Governor, painfully aware of his own weakness, surrendered, and Gibraltar the impregnable was ours. Once more it was demonstrated that no place can be regarded as impregnable of itself; that it is only the proper use of great natural advantages by courage and intelligence that can make it so; and that perhaps the most fatal thing for a great fortress is that there should settle down upon it that deadly slumberous confidence which springs from the word "impregnable." But if ever a place seemed worthy of the name to those who now had taken it, it was this same Gibraltar; for threading its winding passages and steep ascents, and viewing its vast and bristling batteries, our officers declared that 50 men might have held it against a host.

Ere another month had passed away, Rooke had accomplished the wish of his heart; he had at last met the great Toulon fleet, and had defeated it.

Rooke's victory off Malaga, 1704.

The French fleet, under the Comte de Toulouse, was sighted on August 9th, its strength consisting of 50 ships of the line and 24 galleys, and was chased by our fleet of 53 vessels until the morning of Sunday the 13th, when they hove to off Malaga and waited for us. The *Royal Katherine*, Rooke's flag-ship, the *St. George*, and the *Shrewsbury* led the way into the enemy's line, suffering much from his concentrated fire, but backed up by the other vessels as they came on, firing with a rapidity which the French found it impossible to imitate. The fight lasted from about 10 A.M. until dark, when the enemy retreated, and could not again be induced to renew the action. Superior in actual numbers, they had also a great advantage in their galleys, which moved rapidly about supplying their disabled ships with fresh crews or towing them away into safety. As to the number of ships destroyed there is no agreement. The French deny that they lost any, and assert that two of ours sank; but at the end of the day we had the same number of ships as at 10 A.M., while five of their vessels never again entered a French port. It is a fact that Louis ordered a Te Deum to be sung in public thanksgiving, and that a medal was struck commemorating the "Defeat of the English and Dutch fleets off Malaga." But it is also a fact that Louis never again sent a large French fleet to sea.

Attempts to retake Gibraltar, 1704, 1705.

But neither Spaniards nor French were content to acquiesce quietly in our possession of Gibraltar. Twice, in 1704 and 1705, they made strenuous efforts to retake it; twice it was in most imminent peril; twice Sir John Leake came gallantly to its rescue and drove them off. We say Sir John Leake, for Sir George Rooke had gone home after his triumph at Malaga and had been received by the country as a hero; but, being made the victim of political jealousy, had been removed from his command, and was never again employed. His place in the Mediterranean was taken by the ill-fated Sir Cloudesley Shovel, but, as has been said before, no fleet was sent out to meet him on the high sea. Shovel turned his attention therefore to the coasts of France and Spain, reduced Barcelona, and even bombarded Toulon, which place might have fallen into our hands but for the ineffective co-operation of the land-forces. This was in July 1707. Shortly afterwards he sailed for home with about 20 ships and sighted, as he thought, St. Agnes light at a safe distance on the evening of October 22nd. But some one had made a terrible mistake. That night his ship, the *Association*, struck upon a rock, was rolled over by the very next wave, and was never seen again. The *Eagle*, *Romney*, and *Firebrand* shared the same fate; the *St. George* struck, but was lifted off by the same wave that overwhelmed the flag-ship; the remainder with difficulty escaped. The admiral's body was washed up on the shore next day and buried with great ceremony in Westminster Abbey.

Loss of Sir Cloudesley Shovel, 1707.

Sir John Leake now commanded in the Straits, and ably filled so important a post. His principal exploit was the capture of Minorca, which with its valuable harbour of Port Mahon remained ours until 1782.

Of the minor but no less daring actions in different parts of the globe it is impossible to give a description. Yet it is with genuine regret that we omit the story of how Commodore Wager fought

Du Casse in the West Indies; of Whitaker and Norris in the Mediterranean; of Lord Dursley in the Channel; of Riddell's gallant fight in defence of his convoy; and of many another brave seaman whose deeds must be read elsewhere, for the space of this work is necessarily limited. Yet there is one story which must be told in few words as an instance of how British seamen could do their duty in the face of desperate odds and certain defeat; how they could die at their post uncheered by shouts of victory, but upheld by the consciousness of having done what their country demanded of them. Of all the foes who marked down our commerce as their prey (and there were many such), none were so active, enterprising, and skilful as the Count de Forbin and M. Duguai Trouin. Again and again they had swept off rich prizes of merchantmen returning home with loaded holds; again and again they had been sought and chased, but without avail, and their names were names of terror all over the Channel and its approaches. So great was the fear of them and of the host of other but less daring imitators, that merchant ships dared not leave our coasts except when collected in large numbers under a strong convoy. It is true that the large numbers offered the richer prize, but the protecting force was not lightly to be disregarded. Such a fleet of merchantmen, to the number of 130, sailed on October 9th, 1707, for Lisbon, under the protection of the *Cumberland*, 80 guns, the *Devonshire*, 80 guns, the *Royal Oak*, 76 guns, and the *Chester* and *Ruby* of 50 guns each. The very day after their departure they sailed right into the jaws of MM. de Forbin and Duguai Trouin, who, combining their

Duguai Trouin attacks an English convoy, 1707.

forces, were holding the mouth of the Channel with a fleet of 12 line-of-battle ships. Signalling the merchant fleet to disperse, the *Cumberland* and her four consorts unhesitatingly engaged the overwhelming enemy. The battle began about noon. The *Cumberland*, overpowered by three other vessels, was at length boarded and taken; the *Devonshire*, at one time engaging seven of the enemy and battling till evening against five of them, caught fire and blew up, only two of her 900 men escaping; the *Chester* and the *Ruby* were captured; the *Royal Oak*, after setting one of her opponents on fire, with difficulty escaped into Kinsale. But their task was done; their duty had been carried out to the letter; the entire merchant fleet reached Lisbon in safety.

In 1711 the Emperor of Austria died, and the Archduke Charles, whose claim to the Spanish throne we were then supporting against the pretensions of France, succeeded him. This caused further troubles, for the combination of Spain and Austria under one crown was as undesirable as that of Spain and France. Everything pointed to a settlement by peaceful means; all were weary of the war, and at length the Peace of Utrecht in 1713 brought the struggle to an end. A division of the Spanish possessions was arranged with some show of agreement, and England emerged from the conflict with the prizes of Gibraltar and Minorca, with Nova Scotia and Newfoundland, and with the proud position of the acknowledged mistress of the sea.

<small>Peace of Utrecht, 1713.</small>

CHAPTER VIII

George I.—The "Fifteen"—A Spanish fleet seizes Palermo—Admiral Byng's victory off Cape Passaro—George II.—Jenkins's ear—Admiral Vernon at Porto Bello—Failure at Carthagena and Santiago—Anson takes the great galleon—Matthews and Lestock off Toulon—Loss of the *Victory*—The "Forty-Five"—*Lion* and *Elizabeth*—Anson off Finisterre—Hawke off Brest—Peace of Aix-la-Chapelle—Braddock's defeat and death—The Seven Years' War—French attack Minorca—Byng sent to relieve it—Byng fights and abandons it—Execution of Byng—Attacks on French coast—French prepare to invade—Rodney at Havre—Boscawen and de la Clue off Lagos—Hawke and Conflans in Quiberon Bay—Elliot and Thurot off Isle of Man—George III.—Belleisle taken—Spain makes war—*Hermione* taken—The Havana taken by Pocock—Manila taken—The *Santisima Trinidad* taken.

George I., 1714.

THE death of Queen Anne in less than eighteen months after the Treaty of Utrecht had been signed once more placed the country in jeopardy. The succession passed by Act of Parliament to George of Hanover, who was at once proclaimed King. But to the devoted partisans of the Stuarts and to all who had reason to be discontented with the existing government, this seemed a providential opportunity for a general rising, to be followed by the restoration of the old Monarchy. When the Tories found themselves turned out of office, when the Whigs scattered impeachments right and left among their leaders, when the Court teemed with Hanoverian nobles whose language and manners were equally offensive to us, when the King himself shared the unpopularity of his countrymen, it was no matter of wonder that many an old family, especially in Scotland and the north, rushed to arms for James III. But from the Pretender downwards all the Jacobite leaders seem to have been singularly incapable. He himself only came to Scotland after the battle of Sheriffmuir had been fought and lost; and only escaped from the fleet, which was keenly watching for him on his return, by embarking at Montrose in a "clean tallowed French snow," whose small size and shallow draught enabled her to hug the coast and avoid the heavier vessels in pursuit of her.

First Jacobite Rising, 1715.

As in the days of Elizabeth, though outwardly at peace with Spain, the mutual feeling of hostility between ourselves and that country was very great. At last when Philip V., deeply dissatisfied with the partition of Spanish territory, and urged on by his minister Alberoni, a man of boundless ambition, suddenly, without any warning, seized Sardinia by force, and fitted out a vast naval and military expedition against Sicily, we felt it our duty to interfere, and at once ordered Admiral Byng with a powerful fleet into the Mediterranean. There was no declaration of war on our side; again and again we urged Philip to pause; again and again we warned him of our intentions should he proceed. He took no notice. The Spanish fleet, 29 men-of-war escorting 35,000 troops, attacked Sicily, took Palermo, and proceeded to besiege Messina. Off that town Byng shortly afterwards arrived, made one more attempt to stay the proceedings, and finding his efforts disdained, made a determined attack on the Spanish fleet off

Philip V. of Spain attacks Sicily.

Battle off Cape Passaro, 11th August 1718.

Cape Passaro on August 11th, 1718. His own force, 21 ships of the line, was inferior in point of numbers, but superior in guns, in seamanship, and in discipline. The result of the action was such as might have been expected. Don Antonio de Castaneta and two other admirals were taken with their flagships; in all, out of the 29 vessels which composed the Spanish fleet, 13 were taken at the time, three were burnt, and four others, which had escaped for the moment, were either captured or sunk shortly after. This was our last fight with a great Spanish fleet for many years to come; indeed, it was not until the year 1797 that we again encountered them in any great force at sea. The ill-feeling between Spain and England was naturally not abated by the battle off Cape Passaro, and though there was still no declaration of war, English and Spaniards fought and worried each other wherever opportunity offered. In 1726 Philip made another effort to regain Gibraltar; but it was to no purpose, and his 20,000 troops were driven away by Sir Charles Wager ere they could attempt a landing.

In 1727 George I. was succeeded by his son George II., and two years afterwards Philip was induced to sign a treaty of peace at Seville. But peace between two governments does not necessarily imply a similar feeling between their respective countries. Contempt for their broken power led our traders and adventurers at sea to set aside their fiscal regulations, to carry on a wholesale system of smuggling, and even at times to resort to violence.

Episode of Jenkins's ear, 1738.

Quarrels and reprisals were frequent, and when at last one Jenkins, a merchant captain, appeared before the House of Commons with his head swathed in bandages, and with a box in his hand which was understood to contain his ear, cut off by a Spanish officer with the remark that he would like to serve his Majesty in the same manner, the nation clamoured loudly and excitedly for a renewal of the war. Walpole, the Prime Minister, was powerless to stem the tide of popular feeling, and in 1739 war was declared; a war entered into with the highest enthusiasm by the nation, and conducted by the Government with feverish but ill-directed energy. Dazzled and carried away by a bombastic speech made in the House of Commons by a Captain Vernon, whose sole claim to consideration seems to have rested on the fact that he was a member of Parliament with a loud and overbearing manner, the Government passed over their tried and trusty officers, promoted Vernon at once to the rank of vice-admiral, and gave him command of a squadron with orders to sail at once and carry havoc among the Spanish possessions in South America. His first aim was Porto Bello, a place of such exceptional strength as to be regarded as almost impregnable. Luck favoured him. He himself carried thither the first tidings of the war. The Spaniards were taken by surprise; the forts were only half-armed; the garrison was scanty, ammunition was wanting; and the place surrendered after a short bombardment with a loss to us of seven men! Enthusiasm rose to the highest pitch. Never had we had such an admiral as Vernon! Reinforcements were hurried out to him, till 124 ships (men-of-war and transports) and 12,000 troops swelled his force. Then the bubble burst. He brought his huge array before Cartagena but, swollen with conceit, impatient of advice, and incapable of organisation, he grossly

Vernon takes Porto Bello, 1739.

Vernon fails at Cartagena and Santiago, 1741.

misconducted the attack, neglected his opportunities, pressed on where he should have waited, hesitated where he should have acted, quarrelled bitterly with the general in command of the troops, thwarted him in every imaginable way, viciously denied him food and water, and at length drew off his armament to Jamaica, having accomplished absolutely nothing. An attack on Santiago de Cuba ended in an even more miserable fiasco, and Vernon returned disgraced to England, where, after an acrimonious correspondence with the Admiralty, his name was removed from the navy list.

But this was not the only expedition which we had sent out to prey upon the Spanish colonies. Vernon's object was the Atlantic shore of South America; a second squadron was to carry war into the Pacific. In the choice of a commander the Government made an admirable selection, Commodore George Anson, in every way a complete contrast to Vernon; in their choice of material with which to supply him they did all in their power to negative his excellence. They gave him six ships: the *Centurion*, of 60 guns; two of 50 guns, one of 40, one of 28, and lastly, one of eight guns! This last was called the *Trial*, a singularly appropriate name as it proved. These, we must remember, were to weather the dreaded Horn and the storms of the falsely named Pacific, and to face the power of Spain in waters far removed from any friendly help. The crews of this squadron were composed principally of invalids from Chelsea Hospital, including one veteran of some seventy years of age who had been wounded fifty years before at the Battle of the Boyne. Half

Anson sent to the Pacific, 1740.

of this feeble crew deserted ere the ships sailed. Even in the time of despatching the expedition the authorities were singularly ill-advised, for it started on September 18th, 1740, plunged at once into the thick of the equinoctial gales, and when, after unusual hardships and perils, Anson arrived on his station, the *Centurion* was alone. Alone she reached the island of Juan Fernandez on June 9th, 1741, and when with great difficulty she made the anchorage, she had eight men fit for duty. Next day, however, she was joined by the little *Trial*, and, eleven days later, the *Gloucester*, of 50 guns, hove in sight, but so scurvy-stricken was the miserable remnant of her crew, of whom two-thirds had been already committed to the deep, that *she was one month from the day on which she was sighted before she reached the anchorage*. When at length Anson was ready to sail once more, out of 961 men who had formed the crews of the squadron, only 335 remained. Again he put to sea, but soon had to destroy the *Trial* as utterly rotten. With his two remaining ships he took several rich prizes and plundered the coast of Peru. Again disaster overtook him. On July 26th, 1742, the *Gloucester* was dismasted in a gale, sprang a dangerous leak, and shared the fate of the *Trial*. The *Centurion* now alone, leaking at every seam, with her rigging rotten, her spars sprung, and her crew perishing of scurvy " in heaps," bore away for the Ladrones, and barely managed to reach Tinian, the largest of the group. But Anson's troubles were by no means over. While he himself and the weakest of the sick were on shore for the recovery of their health, a terrific storm burst upon them in the night, and when the morning dawned the *Centurion* was gone. For nineteen days Anson and his invalids regarded her as lost, when to their inexpressible delight she once more hove in sight, and at last came to an anchor. The storm had carried away her cables and driven her far out to sea. Again he sailed,—to hurry home as best he might with his coffin ship and his scarecrow crew? No, to make a last effort to attain the great object which he had in view all the miserable time,—to seize the Spanish treasure-ship, the great galleon *Nuestra Señora de Cobadonga*, which he well knew had sailed from Acapulco on the Mexican coast for Manila in the Philippines. Getting with great difficulty some sort of a refit at Macao on the coast of China, he once more stood out to sea, and on June 20th, 1743, to the delight of all, he sighted the great galleon. She carried 550 men to his miserable remnant of 201 all told; she mounted 70 guns, great and small, to his 60, and she meant fighting. But he placed himself across her bows at twenty yards off, and raked her incessantly with a fierceness of fire that she could not attempt to equal, until her flag fluttered down and she surrendered. The prize for which he had endured three years of untold misery was his at last. But even as the cheers of his men were ringing in his ears, and congratulations were being showered on him by his officers, the ominous cry was raised that the *Centurion* herself was on fire, and that the fire was close to the magazine. It seemed as if all were lost; but again Anson's courage and presence of mind prevailed, and this last great danger was averted. In the hold of the galleon wealth to the

Margin: Anson takes the great galleon, 1743.

amount of over one million and a quarter pounds sterling was found, and transferred to the already richly laden *Centurion*, the prize herself being sold in Canton. At length Anson turned his weather-beaten bow homewards. On June 15th, 1744, after sailing, unknown to himself and them, right through the French fleet in a fog at the mouth of the Channel, he dropped anchor with all his vast accumulation of treasure at Spithead, to be welcomed and honoured like his great predecessor Drake by the acclamations of the entire nation.

While Vernon with all the resources of the nation at his command was bringing disgrace upon our flag in the West Indies, and Anson with his meagre force in the Pacific was enriching the Treasury and covering himself with renown, a large English fleet of 28 line-of-battle ships, under Admirals Matthews and Lestock, was anxiously watching the movements of a combined French and Spanish fleet of equal force, which, under the command of Admiral de Court, was lying in the port of Toulon. On February 8th, 1744, this combined fleet sailed, followed at once by Matthews with the signal to engage the enemy flying at his mast-head. But between Matthews and Lestock there was bitter enmity, and the latter appears to have determined on much the same course of action as that of Kirby and Wade towards Benbow. He disregarded his superior's signal, and did not even take the trouble to repeat it to his squadron. Thus, when on February 11th Admiral Rowley in our van was abreast of the enemy's centre and Matthews himself came up with their rear, Lestock and his squadron were miles astern. Nevertheless, a fierce

Matthews and Lestock off Toulon, 1744.

engagement took place, in which many of our ships were most severely handled. The *Marlborough* was almost reduced to a wreck; the *Namur*, Matthews' flag-ship, was so mauled as to make it necessary for him to shift his flag to the *Russel*. On the other hand, the Spanish flag-ship *El Real Felipe*, of 114 guns, after narrowly escaping destruction by one of our fire-ships, was so utterly crippled as to be forced to be taken in tow by one of her comrades: the *Poder*, of 60 guns, struck her flag to Captain Hawke, and was taken possession of, only to be retaken by the enemy before the close of the day; but not for long, for on the renewal of the chase the next morning she once more fell into our hands, abandoned and on fire. And still Lestock was far astern and making no effort to get into action. Had it not been for his conduct it is certain that a great victory would have crowned our efforts. Yet, when the matter was brought to trial, the gross injustice of political party-feeling, as previously exemplified in the case of Sir George Rooke, was once more demonstrated. Matthews was a member of Parliament, voting, unfortunately for him, on the side of the Opposition; his fate, therefore, in those unscrupulous and corrupt times, was sealed. He was actually cashiered, and his name removed from the navy list; while Lestock, who had never fired a shot, and who should have shared the fate of Kirby and Wade, was honourably acquitted, and was soon after given another command only to behave before Lorient two years later in a similar manner.

At last, in March 1744, war was openly declared between France and England, but no great naval event followed on the declaration. Indeed, the only naval incident worthy of record in the remainder of this year is the terrible disaster to the fleet of Admiral Sir John Balchen in the Bay of Biscay in the month of October. On the 3rd of that month the admiral and his fleet, on their voyage home, were overtaken by a frightful storm, which drove the scattered ships in all directions. The *Exeter* with main and mizen masts gone, only saved herself from foundering by throwing some of her guns overboard; the *Duke*, with every sail blown to rags, lay wallowing in the trough of the sea with ten feet of water in her hold; but the *Victory*, said to be the finest line-of-battle ship in the world, with 110 guns, with 1100 seamen, and with one of the best admirals in the British service, was never seen again. She is supposed to have struck upon the Caskets off Alderney, but no certain information as to her fate was ever obtained.

<small>Loss of Admiral Balchen in the *Victory*, 1744.</small>

The year 1745 is ever remembered as that of the last Jacobite Rebellion. As in "the Fifteen" it was French aid that made it possible, and it was a French frigate, the *Doutelle*, which landed Prince Charlie on the shore of the Western Highlands. But ere she reached that point she and her consort the *Elizabeth*, of 64 guns, had a narrow escape from capture by Captain Brett, who, in the *Lion*, of 58 guns, fought the *Elizabeth* for five hours, and finally drove her to seek refuge on the coast of France.

<small>Second Jacobite Rebellion, 1745.</small>

But it was not only in Europe that we had to encounter the enemy. India and America were each in turn the scene of conflicts between the rival forces; and in 1747 the French fitted out at Brest a squadron, half of which was to reinforce their arms on the coasts of Nova Scotia and Newfoundland, while the other part was to assist the efforts of Labourdonnais and Dupleix in India. In order to render their errand impossible, Admirals Anson and Warren were ordered to lie in wait for them and intercept them at the very commencement of their voyage. This duty they ably carried out, and on May 3rd, 1747, they met them off Cape Finisterre apparently in strong force. The greater part of the ships, however, were store ships, and of the 38 sail at first reported, only nine reduced their canvas and prepared to fight. Of these nine, only five were of the line, the others consisting of frigates; and it is no matter of wonder that at the end of the action every French ship engaged was taken and the two admirals were prisoners in our hands. They had, however, made a gallant resistance, fighting for three hours, and losing 700 men, but in that three hours' fight securing the safety of all but two of their convoy. Still the blow to France must have been heavy, since, in addition to loss of the ships themselves, it required a train of twenty waggons to carry the money found in the prizes to the city of London.

Anson's victory off Finisterre, 1747.

Again a French armament sailed from Brest, this time for the West Indies; 250 ships of commerce protected by nine line-of-battle ships and some frigates, under the flag of Admiral de l'Etendeur. Again an English fleet swept down on them, 14 ships of the line under the command of Admiral Hawke, whose flag flew in the *Devonshire*, 66. They overtook their quarry some distance off Brest on October 14th, and the French admiral at once gallantly prepared to protect his valuable convoy.

Hawke's Victory off Brest, 1747.

He had more reasonable hope of success than might at first appear, for though his vessels numbered only nine to our 14, most of them were individually far superior in size and guns to ours. Still, the result of the action was never a matter of doubt. At the close of the day M. de l'Etendeur, with only one ship remaining besides his flag-ship, made good his escape and that of his huge convoy, at the cost of seven ships of the line, leaving us so crippled as to be totally incapable of pursuit for many hours.

A curious instance of the uncertainty of justice comes in here. Three years before this Lestock was tried by court-martial for disobedience of orders. The same fate now overtook Captain Fox of the *Kent*. Lestock, suspected of cowardice, had never fired a shot. Fox had taken an enemy's ship of equal size, while his own ship was knocked to pieces. Lestock was honourably acquitted. Fox was dismissed his ship. Yet it was proved that he had been utterly misled in the matter by the positive assertions of two of his officers. His offence consisted in "not relying upon his own judgment"!

This was practically the end of the war; but news travelled slowly in those days, and Admiral Boscawen on the Coromandel coast and Admiral Knowles in the West Indies were still carrying on active operations with no very brilliant success, when the Peace of Aix-la-Chapelle in October 1748 brought hostilities once more to an end. There was but little breathing space ere the commencement of the next war; for it is to be noticed that from the war of the Austrian Succession to the year 1815, the periods of peace which we enjoyed were but as it were a few minutes' interval in which to

Peace of Aix-la-Chapelle, 1748.

snatch a hurried rest before commencing the struggle afresh. As a curious instance of a calculation in profit and loss resulting from this war, Dr. Campbell mentions that during its continuance we took from the French 2185 vessels of all classes, from the Spaniards 1249 vessels, while our own losses to both nations were 3238, leaving us a meagre margin of 96 prizes to the good!

As has been already said the Peace of Aix-la-Chapelle proved to be merely a short breathing space ere the war broke out again with greater violence than ever. The causes, however, were very different. In the far East and in the West a silent rivalry was going on between France and England. In India the French and English East India Companies, watching each other with jealous eyes, espoused, unsupported by their respective governments, the rival claims of native chiefs to the sovereignty of the Karnatic, and were actually in arms against each other, while the parent countries were at peace. In America the French and English colonists, equally jealous of each other, were also in a state of hostility over the ill-defined limits of their territories. But such a state of things could not long continue without interference from Europe. When General Braddock, sent by the Duke of Newcastle to attack the French frontier forts, was surrounded and killed in 1755, hostilities between the two great naval Powers of Europe could no longer be avoided, and in 1756 war was once more openly declared. The movements of a large fleet sent by the French to North American waters were checked by an English fleet of slightly superior force, without any great engagement being fought;

Defeat of General Braddock, 1755.

Seven years' war begins, 1756.

but it was in European waters that the French proposed to make their greatest effort.

The presence of the English in the Mediterranean was resented by the French and Spaniards alike. We had no right there; we were altogether intruders; we had not an acre of British soil, properly so called, within the confines of the Mediterranean; our possession of Gibraltar was an impertinence; our retention of Minorca was an outrage. To the recapture of this latter place, therefore, the French determined to devote their whole energy. In order to divert our attention from their real object, they made it appear that their purpose was to invade our shores; while at Toulon a powerful fleet under M. de la Galissoniere was being equipped with all speed, to make a descent upon our latest Mediterranean stronghold in co-operation with a large military force.

Not until too late did we learn the true aim of the expedition. Then, in all haste, Admiral Byng was sent out from England to frustrate the attack, in command of a fleet badly equipped, poorly manned, and incompletely furnished with stores. Arriving at Gibraltar he learned from an English frigate that the French fleet of 12 ships of the line with 16,000 troops was already besieging Port Mahon. When he reached that place on May 19th, 1756, the French bomb vessels were actively playing on the defences, which were held by a garrison of but 3000 men, commanded by General Blakeney, a veteran eighty-two years of age. The port had been barred by ships sunk across the channel. Nominally the two fleets were equal, each consisting of 12 line-of-battle ships; but the French were superior to us by 24 guns and by 2600 men. On May 20th

Admiral Byng sent to protect Minorca.

Byng and La Galissoniere off Minorca, 1756.

Byng, with the advantage of the wind, bore down upon the enemy, apparently determined to do or die. Admiral West, the second in command, was far ahead of his chief, and opened the fight with great vigour and effect, throwing the French line into confusion and inflicting, as also receiving, considerable damage. Had Byng acted with equal energy a great victory had assuredly been ours; but he was easily daunted. One of West's division, the *Intrepid*, becoming disabled, drifted down on Byng's advancing line and threw it into some disorder, thereby giving M. de la Galissoniere an opportunity of retreat, of which he immediately availed himself. This alone should have inspired Byng to press on, but he did nothing of the kind. Finding three of his ships badly damaged, he laid to and called a council of war. The very fact of calling such a council proves indecision, and it is rarely that it advocates determined measures. It will be remembered that just one year later, Clive on the eve of Plassey called his first and only council of war; that it strongly condemned the idea of fighting against such enormous odds, that Clive announced his entire concurrence with its decision, that nevertheless he fought next day and gained the greatest victory which has ever been won on Indian soil. The decision of Byng's council strikes us now as almost incredible. It resolved, "That an attack on the French fleet would not relieve Minorca; that even were there no French fleet they could not help the garrison; that any accident to the English fleet would imperil Gibraltar; that Gibraltar would be endangered if, in their present state, they attacked the French fleet at all; and that they ought at once to sail to Gibraltar." Accordingly to Gibraltar they sailed and left Minorca, its 3000 troops, and its veteran general to their fate. For more than a month Blakeney held out hoping against hope, and at last, on June 29th, he surrendered. Then the national indignation rose beyond all bounds. Byng and West were superseded, and ordered home to be tried by court-martial. When West's gallant conduct in the fight became known general opinion exonerated him from a share in the blame; but upon Byng the whole weight of popular odium fell with crushing force. The people clamoured loudly and ceaselessly for his death; and Newcastle, fearing lest the rage of the populace might turn against himself, promised that he should be immediately hanged. The trial was in many ways a shameful one, for Byng's despatches were altered and garbled lest Ministers also should incur blame for the failure; yet in the end Byng was acquitted of cowardice and found guilty simply of an "error in judgment." Nevertheless the sentence of the court was death, though he was strongly recommended to mercy. By this time a revulsion of feeling had set in, and Byng's sympathisers were many. The King was petitioned to pardon the unfortunate officer, but the King was inexorable. In spite of appeals from men of all parties, in spite of the recommendation of the court, of the testimony of West, of the decision of the council of war, of the full concurrence in that decision of the garrison at Gibraltar, Byng's sentence was carried out, and he was shot on board the *Monarch* at Portsmouth on March 14th, 1757.

Minorca surrenders.

Byng shot, 14th March 1757.

Byng's vacant place was taken by Hawke, but the war degenerated for a while into a series of attacks by combined naval and military forces on various portions of the enemy's coast, attacks stigmatised by Fox as "breaking windows with guineas," so much did the expense of the expedition exceed the damage to the foe. In some of these, however, we were eminently successful, as when, in April 1758, Hawke attacked Rochefort, took the isle of Aix, and forced the French squadron to heave their guns overboard and run ashore; or when in August of the same year Howe totally destroyed Cherbourg. Others again through shameful mismanagement ended in disaster, as when in September 1758 we were driven off with loss at St. Malo. Far away, however, on the other side of the oceans, Watson and Pocock in the East, Forrest and Suckling in the West Indies were gallantly upholding the honour of the British flag. Now, too, was born, in an obscure Norfolk parsonage, Horatio Nelson, the nephew of that very Captain Suckling whom we have just mentioned, and whose great action in the West Indies was fought on the 21st of October 1757, anticipating thereby the date of the triumphant victory of his brilliant nephew then unborn.

Nelson born, 29th September 1758.

But in 1759 the war entered on another and more acute phase. The invasion of England was determined on by the French, not now as a blind for an attack in some other quarter, but in deep and vengeful earnest. A large military force was concentrated at Havre in readiness to embark at any moment. The Toulon fleet of 12 line-of-battle ships under Admiral de la Clue, the Brest fleet of 21 ships of the line under Admiral Conflans, were to act in concert, were to unite, to sweep the Channel, to convoy the troops across, to cover the

France proposes to invade, 1759.

landing; while M. Thurot, with a squadron of frigates at Dunkirk, was to watch his opportunity to make a similar landing in Scotland or Ireland. That was the French view of the situation. Let us look at our side of the question. Close outside Brest Hawke was patrolling with 23 ships of the line; off Toulon, with 14, lay Boscawen eagerly watching to pounce down on M. de la Clue; off Dunkirk hovered Commodore Boys with a squadron of frigates; and neither French fleet dared to put to sea. In the meanwhile Admiral Rodney with five ships of the line and five frigates entered the port of Havre, bombarded the fortifications, sunk the transports, burned the flat boats, destroyed the stores, and set fire to the town itself, carrying consternation and dismay among the troops assembled there. In vain, however, did Boscawen try to tempt De la Clue to come out of his lair at Toulon and fight him in the open. In despair he even tried to force him out by making an attack with part of his fleet upon vessels inside the harbour mouth; but met with such damage himself as to force him to retire to Gibraltar for repair. Well was it for him that we had such a shelter to retire to, otherwise Plymouth Sound, 1500 miles away, would have offered the nearest harbour, and the dreaded junction between De la Clue and Conflans might possibly have taken place. But while repairing at Gibraltar Boscawen kept two frigates cruising in the Straits; nothing could pass in or out without their knowledge, and Gibraltar itself was close at hand. So it happened that on August 17th one of the frigates ran in with the signal flying "enemy in sight"; De la Clue had slipped out of Toulon and hoped to pass the

Rodney bombards Havre, 1759.

Straits unobserved. Boscawen lost not a moment; he at once weighed and went in hot pursuit. De la Clue was unfortunate; five of his ships either through fear or error made for Cadiz, and when Boscawen caught him up on August 18th off Lagos, he had only seven ships of the line with him. Nevertheless he made a gallant fight. Boscawen in the *Namur* was so severely handled by the French admiral in the *Océan*, that he was forced to shift his flag to the *Newark*, while De la Clue took advantage of the pause to escape to the shelter of the Portuguese coast. Here he himself, badly wounded, was carried on shore, but his ship was burned; the *Redoutable* shared the same fate; three other ships of the line were taken; and the junction of the two French fleets was rendered impossible.

<small>Boscawen and De la Clue off Lagos, 1759.</small>

Meanwhile with equal vigilance Hawke was keeping guard off Brest; but Conflans had no more intention of coming out to fight than had De la Clue at Toulon. From May till November Hawke hovered round the port, but the Frenchman made no move; then a great gale of wind sprang up, and Hawke, driven off to get sea-room, was forced into Plymouth. When, on the weather moderating, he again sailed for Brest, a frigate signalled him that Conflans had escaped. He at once divined his intention. A large convoy was at Quiberon: Conflans had gone to protect it; and with every stitch of canvas set to an ever-increasing wind, Hawke swooped down after his quarry. His instinct was correct; he found the French fleet chasing a small squadron of British frigates, which were watching the merchant ships with hostile intent. Conflans, on finding himself pursued, abandoned the chase, and, dashing in among the rocks and shoals to the south of Belleisle, sought to lead his enemy among dangers which none but French pilots, as he thought, would dare to face. But Hawke was not the man to be daunted; though he was now upon a lee shore, though the wind had risen to a gale, and though he was fully aware of the terrible risk which he ran, he considered that where French ships could go British ships could follow. His own pilot remonstrated, but Hawke silenced him. "You have done your duty in pointing out the danger; you are now to obey my commands and lay me alongside of the *Soleil Royal*." This was done; but ere the *Royal George* could range up alongside the French flag-ship, the *Thésée*, a French 74, interposed to protect her admiral. She almost immediately foundered, either from the effect of a single broadside from the British three-decker, or swamped by a mountainous sea which rushed into her lower deck ports. The *Superbe*, of 70 guns, also foundered in the heavy sea: the *Héros* and the *Formidable* surrendered, the latter with not one single officer left on board alive; and, night coming on, Hawke anchored under the lee of Dumet Island full of anxiety for the safety of his fleet. All night long he lay rolling and wallowing at his anchors, surrounded on all sides by rocks and shoals, the wind howling through his rigging, minute-guns booming and flashing through the roar and darkness of the gale, not knowing who it might be in distress, whether friend or foe, or whether his own turn might not come next. When morning dawned his fears were realised. The *Héros*, taken the day before, and the French flag-ship were ashore on one bank:

Hawke and Conflans in Quiberon Bay, 1759.

on another the *Resolution*, a British 74, was hopelessly wrecked; and the *Essex*, 64, going to her assistance, only shared her fate. The two French ships were burned; the two English ones were knocked to pieces, but the greater part of their men were rescued. The remainder of the French fleet, throwing all their guns overboard, fled up the river Vilaine as far as they could possibly reach in their lightened condition, and were there run ashore with such good will that, with the exception of three, they could never afterwards be got off, and were broken up by their own people. Thus the second and larger of the two fleets for the invasion of England was in its turn destroyed; a further proof, if proof were still required, that the defence of an island consists in never permitting the enemy to reach its shores.

But there was still Thurot's squadron to be reckoned with. On the same day that Conflans escaped from Brest, Thurot slipped out of Dunkirk; but he was so hotly pursued by Boys that he fled into the Baltic, and it was some time ere he dared to emerge from its shelter. After all, of the three French expeditions, his had the largest share of success and the most complete defeat. Early in the year 1760 he effected a landing in Ireland, and actually took the town of Carrickfergus, forcing the garrison to surrender; but, a few hours afterwards, encountering Captain Elliot with an equal number of frigates off the Isle of Man, he himself was killed and all his squadron taken.

Thurot and Elliot off the Isle of Man, 1760.

George III., 1760.

In October 1760 George II. died and was succeeded by his grandson George III., but this change of Sovereigns had no effect on the conduct of the war. All fear of invasion being now removed, and French aggression in North America having been checkmated by the fall of Quebec and other successes on our side, Pitt determined on a counter-stroke which should both wound the French in their most vulnerable point, their national pride, and which, if successful, should give us something which we might turn to good account when the time came for arranging terms of peace. This was an attack upon the island of Belleisle which, if it fell into our hands, might possibly be restored by us in exchange for Minorca. Belleisle, though small, was strongly fortified, and was under the command of a man who well knew how to uphold the honour of his country, —M. de St. Croix. Our armament, however, would appear to have been even more than ample for such a purpose; 10 ships of the line, eight frigates, 10,000 troops under the command of Commodore Keppel and General Hodgson. Yet, at their first landing they were driven off with the loss of 500 killed, and many prisoners; nor was it until he had endured a two months' siege that M. de St. Croix at length surrendered the citadel at Port Andro, after having captured one of our generals and his staff and sent them prisoners to Paris. Belleisle was taken on June 7th, 1761; on the 4th of that month Dominica had fallen in the West Indies; Pondicherri, the French settlement in the Karnatic, had surrendered earlier in the same year; Guadaloupe had been ours for nearly two years; Canada had also passed into our hands. The French were now heartily sick of the war, and both countries were eager for peace; when a fresh complication was caused by Spain throwing in her lot with *Belleisle taken, 1761.*

Spain joins France, 1762.

France once more and declaring war against us in January 1762. Had she done this at the commencement of the struggle, when the naval power of France was yet unbroken, her alliance might have been of material aid to that country, and of serious moment to us; but, coming at a time when the French power at sea was already crushed, her declaration of war was merely courting her own destruction. We determined at once to attack her West Indian possessions, but, mindful of our mismanagement in 1740, to select capable and well-tried commanders, and to strike straight at the centre of her wealth and power in the West Indies; at her splendid seaport of Havana, the rendezvous of all the great galleons whose freight of gold and silver ingots offered such a dazzling prize to our brave but underpaid seamen. Before the expedition which we at once fitted out for that purpose could sail, the great French possession in those waters, the island of Martinique, had fallen before the gallantry and perseverance of our seamen and soldiers who, led by Rodney and General Monkton, performed wonders of daring and endurance in the attack. With Martinique fell all the smaller French islands; and we were thus left free to devote our whole strength and attention to the encounter with our fresh foes, while they had no friend to whom to look for support.

Hermione treasure-ship taken, 1762.

The first blow which we struck at them was equally unexpected on both sides. The *Acteon*, 28, and the *Favourite*, 18, were cruising off Cadiz in May, when right into their very mouths sailed the great treasure-galleon *Hermione*, homeward bound from Lima, unconscious of the existence of war and quite unprepared for action. No prize ever submitted more quickly or more quietly; and it was not until her captors had begun to overhaul her hold that the true state of the case dawned upon their dazzled senses. To each man of the two ships in his class the prize of that May morning meant wealth, almost independence for life. The shares of the admiral and the two captains amounted to £65,000 apiece; each lieutenant had £13,000, each warrant officer £4000, each petty officer £2000, each bluejacket £500. Of what the officers did with their share no record is found; but we know from the pages of Yonge's *History of the British Navy* that the bluejackets squandered theirs in the maddest manner. They bought up all the watches in Portsmouth; and to show how little value they attached to them when bought, they fried them in fat over the galley fire. They passed a resolution making a gold-laced hat an indispensable portion of the uniform of each one of the two crews; and they very nearly executed summary vengeance upon one of their number who had the audacity to appear in a hat only ornamented with silver lace. They acquitted him, however, on his explaining that, failing to get a gold-laced hat on account of their having been all bought up, he had insisted on paying the same price for the hat which he then wore, as they had paid for theirs. In such and similar follies was the lightly earned wealth of the *Hermione* squandered by our seamen. The only people who reaped a harvest from it were the hordes of Jews, crimps, and villains of every description who infested our naval ports, lying ever in wait for poor foolish Jack, whose life at sea was one of the sternest discipline and hardship, whose life on shore was a short, frantic riot, begun one day under a press of apparently inexhaustible wealth, ended the next in absolute penury.

Expedition against the Havana, 1762.

The expedition against the Havana sailed from Portsmouth on March 5th, 1762, under the command of Admiral Pocock, a bare mention of whose name has previously been made as gallantly fighting the French on the Coromandel coast. He was given a fleet of 12 ships of the line and 15 frigates, and he carried out 14,000 troops for the operations on shore. The Havana has one of the most magnificent harbours in the world, said to be capable of sheltering 1000 sail from every wind that blows. Its artificial defences were very strong and garrisoned by 20,000 men, and in the harbour itself lay 12 ships of the line. Yet on the arrival of the British fleet the Spaniards sank three of these across the mouth of the harbour to prevent our entrance, and thus locked up the others inside where they could be of little or no service. It is not within our scope to give a detailed account of a siege which, though largely aided by the naval force, was principally conducted by the troops on shore. Suffice it to say that after terrible hardships, after losing numbers of men by heat, thirst, and fatigue, after the total destruction of our great battery ashore by fire, after our force had been reduced to half its numbers by sickness, want of water, and provisions, the Havana at length surrendered in August, and a deadly blow had been struck at the very source of Spanish wealth.

Expedition against Manila, 1762.

There remained one more point at which to strike. In the Eastern seas was another centre of wealth and trade, Manila, the capital of the Philippine Islands; and it was against Manila that we next determined to direct our efforts. Admiral Cornish and Colonel Coote (of Indian fame) were sent out with seven ships of the line, three frigates, and 13,000 men, to make conquest of this eastern Havana; and they carried out their orders in the same splendid manner as their comrades in the west. In spite of heavy surf, of tropical rains, of frightful storms, of fierce savages; in spite of the true Spanish gallantry of the Marquis de Villa Medina, and the truly Spanish arrogance of the Archbishop of Manila; in spite of the irrational courage of the Spanish guard who refused quarter and were cut to pieces; Manila surrendered on October 6th, 1762. Before the month was ended the Spanish treasury suffered a loss similar to that by which their declaration of war had been followed in the spring of the year. To two of Admiral Cornish's fleet, the *Panther*, 60, and the *Argo*, frigate, there appeared, as they cruised off the Philippines, an immense galleon evidently making for Manila. With some difficulty they overtook her. An attack was made upon her by the *Panther*, to which she offered a dull and stolid resistance, her guns replying slowly and feebly to our fire, and her whole defence, though sullen and persistent, being quite unworthy of a vessel of such enormous size. When at length she was taken, the mystery was solved. Though pierced for 60 guns she mounted only 13; but her sides were of such extraordinary thickness that, except in her upper works, our shot were quite unable to penetrate them. She was called the *Santisima Trinidad*, was manned by 800 men, and her cargo was valued at three millions of dollars.

<small>The *Santisima Trinidad* treasure-ship taken, 1762.</small>

By this time Spain also had had enough of the

Peace of Paris, 1763.

war on which she had so rashly and wantonly embarked. Negotiations for peace were set on foot ; and on February 10th, 1763, the Peace of Paris was signed between France, Spain, and England. Minorca once more became ours, exchanged, thanks to Pitt's foresight, for Belleisle ; Canada, Nova Scotia, and Cape Breton were permanently ceded to us. Henceforth English was to be the prevailing language of the great North American Continent : the English were to be the dominant race in the vast Indian Empire ; and, perhaps of more value than all, the supremacy of the British nation at sea had been asserted beyond power of contradiction.

CHAPTER IX

The tea tax—Sir Peter Parker at Norfolk, Virginia—Attack on Charleston repulsed—Lord Howe in the *Eagle*—Bushnell's torpedo—Douglas' squadron on Lake Champlain—French declare war—Howe and D'Estaing at Rhode Island—Barrington and D'Estaing—Keppel and D'Orvilliers off Brest—Spain joins France—Byron and D'Estaing—France and Spain prepare to invade—Huge fleet off Plymouth—Rodney and De Langara off St. Vincent—Gibraltar relieved—Rodney and De Guichen in the West Indies—Great hurricane—Nelson at San Juan—Second relief of Gibraltar by Admiral Darby—Parker and Zoutman off the Dogger Bank—De Grasse and Hood at Fort Royal—De Grasse and Graves off the Chesapeake—De Grasse and Rodney off Martinique—Lord Howe prepares to relieve Gibraltar again—Loss of the *Royal George*—The great attack on Gibraltar—Sir Edward Hughes and M. de Suffren in the East Indies—Treaty of Versailles.

SOME twelve years were now to elapse ere we found ourselves again in actual war; yet it is not to be supposed that, with France and Spain still smarting from the blows which we had inflicted, all jealousy and ill-feeling could subside at the voice of the ambassadors who signed the Treaty of Paris. In the West Indies the French were ever on the lookout to infringe the articles of that treaty should an occasion offer, while a totally unprovoked and unjustifiable attack by a Spanish squadron on the Falkland Islands almost involved us afresh in war with that country. This time of peace, this short breathing-space before the next great struggle began, was employed by our Government in fitting out various expeditions for discovery and investigation in distant seas. Byron with the *Dolphin* and *Tamar* made a voyage round the world; Wallis and Cartaret added much to our scanty knowledge of the vast Pacific; Cook, starting in life as a draper's apprentice, made for himself an undying name by the courage, the skill, and the perseverance with which he conducted his three great voyages in the same waters; and an expedition was sent to the Arctic seas in which young Nelson gave some signs of the fearlessness and determination which were among his chief characteristics in after-life.

But already a cloud was threatening to burst upon us from a quarter whence we had looked for no such serious disturbance. The last war with France had been undertaken for the protection of our American colonies. The mother country had earned the gratitude of her children at the cost of many millions, and she thought it only fair to call upon them to bear their part of the burden. This she did by the imposition in 1765 of a duty on stamps used in legal documents, a duty only calculated to bring in a comparatively small sum to the exchequer. But the colonies were unwilling to take even this small burden on their shoulders, and so loud was their clamour that the Stamp Act was withdrawn. But the matter was not to be so easily settled. The colonies chafed against all taxation imposed by England; and when at length Lord North's tea-ships entered Boston harbour the popular indignation broke out in an attack upon the ships and the destruction of their cargo. This was in 1773. In 1774 the ill-feeling was spreading like an insidious

Stamp Act, 1765.

The Tea Ships, 1773.

disease. In 1775 it broke out into open acts of war, and we found ourselves fairly engaged in a struggle with our American colonies—a struggle which we regarded and spoke of as against rebellion, and about the ultimate issue of which we had not the slightest misgiving; but which, by stirring up the whole nest of hornets round our ears, was destined to tax our powers to the very utmost, and to leave us in the end despoiled of our great North American possessions, though triumphant over our enemies at sea. *War with American colonies, 1775.*

At the end of the year 1775 Commodore Sir Peter Parker was sent out from Portsmouth to assist our land forces in putting down the rebellion. His was but a small force,—two ships of 50 guns, four frigates, and a few small craft; but we had only the revolted colonists to deal with,—they had no navy to speak of,—a few frigates and sloops,—that was all, and the whole affair would soon be over. The first of January 1776 saw Norfolk, Virginia, bombarded and burned by our naval force, and then Sir Peter Parker moved southwards to co-operate with General Clinton at Charleston. But here, at the very commencement, the lesson of Bunker's Hill was once more enforced; the "despicable rabble" more than held their own. Our frigates failed to master the intricacies of the channel, ran aground, and were so hardly used by the rebel batteries that we were obliged to burn one as she lay, and with great difficulty floated the others off grievously damaged. For nine or ten hours the contest raged so hotly that at one time the commodore was the only officer left alive on the quarter-deck of his flag-ship, the *Bristol;* and eventually we retired to New York *Sir Peter Parker repulsed at Charleston, 1776.*

strongly impressed by the fact that we had been fighting against our own flesh and blood, and had, at least, gained no advantage over them. This was on June 28th, and six days later the famous Declaration of Independence was published to the world.

Declaration of Independence, 4th July 1776.

In the meanwhile Lord Howe had been despatched from England with a squadron deemed ample for every emergency, and was joined at Sandy Hook by Sir Peter Parker and his diminished force. Here he remained, co-operating as best he might with the troops ashore, and here, in his flag-ship, the *Eagle*, of 64 guns, he was the object of the first torpedo attack ever made upon a ship of the British navy. One David Bushnell, a native of the State of Maine, built for this purpose a submarine boat which has been compared in appearance to a gigantic walnut, so short and bulky was she in proportion to her length. Her mode of propulsion is a matter of doubt. Some authorities assert that she was propelled by a simple stern oar; others say that, like Fulton's boat of twenty years later, she was driven by a horizontal screw worked by hand, while a second screw placed vertically controlled her powers of descent and ascent. The main difficulty lay in the fact that an explosive clock-work machine had to be attached to the bottom of a ship by a man closely shut up within the submarine boat. Bushnell is said to have spent a considerable time, unsuspected and unseen, under the bottom of the *Eagle* vainly trying to fix his petard; obliged to come to the surface for air, he was discovered and fired at, but escaped by diving again. Eventually his boat was destroyed while on board a vessel which fell as a prize into our hands.

Bushnell tries to torpedo the Eagle, 1776.

It is interesting also to notice that our naval operations were not confined to the open sea or the bays and inlets of the coast. On Lake Champlain, connected with the St. Lawrence by the River Richelieu, the Americans had already a number of small vessels of war, sloops and others, which gave them the command of both sides of the lake, and enabled them to annoy our troops with comparative impunity. Captain Douglas, of the *Isis*, determined to put an end to this. Aided by frames sent out from England to Quebec, he quickly built a squadron, the largest of which was the *Inflexible*, ship-rigged and carrying 18 guns, and encountering the rebel fleet on October 12th he entirely defeated and destroyed it. *Fight on Lake Champlain, 12th October 1776.*

The year 1777 added little to the renown of our naval force; indeed, the navy found itself at this time with no proper antagonists to combat. Its operations were confined to assisting our land forces by entering the Delaware and other rivers, bombarding batteries, and destroying storehouses and magazines. The disastrous surrender of General Burgoyne with all his troops at Saratoga in this year was another and still graver warning against the contempt which we expressed for our opponents at the beginning of the war. But in 1778 matters assumed a much more serious aspect. From the beginning of the troubles the sympathies of the French nation had been, perhaps reasonably enough, with our colonies. Now our ancient rivals openly recognised the independence of the United States, made an alliance with them, and sent the Comte d'Estaing across the Atlantic with a fleet of 12 ships of the line and four frigates to render them that aid by *General Burgoyne surrenders, 1777. France joins the Americans and sends a fleet to their aid, 1778.*

K

sea which they were unable to provide for themselves. The tables were at once turned upon us, and Lord Howe with 11 small ships of the line was now obliged to stand on the defensive. On July 12th D'Estaing found the English drawn up inside Sandy Hook, far inferior in guns and men, but in so strong a position that he dared not attack. Howe's lack of men, moreover, was quickly supplied; volunteers from the merchant ships and transports flocked so eagerly and enthusiastically to him, that his main difficulty was to avoid being overcrowded. D'Estaing made off to Rhode Island, and had hardly done so when a portion of a squadron sent out under Admiral Byron to reinforce Lord Howe arrived off Sandy Hook. At once Lord Howe was off in pursuit. He found his enemy on August 9th in Narragansett harbour. The French admiral came boldly out to meet him, but finding him stronger than he expected sheered off, and both fleets spent the next two days in manœuvring for the weather-gage. These movements were interrupted on the 11th by a terrible gale, in which the ships of each fleet received serious damage and were greatly scattered; but on the 13th the *Renown*, 50, fell in with D'Estaing's flag-ship, the *Languedoc*, of 90 guns, totally dismasted, and at once attacked her. Had it not been for the arrival of six French 74's the admiral and his ship must have been taken. The *Tonnant*, 80, had a similar narrow escape, and the *César*, 74, was with difficulty rescued from a most determined attack at close quarters by the *Isis*, 50. Gathering his fleet round him, D'Estaing made off to Boston for repairs. We followed, but encountering a second gale while the French lay snug at their anchors, and being greatly in need of repair ourselves, we returned to Sandy Hook, Lord Howe having resigned the command to Admiral Byron.

And now the scene of naval operations was shifted from the American coast to the West Indies. The French had already seized our island of Dominica, and D'Estaing, quitting Boston in December, hastened to a field which seemed for the moment to offer an easier conquest. He found Admiral Barrington, with a force just half of his own, attacking the French island of St. Lucia. Trusting to his immense superiority, he advanced at once to the assistance of his countrymen; but Barrington drew up his small squadron in so threatening a manner that, after two failures, D'Estaing abandoned St. Lucia to its fate. *Barrington and D'Estaing at St. Lucia, 1778.*

But the war was no longer confined to the western shore of the Atlantic. No sooner had the French treaty with our colonies been made known than Admiral Keppel, with a fine fleet of 23 sail of the line, was ordered to cruise off Brest, his force being considered ample for any contingencies. But an enemy's frigate falling into his hands, he learned to his surprise and almost consternation that the French fleet at Brest amounted to 32 ships of the line and 12 frigates. Feeling himself too weak to risk an encounter with so superior a force, he at once returned to Spithead. On July 9th he again put to sea with an increased fleet of 30 ships of the line and four frigates. He was just one day late. The French, under the Comte d'Orvilliers had already sailed. For some days he searched for them in vain, running into a thick fog which seemed likely to destroy his last hope of overhauling them; but *Keppel and D'Orvilliers off Brest, 27th July 1778.*

on the 23rd July the fog suddenly cleared off and he found himself about thirty-five leagues west of Brest with the French fleet full in sight. Unfortunately for him the enemy had the weather-gage, and for three days made use of this advantage to decline action and make off, a course in which their superior speed greatly assisted them. But on July 27th a slight shift of wind gave us the superior position, and the combat could no longer be delayed. The chase, however, had been long, and the British fleet was much scattered. Nevertheless Admiral Harland, in the *Queen*, led the van into action, followed by Keppel himself, in the *Victory*, with the centre ; while Sir Hugh Palliser, in the *Formidable*, though at one time far to leeward with the rear squadron, seems to have hurried up as soon as possible to support his chief. The fighting, though only lasting from two to three hours, was very hot. The *Formidable* suffered so severely as to be obliged to quit the line of battle ; the *Victory* and several others were almost crippled on account of the invariable custom of the French of firing at an enemy's masts and rigging, while we always preferred to aim at the hull,—a distinction possibly due also in great measure to the fact that our men were taught to fire on the downward roll, while the French adopted the opposite plan.

But now Keppel, in order to enable him to continue the action with advantage, hoisted a signal, which Sir Hugh Palliser not only ignored himself, but which, by failing to repeat it, he prevented the whole of his squadron from obeying. His excuse was that the *Formidable* was too severely injured to make it possible for her to obey; but the excuse could hardly extend to the other ships under his command. The order being enforced by a frigate specially sent for that purpose, Sir Hugh gave a tardy obedience. But it was now too late; night had fallen, and the French took advantage of the darkness to make their escape, leaving three of their fastest vessels to decoy us in the wrong direction by means of false lights. When morning dawned we discovered our mistake, but the enemy was no longer in sight. Though not mentioned by Admiral Keppel in his despatch, the conduct of Sir Hugh Palliser gave rise to a long controversy, which culminated in Sir Hugh accusing his commander-in-chief of incompetence in the management of the fleet under his command. A court-martial was called, and Admiral Keppel was put on his trial. As usual the matter was made a political question. Both admirals were members of Parliament, Palliser on the side of the Government, Keppel on that of the Opposition. Keppel, however, was unanimously acquitted, a verdict which made it absolutely necessary for Palliser in his turn to be put on trial. He also was acquitted; a sufficient proof that a little good feeling and self-command on both sides might have avoided the scandal altogether. Keppel was raised to the peerage and afterwards made head of the Admiralty; but he resigned his command of the fleet and never went to sea again. *Keppel is tried and acquitted.*

It is to Keppel's initiative that the practice of coppering our ships of war became universally adopted. It dates in our navy from the year 1761, but was then only in an experimental stage. It was reserved for Keppel to advocate it for general use; and its *Keppel adopts the use of copper.*

adoption made a vast improvement in the speed of our vessels which, accustomed to keep the sea so much longer than those of the French, had again and again been unable to overhaul them from the accumulation of weed and barnacles upon their bottoms. Moreover, the copper proved an admirable protection from the worms which, especially in hot latitudes, destroyed the planking of our ships and rendered them unseaworthy.

Spain declares war, 1779.

The year 1779 brought fresh foes into the field. Spain, seeing us hard pushed on shore by our own colonies and at sea by the French, could not resist the temptation of another attempt to regain Gibraltar. After silently fitting out fleets, the object of which was quite unknown to us, she threw in her lot once more with France, and trusting to her ancient ally to keep our fleets employed, she addressed herself with all her might to the reduction of the great fortress, by famine if possible, if not by more violent methods. There we must leave the Spaniards for a time while we see what was going on in the West Indies. It will be remembered that we left the British fleet at the close of the year 1778 refitting at Sandy Hook. So soon as Admiral Byron heard that D'Estaing had left Boston for the West Indies, he at once sailed for the same waters, gathered up Admiral Barrington's squadron with his own, and took command, making St. Lucia generally his headquarters. D'Estaing, though the more powerful, rather avoided than sought an action; but at length Byron, moving

Byron and D'Estaing off Grenada, 1779.

up with the hope of relieving Grenada, which was then closely pressed by the enemy, came in sight of the French fleet on July 6th, 1779, too late to save the island, but not too late to bring the French to action. D'Estaing, however, was still unwilling to fight, though he had 25 ships of the line to our 21 and 12 frigates to our one. He moved out indeed to meet us boldly enough at first; yet, though the wind was in his favour, he avoided a general action and kept up a running fight from noon till sunset in which only a portion of our fleet was able to take part, disappearing during the night and leaving, as usual, many of our ships severely crippled aloft, but having lost five times as many men as ourselves. Shortly after this Admiral Byron returned to England, being superseded by Sir Hyde Parker; and the only other action of note on the western side of the Atlantic during this year was the capture or destruction of a large force of American ships of war by Commodore Sir George Collier at Penobscot, which though far superior to us in number of guns was so completely overpowered that every vessel was either taken or burned. *Collier at Penobscot, August 1779*

We must now return to European waters where Spain and France were concentrating their efforts to crush our naval supremacy. After the failure of an attack on the island of Jersey, which involved the almost total destruction of the force employed, the French once again bent their thoughts towards the ever recurring scheme of the invasion of England. *France prepares to invade, 1779.* All this time Gibraltar was closely invested both by land and sea, and the necessity of providing for the safety of our own shores prevented, as our enemies intended it should, any efforts for its relief. The preparations for the invasion were pushed rapidly forward; 50,000 troops were concentrated at St. Malo, and an enormous combined French and Spanish fleet actually appeared off Plymouth on August 15th, *A French and Spanish fleet of sixty-six ships off Plymouth, 1779.*

numbering no less than 66 ships of the line!
It was the Armada over again. Panic seized our
coasts: people hurriedly packed up their goods,
deserted their houses, and fled inland; and it is
related that during Divine Service in one of the
churches of a southern county the cry "The French
have landed!" made the whole congregation rise in
terror, scramble over the backs of the pews, and fly
for safety, leaving the parson in the pulpit horror-
stricken and alone.

To oppose this huge fleet we had no force of anything like equal size. The most we could do was to
send Admiral Sir Charles Hardy, a veteran whose
best days were over, with a fleet which at its greatest
did not exceed 46 ships of the line, to face the apparently overwhelming force of the enemy. But our
alarm was needless. Our great defence was the incompetence and divided counsels of the leaders of
the combined fleet. Its only exploit was the capture
of a hapless 64 which sailed into the midst of it
unawares. It missed a vast fleet of West Indian
vessels which would have made its fortune and well-
nigh ruined us: its leaders quarrelled over what
should be done, and ended in doing nothing; and
eventually they retired to their own respective ports
fearing the approach of the equinox and the fate of
the first Armada.

But while the French and Spaniards were making
so threatening a show in the Channel, and while
England was echoing with rumours of invasion, our
gallant troops in Gibraltar were slowly starving—
starving, that is to say, in the sense that they were
reduced to eating rats and other vermin. If the Rock
was to be saved it must be done at once. We were

already preparing a fleet to strengthen our position in the West Indies, the command of which was to be entrusted to Sir George Rodney. He was now ordered to take Gibraltar on his way and at all hazards to carry supplies of food to the beleaguered garrison. Accordingly he sailed with that object, his force consisting of 21 ships of the line and nine frigates with a convoy of vessels full of stores of all sorts. His voyage was most fortunate. Not far from Finisterre a Spanish convoy laden with provisions fell into his hands, and was at once added to his own for the relief of Gibraltar, a destination far other than that intended for it by the Spaniards. On January 16th, 1780, off Cape St. Vincent, part of the Spanish fleet engaged in the blockade of Gibraltar hove in sight. It consisted of nine ships of the line and two frigates. Rodney at once bore down, his coppered ships easily taking the lead. The Spaniards naturally fled, and a stern chase is invariably a long one. It was late in the afternoon before he succeeded in overhauling them; darkness was already setting in, and the day was wild and stormy. Nevertheless he pressed his attack, fearing lest they might make a Spanish port. The Spaniards fought gallantly, but the odds were such as to make defeat a certainty. In half an hour the *San Domingo*, of 70 guns, blew up with all on board. Through the dark hours of that wild tempestuous night they fought until, at 2 A.M., the *Monarca* struck to the *Sandwich*, Rodney's flag-ship, at the first broadside which she received from her; and when day enabled us to see the extent of our victory, we found that only two of the enemy's line had escaped, and that Don Juan de Langara and his flagship were in our hands.

Rodney sails to relieve Gibraltar, 1780.

Rodney defeats De Langara off Cape St. Vincent, 16th January 1780.

The relief of Gibraltar was now only delayed by the weather, which for a time placed Rodney's fleet in great jeopardy and even wrecked two of his prizes. At length the fleet and convoy were brought safely up in Gibraltar Bay under the shadow of the great rock, amid general rejoicing from the starving garrison, and with no little amusement at the thought that the Spaniards should themselves have contributed so largely to the replenishing of their empty store-rooms.

Gibraltar relieved first time, 1780.

Minorca also, which, still further cut off from help, had shared the trials of the garrison of Gibraltar, was revictualled at the same time, and, having thus fulfilled his orders in the Mediterranean, Rodney sailed at once for his station in the West Indies. His presence there was urgently needed. When he arrived he found Sir Hyde Parker closely blockaded at St. Lucia by the Comte de Guichen (who had relieved D'Estaing) with 25 ships of the line, and though his own fleet was inferior both in numbers and size he pushed eagerly forward to an encounter. But an encounter was apparently the last thing which the French admiral desired, unless his own force was immensely superior to ours. He at once took shelter in the harbour of Fort Royal, Martinique, which formed the headquarters of the French fleet in the West Indies, as did St. Lucia of the British, during the operations of this war. To Fort Royal also Rodney followed, but could not tempt his enemy to come out. In vain he cruised up and down outside as a challenge to the French fleet; in vain he sailed boldly within shot of the batteries, and even counted their guns to shame him into action. The Frenchman would not stir, and Rodney at last returned to St. Lucia to await the next move. Hardly had he reached it,

ADMIRAL LORD RODNEY.

when the enemy stole out by night, 23 ships of the line and some frigates. But Rodney was not asleep. Informed of their departure by small fast

Rodney and De Guichen. 1780.

vessels specially left for that purpose, he was under way and after them in a moment, and sighted them the very next day off the Pearl Rock. On April 17th, 1780, his great opportunity had apparently come. The enemy was close under his lee, and nothing could prevent a general action. No doubts harassed his mind as to the result; his dispositions were made; it would be a glorious victory. But it was not to be. Nor was it now any reluctance on the part of the enemy which balked all his plans. It was the spirit of neglect and insubordination in his own fleet; a spirit which had already betrayed itself while the fleet was yet fitting out, and which had been still further displayed in his action with the Spaniard off St. Vincent. Rodney's proposed evolution was somewhat similar to that employed by Nelson five and twenty years afterwards with such crushing effect at Trafalgar. He had the wind; he would bear down on his adversary's line, would cut it in two, and would overwhelm the latter half with all his force ere the van could put about and come to the rescue. To carry out such a manœuvre signals must be obeyed with absolute precision. Unfortunately the very opposite happened. Disregarding the signal to bear down on the ship directly opposite her, the *Stirling Castle* pressed on to the far distant head of the French line. She lost valuable time in doing so, led a large number of other ships after her, caused the whole fleet to be widely scattered, and made Rodney's scheme utterly impossible. Disappointed and indignant, Rodney tried to make up for the disobedience of his captains by his own magnificent courage. Plunging with his flag-ship into the thick of the French centre, and nobly followed by eight other vessels, he engaged single-handed with three of the enemy, and threw the French line into great confusion. But no sooner had he driven off his three antagonists than their place was taken by De Guichen himself and two others. Nothing daunted, Rodney treated these fresh foes as the others; and at length, though battered and exhausted, seventy of his men killed, his foremast gone, his ship leaking dangerously, he compelled them to sheer off. De Guichen gathered his ships together and made for Fort Royal. Damaged as he was, Rodney was determined to keep him out of so desirable a shelter, and drove him to Guadaloupe, while he himself refitted in all haste at St. Lucia lest he might miss a second opportunity. But two years were to elapse before that opportunity came, before he was to find the French fleet once more at his mercy, and at the end of the day a French admiral prisoner in his after-cabin. Patiently and persistently he watched and waited for them: twice he got so near as to bring on a distant skirmish; but they were determined to avoid a general action, and the superior speed of their ships, coupled with the deplorable condition of many of his own, made all his efforts unavailing. He occupied his time in so perfecting his officers in fleet-manœuvres that when next they met the enemy nothing might prevent the working of the fleet with thorough unanimity.

But his anxieties as to the efficiency of his force were now to be enormously increased. A Spanish fleet arrived in the West Indies, formed a junction with the French, and raised the number of ships of the line under De Guichen's orders to 36. To oppose this combination of enemies, Rodney had now but 17 ships of the line and two of 50 guns. To meet them in line of battle at sea was obviously to expose himself to almost certain disaster; but he drew up his vessels at St. Lucia in so strong a position that even the immense superiority of the French did not seem to them to justify an attack. Rodney's great fear was that an attempt would be made on our most valuable island, Jamaica, before reinforcements could reach him from home; but the danger was not so great as it seemed. Disease broke out among the Spaniards; the French and Spanish commanders quarrelled and went each his own way,—the Spaniard to the Havana, De Guichen, after a short delay, to join D'Estaing at Cadiz. Thus relieved of his most pressing apprehension, Rodney sent Admiral Rowley with 10 ships of the line to guard Jamaica, while he himself with the rest left the West Indies for New York, whither he wrongly suspected that De Guichen was also bound. By this movement on his part he was providentially saved from the ravages of a terrible hurricane, which in the month of October caused the most frightful destruction of life and property among the West India islands, and the loss of 13 of our men-of-war, great and small, including the *Thunderer*, 74, and the *Stirling Castle*, 64, with many men.

Great hurricane, October 1780.

Among the smaller expeditions of the year 1780 in these waters it is right to mention that conducted by Captain H. Nelson up the San Juan river against the fort of that name at the entrance of Lake Nicaragua. He was then a post-captain, only twenty-two years old, in command of his first ship the *Hinchinbrook*, 28. Finding the military officer incapable, he took upon himself the conduct of the whole affair, brought it, in spite of great difficulties, to a

Nelson at San Juan, 1780.

triumphant termination, but returned with his force decimated by disease and with his own health so broken down that his life for long hung in the balance, and his return to England was a matter of absolute necessity.

The last month of 1780 added yet another enemy to our list,—an enemy with whom we had had many a terrible bout in the past, and who, even now, was by no means to be despised. This was Holland, whose bearing towards us was of so unfriendly and threatening a character that, full as our hands already were, we declared war against her rather than have her silently and stealthily assisting our open enemies.

War with Holland, 1780.

Thus the year 1781 found us at war with our American colonies, with France, with Spain, and with Holland. The sea-power of the latter was indeed nothing compared to that of the days when Van Tromp and De Ruyter flew her flag; yet, in conjunction with the other two great naval nations, she was a serious addition to our anxieties and necessitated the employment of an additional fleet under Sir Hyde Parker in the North Sea to guard our eastern coast.

Meanwhile the garrison of Gibraltar was again in a starving condition. The provisions which Rodney had thrown into the fortress were well-nigh exhausted, for on his departure for the West Indies the leaguer by land and sea had been drawn closer than ever. Dr. Campbell tells us of the straits to which the garrison were reduced at the end of the year 1780; how bad ship-biscuit full of worms fetched 1s. a pound; how the worst salt, half dirt, was sold at 8d., and old Irish butter, completely rancid, at 2s. 6d. a pound; and how, when by any chance a boat managed to steal in with market produce, a turkey would fetch £3, 12s. 6d., and a small hen 9s. These, however, were luxuries only possible for those who could afford such prices; the condition of the private soldiers was infinitely worse. Relief was again absolutely necessary; but the strain upon the navy was now so great that it was with difficulty that an adequate force could be got together. It was known that a large French fleet lay at Brest, and a still larger Spanish fleet at Cadiz. The two combined would amount to more than 50 ships of the line; yet we could but raise a fleet of 28 of the line for the relief of Gibraltar, and it was with great misgiving that it was despatched on March 13th, 1781, under the command of Admiral Darby. Fortune, however, was on our side. We avoided the French fleet; the Spaniards in Cadiz were unprepared for our arrival; Gibraltar was once more rescued from famine; but the blockade and the bombardment were resumed as before upon the departure of the relieving force.

Gibraltar relieved second time, 1781.

One other important incident took place in European waters during this year. Admiral Sir Hyde Parker fell foul of the Dutch in the North Sea, and there ensued a battle such as one would be led to expect from our previous experience of these sturdy seamen. In numbers the squadrons were nearly equal, though even here Admiral Zoutman was slightly superior; but in actual ships there was no comparison. The Dutch had no such strain on their resources as we had; their ships were strong, seaworthy, well armed, fully manned; our North Sea fleet was a collection gathered in great measure from "Rotten Row," as the long line of old and decaying hulks in our great naval ports is called. An old 80-gun ship with small obsolete guns, an old 60 long since condemned but now patched up, a 50 and a 44 doing duty as vessels of the line,—seven in all with four frigates, these were the best with which we could supply Admiral Parker; while the Dutchman had eight good two-decked ships under his command. They met on August 9th, 1781, off the Dogger Bank. Parker had the wind; he bore down instantly; not a gun was fired till the fleets were about fifty yards apart, when both sides opened fire with incredible fury, and kept it up incessantly for three hours and a half. Then neither fleet was in a condition to continue the action; both equally exhausted and disabled, neither could take advantage of the other, for neither could move. Hurriedly they repaired their damages aloft, anxiously watching each other the while. The Dutchman was the first to make sail. For a moment it looked as if he would renew the combat, but he bore away for the Texel leaving Parker still immovable. Ere Zoutman could reach his port, however, the *Hollandia*, 64, foundered from her injuries, with all her wounded on board. *Parker defeats the Dutch, off the Dogger Bank, 9th August 1781.*

Again we must turn to the West Indies. Rodney had already been warned by the Government of the rupture with Holland. He had returned to the West Indies and had seized the Dutch island of St. Eustatius, north-west of Guadaloupe, an island which, though of insignificant size, had for long been used as a storehouse for our enemies, but which, while nominal peace reigned between the Dutch and ourselves, we were unable to touch. This island now, with six ships of war and 150 merchantmen, became a most valuable *Rodney seizes Dutch West India Islands, 1781.*

prize, and Rodney was proceeding against other Dutch possessions in these waters when he heard that a large French fleet under the Comte de Grasse was already on its way from Europe. Assured that they would make for Martinique, where a British squadron of nine ships was holding some few French vessels blockaded, he detached Admiral Hood with nine more to strengthen that force, assuming that 18 ships of the line would be ample for any fleet that the French would be likely to send. But the French were far stronger than he suspected. De Grasse's fleet consisted of 20 very powerful ships of the line with one of 50 guns, and the French admiral looked for no opposition to his entrance into Fort Royal. But Hood had no idea of retiring; he drew up his fleet off the port to receive De Grasse, and at the same time to prevent the escape of the blockaded ships. That, however, was impossible. De Grasse fought as usual at a distance, and while Hood manœuvred in order to close with him, the blockaded ships made sail and slipped out, thus making the superiority of the French greater than ever. But even this did not stimulate De Grasse to make the action general, and after many attempts to crush us in detail, attempts which Hood's admirable seamanship entirely frustrated, he at length retired into Fort Royal harbour. The danger, however, was too pressing for Hood not to ask for aid. The French fleet was more numerous, its ships far bigger, its guns far heavier than ours; and the *Russel*, badly damaged, was sent to Rodney at St. Eustatius. He answered the call in person; but his health was now giving way; De Grasse would not come out; and Rodney was obliged to resign his command and go

Marginal note: Hood and De Grasse off Martinique, April 1781.

home, leaving Sir Samuel Hood in charge. This was in July; the hurricane months were now coming on, and the rival admirals, dreading a repetition of the disaster of the previous year, transferred themselves and the greater part of their respective fleets to the American coast. We find Hood accordingly, in August, placing himself under the orders of Admiral Graves at Sandy Hook, where the two squadrons together numbered 19 ships of the line. On September 5th the English fleet encountered De Grasse with 24 off the mouth of the Chesapeake and fought another of those partial engagements in which neither side can claim any marked advantage, while many vessels on both sides are damaged and many lives lost. The French, however, were again far superior to us in force, by five more ships, by 400 guns, and by 7000 men; yet in little more than an hour De Grasse drew off, having suffered double the loss in men that he had inflicted, but having, as usual, crippled many of our ships severely. Shortly after this the French force was raised by reinforcements to 32 sail of the line: our admirals were too weak to venture upon another attack; and the immediate result was that Lord Cornwallis with the whole of his force was obliged to surrender at Yorktown.

Graves and De Grasse off the Chesapeake, 5th September 1781.

Cornwallis surrenders at Yorktown, 1781.

With the surrender of this second British force the fighting ashore was practically over; the cause of the colonists was won, and the British Government now recognised the hopelessness of the struggle. But afloat our supremacy of the sea was still at stake; it was absolutely necessary that it should be asserted as decidedly as ever if Great Britain was not to sink back into that insignificance from which she had slowly risen after long centuries of struggle. Nor was it only ourselves who recognised that the crisis had come. France and Spain saw it and rejoiced, and each prepared to put forth her greatest strength for the humbling of England. De Grasse was heavily reinforced in the West Indies, so heavily that Hood, who had returned to the islands, dared not face him in the open, though he outwitted him at St. Kitts, drew him out of his snug anchorage to fight, and then sailing round him dropped anchor in the very berth which the Frenchman had just quitted, and from which all the furious efforts of De Grasse failed to dislodge him. He could not, however, save the island from falling into the hands of the French, whose superiority was so great that it seemed as if they would sweep all before them. Island after island surrendered to them, till at last but four of all our settlements remained to us.

French heavily reinforced in the West Indies.

The crisis had indeed come. Jamaica once lost, our existence in the West Indies would be impossible. The two nations determined to reduce it. But Rodney had partially recovered his health and was even now hurrying out to his old battle-ground with reinforcements. The fate of the Empire was in his hands, and he did not shrink from a responsibility which will often daunt the bravest. At Barbados he met Hood, and his fleet then amounted to 36 sail of the line. As of old he took his station at St. Lucia; De Grasse was at Fort Royal, the Spaniards at San Domingo; he must crush one before the two could combine. On April 8th, 1782, De Grasse put to sea. Rodney was instantly under way and in pursuit. Ere they reached Dominica he was close upon them. But the wind fell; his rear got becalmed and lay helpless miles astern. Now was the Frenchman's chance. Had he fallen on our van with all his fleet, —34 splendid ships of the line—he might have inflicted a heavy blow, perhaps a crushing defeat. But he was too wary: he was content to engage at a great distance; and though his heavy guns caused considerable damage there was no danger of disaster, and when our tardy rear came up he ceased firing and held on his course. For the next two days both fleets manœuvred for the better position; in seamanship we were ever superior to the French, and at daybreak of the 12th of April Rodney found himself once more in possession of the wind, able to force on a fight at any moment, whether the foe was willing or not. The foe was by no means unwilling. Though less by two in actual number of ships he considered himself the more powerful, but he could no longer select his distance; he would have to fight now after the British fashion at close quarters. It was a battle of giants: 36 ships of the line against 34; and its duration was worthy of such combatants. For twelve terrible hours it lasted, far longer than any battle since those furious encounters with the Dutch in the previous century. The action commenced shortly after 7 A.M. and continued without the least cessation until evening. The French moved in one long line ahead; Rodney's fleet was parallel to them, and for some five hours it was a ding-dong fight ship to ship. The wind, killed by the concussion, failed; the smoke hung like a white pall over the double line; no ships could be distinguished, no signals seen. At noon a breeze sprang up, the smoke blew away, the position could be taken in at a glance. The French line was disordered; there was an obvious gap

Rodney defeat De Grasse off Martinique, 12th April 1782.

in the centre; the time had come for Rodney's scheme of "doubling" on the enemy, of overwhelming part of their force with the whole of his own, a plan which, it will be remembered, had been balked two years before by the misconduct of his captains. Now, however, the discipline of his fleet was perfect. Followed by the whole of his division Rodney, in the *Formidable*, pushed through the gap. Once through he turned, and leading his ships along the rear half of the French line on its disengaged side he placed it between two fires, ensuring its destruction ere the enemy's van could come to its rescue. De Grasse saw the impending catastrophe and, powerless to remedy it, endeavoured to make up for it by the splendid gallantry of his own flag-ship, the *Ville de Paris*. Built by the city of Paris, and presented by its people to Louis XV., she was the largest and most magnificent ship in the French navy, carrying 110 guns of the heaviest calibre, far heavier than any of ours. So little did De Grasse spare her that her list of killed alone was larger than that of the whole British fleet. It was a magnificent but hopeless attempt on his part; and when at length about sunset he surrendered, there were only two men on deck beside himself uninjured. The flag-ship was the last to strike; the *Diadème*, attempting to protect her, had been sunk by a single broadside from Rodney; five were taken that day, and two more shortly after; but of the five the *César* caught fire that same night and blew up with all her prize crew and the greater part of her own men. The fate of the other prizes was equally melancholy, and reminds us of a similar disaster after the battle of Trafalgar. They were sent home with a small squadron of damaged ships under Admiral Graves. In mid-ocean they encountered a hurricane; the *Caton* fled before it and reached the American coast a wreck; the splendid *Ville de Paris*, the *Hector*, and the *Glorieux* foundered with the whole of their crews; only the *Jason* and the *Ardent* with great difficulty reached England.

<small>Rodney's prizes lost, September 1782.</small>

Meanwhile party feeling at home had been undermining Rodney, and he had actually been already superseded by the Admiralty, when the news arrived of his glorious victory, a victory which turned the wavering scale indisputably in our favour, and once more established the naval supremacy of England. It was too late to recall his successor; but it is satisfactory to know that he was honoured as he deserved, and that both he and Hood were created Peers of the Realm.

Once more we must turn to Gibraltar which just a year ago had been revictualled by Admiral Darby, but which was again suffering from want of provisions and must at all hazards be relieved. The combined operations of the French and Spaniards against it were now rapidly approaching an acute stage; defeated elsewhere, the two nations had staked their reputation on the fall of the great fortress. A third time a fleet was equipped for its succour,—a fleet far larger than either of the two which had preceded it, consisting of 36 ships of the line under the chief command of Lord Howe, with three other admirals. This fleet was fitting out at Portsmouth in all haste to proceed to the help of our long-suffering garrison, when it was found that the *Royal George*, of 108 guns, flying the flag of Admiral Kempenfeldt, had something wrong with a pipe far below the

<small>Gibraltar again starving, 1782.</small>

<small>Loss of the *Royal George*, 29th August 1782.</small>

waterline. There was no time to dock her; the defect might be reached by heeling her over as far as possible. The day, August 29th, was bright and calm, the water smooth, no danger was apprehended. All were on board; the admiral writing in his cabin, the bluejackets at their work, the carpenters over the side, the decks swarming with wives and children, as was then the common custom on the eve of sailing; tradesmen, Jews, crimps, all the heterogeneous following of an old-time man-of-war were there—when, without a moment's warning, pressed down by a sudden puff of wind, the great ship suddenly rolled over, filled, and sank, carrying down a dockyard lighter with her. The admiral, many of the officers, and three-fourths of the ship's company were lost; most of those on the upper deck were picked up, but those below, including the helpless women and children, were drowned. Though more than a century has passed, the loss of the *Royal George* still stands out in terrible relief in the history of our navy, while many another disaster of equal or even greater horror has been buried in the oblivion of years.

But none the less must the fleet sail for Gibraltar; and sail it did on September 11th with transports, victuallers, and store-ships, ignorant of the fact that the great attack was then almost in the act of commencing, and would be ended and defeated ere they had cleared the Channel. Although not strictly a naval matter, one or two details of this last tremendous effort to regain Gibraltar will hardly be out of place. The combination against the fortress was imposing; a great Spanish army aided by 12,000 French troops, batteries mounting 300 guns ashore, a combined French and Spanish fleet of 48 sail of the line, a multitude of frigates, a countless host of gun and mortar boats, and lastly, 10 huge battering vessels constructed specially for this duty. These last were line-of-battle ships cut down, housed in with bombproof roofs, with sides impenetrable by reason of their thickness, and incombustible by reason of a contrivance of waterpipes within, armed with new brass guns of great size fired simultaneously by a mechanical arrangement.

On September 13th, two days after Lord Howe had sailed, the great attack took place. The batteries, the fleet, the frigates, the gunboats, the bomb vessels, and the ten great battering machines opened fire at once upon the devoted garrison. General Elliot relied principally on his red-hot shot, and had erected furnaces in every quarter for this purpose. His chief fire was directed against the battering machines, these being considered the most formidable. For many hours they seemed to suffer no injury from the storm of red-hot shot which he poured upon them. At last, from the admiral's battering ship there was seen to rise a thin column of smoke. Presently a similar column was observed from the next in the line. The pipes had failed to act; the sides were so thick that the red-hot shot could neither be cut out nor extinguished. During the night the flames burst forth fiercely, but the fiery hail never ceased. Rockets were sent up for help, but no help could be given under such a withering storm of shot and shell. The battering-ships became objects of terror to their friends, and burned with such appalling fierceness that they did not dare approach. Daylight found their crews in a pitiable

The combined attack on Gibraltar, 13th September 1782.

and awful plight, exposed to the triple danger of their own conflagration, of death by drowning, and of being shot by the British. Their friends dared not render them any assistance; but it was from their enemies that help came at last. When their piteous condition was seen from the Rock, General Elliot gave orders to cease firing. At once the British gunboats dashed in to the rescue, at their own most imminent peril, for the vessels were blowing up and heated guns going off in all directions. More than 400 of the enemy were thus saved from their terrible situation. Of the ten great battering machines nine blew up, and the tenth was burnt by us after the engagement. The great attack had taken place, and had resulted in a great failure. The garrison had earned the deepest and most heartfelt thanks of the entire nation; but they were still starving, and it was not until a month afterwards that Lord Howe's fleet arrived through the Straits, and brought provisions to the fortress. Then so cowed and dispirited were the fleets of France and Spain, that though lying in Algeciras Bay at the time of Howe's arrival, and though counting as many as 44 sail of the line, five of which mounted 110 guns, and one 120, they avoided a conflict, sailed away, and having the weather-gage, defeated all our efforts to bring them to a close action.

Gibraltar relieved the third time, 11th October 1782.

It is impossible to close this account of the war without referring to the services of a detached squadron under Sir Edward Hughes in the East Indies. This force, composed of eight ships of the line and some smaller vessels, was opposed on the Coromandel coast by a French fleet of very considerable superiority under Admiral de Suffren, who was

Hughes and Suffren in the East Indies.

combining with Hyder Ali of Mysore to drive us out of the Karnatic. Four times in the year 1782, and once in 1783 did these two meet between Madras and Trincomalee. Five times they fought a hard and determined battle: five times they drew off, each severely damaged, and neither having gained any appreciable advantage over the other; and it is interesting to notice that the second fight of this series of battles in the East Indies took place on the very day on which Rodney inflicted his final defeat upon De Grasse in the West Indies. Both were eagerly preparing for their sixth encounter when the news reached them of the preliminaries for peace. The Treaty of Versailles placed us once more in friendly relations with France, with Spain, and with Holland. It restored to us most of our possessions in the West Indies while depriving us of the island of Minorca; and it acknowledged a new and separate nation across the Atlantic, a nation composed largely of our own flesh and blood, which, in other and happier circumstances might have continued to form one of the great family of the mother country; a great elder son as it were of mature strength and vigour, able to stand alone, yet bound to the parent land by the silken bonds of interest, of sympathy, and of love.

Peace of Versailles, 1783.

CHAPTER X

Mutiny of the *Bounty*—War with the French Republic—Hood at Toulon—Nelson in Corsica—"The glorious First of June"—Martinique and St. Lucia taken—Dutch declare war—Cornwallis escapes from the French fleet—Bridport off Lorient—Hotham in the Gulf of Genoa—*Ça Ira* and *Censeur*—Hotham off Hyères—Attempt on Ireland—Spain joins France—Battle of St. Vincent—The Mutinies—Attacks on Cadiz—Nelson at Santa Cruz—Battle of Camperdown.

FOR a short ten years we again enjoyed the blessing of peace. The time was not wasted. As in the interval before the previous war, expeditions were fitted out to enlarge our knowledge of distant waters; and as before it was the Pacific which offered the largest and most promising field for investigation. It was during this time that Captain Vancouver, searching the western shores of the two Americas, gave his name to the great island, now so well known to us as a promising colony, having many features in common with the British Isles, notably its climate and its coalfields. Now also it was that Captain Bligh, despatched in the little *Bounty*, of 215 tons, to attempt the transplanting of the breadfruit tree from the Society Isles to the West Indies, was turned adrift by his mutinous crew off the Tonga Islands. With an almost incredibly scanty supply of provisions, and with no weapons but four cutlasses, he and 16 others were cast off in a small boat but 23 feet

Mutiny of the *Bounty*, 1789.

long to find their way to the nearest civilised settlement, or to perish by famine, by tempest, by exposure, or by human violence. An interesting relic of their voyage was to be seen in the Naval Exhibition of 1891, consisting of the bullet which served to weigh out their miserable daily ration of one ounce of bread per man; and the tiny horn cup, two inches in depth, which measured their meagre sup of water for some two months ere they reached the island of Timor.

As before also we had again to put down by a firm display of determination the ever-ready insolence of Spain abroad, not this time at the Falklands, but on the coasts of Vancouver Island, which the Spaniards claimed as theirs by Papal gift dating as far back as the fifteenth century.

But though we ourselves maintained peace at home and abroad, and strove by the encouragement of trade and commerce to make up in some small measure for the heavy losses and privations which our incessant wars had inflicted on us, we were kept in a state of the most anxious suspense and apprehension by the unparalleled events which were taking place across the narrow boundary of the Channel.

All France was in a ferment. It was some- *French thing more than a national revolution; it was a Revolution.* volcanic eruption. Maddened by long years of extortion, insolence, and tyranny, the people had at length risen against their rulers. Armed with the strength which comes of insanity, they had proclaimed themselves the enemies of all sovereignty, and the champions of universal liberty and equality had set the example by the murder of their own King, and were now looking round with bloodshot eyes for further victims. Holland was their nearest neighbour; they attacked Holland instantly. England was close at hand, and they had many a grudge against her. On the 1st of February 1793 they declared war upon us also. It came upon us in no way as a surprise. Impending war, like disease, has its own premonitory symptoms. The language of the French Convention was sufficiently explicit, and the *Childers*, sloop-of-war, with English colours displayed, had been already fired on by the batteries at Brest, and no apology had been offered.

<small>War with France, 1793.</small>

The French were confident of their own superiority. Their navy contained vessels far larger and more heavily armed than ours, though numerically less. Their line-of-battle ranged from ships of 120 guns to those of 74 inclusive; ours starting from ships of 100 guns admitted very many of 64; they pronounced themselves publicly to be "the most redoubtable maritime power in Europe."

Besides Holland, Spain as a monarchy was also regarded as an enemy, and the war opened with both these countries as our nominal allies,—allies who were, however, soon to turn into enemies once more.

At once a powerful fleet was placed in the Channel under the command of Lord Howe, whose efforts during the first year of the war were so barren of all result as to excite a considerable amount of popular ridicule and indignation. But attention was more particularly attracted to the Mediterranean. The great French seaport and naval station of Toulon was not yet wholly in the hands of the Republicans. It seemed that with the help of its still loyal inhabitants it might be seized and held by us; and Lord Hood, with a fleet of 20 ships of

<small>Hood holds Toulon.</small>

the line, was sent to co-operate with a Spanish fleet under Admiral De Langara in taking possession of it. This was accomplished with little difficulty. The forts and batteries were occupied, and the large French fleet then lying there was taken over, its action being paralysed by the divided counsels of its commanders. But we had only a handful of troops with which to man the forts; the loyal inhabitants of Toulon were too few to assist us materially; the Spaniards were in every way far more of a hindrance than a help to us; and the Revolutionists were pouring down in thousands to recover their great naval depot of the south. Soon Toulon was surrounded by 60,000 troops, the stories of whose unspeakable cruelty to their own countrymen made the hearts of the ill-fated Loyalists faint within them. It was obvious that a naval force could not alone hold Toulon. Piteous as the decision was, it was determined to abandon it to the Republicans, first destroying all forts, guns, ammunition, stores, and ships which might otherwise fall into their hands, and embarking on board the fleet as many of the royalist French as chose to claim our protection. On December 18th, 1793, the work of destruction was begun in most difficult and dangerous circumstances. The batteries of the French army, skilfully planted by a young captain of artillery, Napoleon Buonaparte, poured storms of shot and shell upon the forts and harbour, while their troops were already taking possession of the town. The Spaniards, who had undertaken part of the work of demolition, most grossly neglected it, exposing our boats to additional and frightful danger. But at length we drew off, carrying 15,000 French citizens into

Toulon evacuated, 18th December 1793.

safety, and having inflicted on the Republicans a very serious blow in the ruin of their defences and the removal or destruction of the greater part of their fleet. The fate of those unhappy French who remained either from choice or necessity was pitiable in the extreme. Men, women, and children were massacred in thousands; every day 200 were guillotined; the population of Toulon shrank from 28,000 to 7000; and this was the handiwork of their own countrymen under the cry of Liberty, Equality, Fraternity!

The following year was to bring us more tangible and satisfactory results. Toulon being abandoned and the French fleet in the Mediterranean almost destroyed, Lord Hood was free to turn his attention elsewhere. His next object of attack was the island of Corsica, whose inhabitants, groaning under the tyranny of the French, were represented as only awaiting the aid of some friendly Power to throw off the yoke. The principal fortified ports of the island were San Fiorenzo, Bastia, and Calvi. San Fiorenzo was presently abandoned by the enemy and occupied by a British military force. Bastia and Calvi were strongly fortified, heavily armed, and well manned by French troops; the British general in command, pronouncing them impregnable, proposed to do, and indeed actually did nothing.

Nelson in Corsica, 1794. Here Nelson steps upon the scene. Since his attack on San Juan in 1780 he had greatly distinguished himself by his extraordinary firmness in stopping the illegal trading in the West Indies, and had then, on paying off, lain idle for several years on half-pay, despairing of further employment. On the outbreak of the war he had been rejoiced at receiv-

ing the command of the *Agamemnon*, 64, one of
the fastest ships of the line in our navy, and had
already signalised himself by an action with a large
squadron of French frigates. Hearing the decision
of the British general, he instantly offered to undertake the matter himself; it was better, he said, to
fail than not to try at all. Lord Hood placed the
conduct of the operations entirely in his hands. He
at once set to work. His ceaseless activity, his inexhaustible resource, his unflagging perseverance
accomplished wonders. His men seemed to be
inspired with the spirit of their little captain. He
pitched a tent for himself ashore, he made roads,
he selected sites for batteries, brought guns and
mortars from his ships, and had them hauled up
heights regarded as barely possible of attainment by human beings. Several times the general
came over from San Fiorenzo to see how he
was getting on, but offered neither advice nor aid;
indeed, he refused both guns and men when they
were demanded of him. In spite of his sneers
Bastia fell on May 22nd. Nelson after a fruitless
cruise with his admiral in pursuit of a French fleet
then turned his attention to Calvi, conducted a similar
attack by similar methods, and in less than a fortnight forced it also to surrender; not, however, without serious consequences to himself, in the loss of
his right eye through a splinter of stone thrown up
by a shot. Calvi surrendered on August 1st, and
Corsica became for a time a British possession.

We must leave the Mediterranean for a while
and see what the Channel fleet under Lord Howe
was doing while Nelson was bombarding Bastia.
A great French fleet of 25 sail of the line and

Lord Howe in the Channel.

17 frigates had been assembled at Brest, under the command of Admiral De Villaret Joyeuse. Twelve months previously he had been but a post-captain, but the Republican Government found themselves in great difficulties as regards their officers and crews. The former had consisted of men of good family connected, perhaps for generations, with naval matters, men of experience, accustomed to command. But the men of good family had fallen on the guillotine and there was nobody to replace them; while the crews, with their ridiculous ideas of liberty and brotherhood, deeply and violently resented any attempt even by their own officers to punish any of their number. Punishment, if necessary, was to be inflicted by vote of the entire ship's company. It was not a hopeful look-out for the admiral, himself inexperienced, his officers often incompetent, his crews undisciplined; the marvel is that they fought so well.

Lord Howe had a treble duty imposed upon him: he was to protect as far as the open ocean a convoy of vessels bound for the West Indies and elsewhere; he was to intercept, if possible, a convoy of French vessels laden with supplies; he was to find and fight the Brest fleet. For the first part of his duty he detached Admiral Montague with eight ships of the line; the other two he undertook himself, considering that where the French merchant fleet was found, there would also be the Brest fleet to protect them. He looked into Brest: the French were gone; and he accordingly cruised beyond the mouth of the Channel, where he thought that the convoy might be expected. Early in the morning of May 28th the Brest fleet hove in sight, both fleets then lying in the open Atlantic, some 350 miles west of Ushant. In numbers they were exactly equal, each consisting of 26 sail of the line. The French at first seemed inclined to wait for us, their orders being to fight at all hazards; but as we drew near they bore away, and Howe signalled his fleet to chase. This at length brought on a partial action, the *Revolutionnaire* of 110 guns, in the extreme rear, being attacked in turn by no less than six of our 74's and retaliating so fiercely that the *Audacious* was badly damaged and compelled to return to Plymouth for repair. But at 10 P.M. the *Revolutionnaire* was herself little better than a wreck. With her mizen-mast gone, followed shortly after by the other two masts, with her captain and great numbers of her men killed, she dropped astern, having, as our men asserted, struck her flag. But when all three masts are shot away it is difficult to assert that the flag has been lowered intentionally; and the *Revolutionnaire*, whether she struck or not, took advantage of the darkness to be towed into Rochefort. The fight was renewed the next day, but again with only partial results, the greater part of our fleet never getting within shot of the enemy; nevertheless three or four of his ships were so crippled by our shot that they had to be taken in tow by their comrades to avoid capture. The 30th of May was marked by a fog so dense that all warlike operations were necessarily suspended, the proximity of the rival fleets and even of individual ships, being at times only known by the sound of bells and foghorns.

On the 31st the weather cleared, and glasses were eagerly levelled at the French fleet to ascertain

Lord Howe's victory, 29th May to 1st June.

their position, and more especially that of the ships dismasted on the 29th, which might reasonably be regarded as likely prizes. There was not a crippled ship to be seen! The French line still numbered 26 ships, but each of these was apparently as fully equipped and as seaworthy as when she left port. The French had achieved a miracle. But the mystery was cleared up afterwards when it was ascertained that during the fog a reinforcement under Admiral Nielly had joined M. de Villaret Joyeuse, who had accordingly sent his damaged ships at once into Brest.

The whole of the 31st of May was spent in the endeavour to get into position for attack; but this was not accomplished until so late that Lord Howe postponed his onset until the following day. This was construed by the French into a desire to avoid a general action, an opinion still further strengthened by the fact that on the 1st of June Lord Howe hove to about 7.30 A.M. in order that the men might get their breakfasts quietly before engaging. A little after 8 A.M. he again filled and bore down in line ahead upon the enemy, who was also sailing in similar order, with the intention of engaging ship to ship all along their line. Some of his ships, notably the *Cæsar*, behaved badly, and showed an indisposition to close with the enemy; but the greater number obeyed his signal with praiseworthy eagerness. Howe himself, in the *Queen Charlotte* of 100 guns, singled out the French flag-ship, the *Montagne* of 120, and, passing so close under her stern that her ensign brushed his shrouds, poured in his broadside through her stern ports with such terrible effect that 300 men fell with their captain; then ranging alongside

Glorious 1st of June, 1794.

he engaged her at close quarters until the Frenchman managed to wriggle clear, leaving the *Queen Charlotte* unable to follow him from the loss of both fore and main topmasts.

But the central incident of this great action was the tremendous fight between the *Vengeur* and the *Brunswick*, both 74's. The *Brunswick*, which had suffered severely before she herself had fired a shot, in attempting to pierce the French line fell foul of the *Vengeur*; her anchors caught in the Frenchman's rigging, and the ships lay grinding together side by side. By reason of this, the French were unable to open their lower deck ports; moreover, where they were open there was no space to use the long-handled rammers for loading the guns. The same objections applied equally to the lower deck guns of the *Brunswick*; but our sailors were men of resource. They blew off the lids of those of their lower deck ports which were closed, by firing the guns through them, and got over the difficulty of loading by the use of flexible rope-rammers; moreover, by alternately elevating and depressing the muzzles of their guns to the full, they poured one broadside into the bottom of the devoted ship, and blew up her decks with the next. While thus engaged, the *Achille*, 74, was seen through the smoke approaching to the aid of the *Vengeur* with the intention of engaging the *Brunswick* on the other side; but one broadside from the British ship brought down all three masts by the board and, instead of aiding her comrade, she struck her flag. After a terrible embrace of three hours the two ships broke away from each other, and the *Ramillies* coming up poured her fire into the *Vengeur*, splitting her rudder, shattering her sternpost, and making an awful gap in her stern. Meanwhile the *Brunswick's* crew, finding to their sorrow that the *Vengeur's* shot had carried away the wooden cocked-hat which crowned the figurehead of their ship, had prevailed upon their brave skipper, Captain John Harvey (who died a few days after of his wounds), to lend them his, which they nailed with great care and pride upon the battered pate of the Duke of Brunswick. Judging from the ordinary size of figureheads it must have been but a poor protection. But now the ill-fated *Vengeur*, her masts gone, her hull shattered and riven in every direction, her lower deck ports going under at every roll, hung a Union Jack over the quarter and implored help. Those ships who had boats capable of floating hurried to her aid; but it was too late to save all her gallant crew, and with 356 men, mostly wounded, on board, she foundered in sight of the whole fleet shortly after 6 P.M.

With the loss of the *Vengeur* the action closed. Six other ships had struck and been taken possession of, and the French admiral was allowed to make off with the rest of his battered fleet without further effort on our part. It is true that many of our ships were also greatly damaged, and that our men were exhausted with the incessant fighting; but three more French ships were absolutely without a mast while two others had but one left standing; and it seems that these might have been added to our list of prizes with but little extra exertion and with small risk in the presence of an already defeated enemy. Within little more than a week after this Admiral Montague, returning from his successful convoy of the merchant ships committed to his care, saw the shattered remains of the French fleet making its slow way back to Brest, but, considering himself not justified in attempting anything against it with his small force, he held on his course.

The result of this action seems to have given equal satisfaction on both sides of the Channel. Equally with ourselves the French proclaimed a victory. We greeted the name of Lord Howe with cheers; they strewed flowers in the path of the official who published the news of the battle. We created our admiral a marquis; they promoted theirs. We feasted our eyes on the six prizes flying the British flag over the tricolour; they read with delight how the British admiral's deck was cleared by a young cadet with a whiff of grapeshot, upon which he set all sail, signalled his ships to follow him, and fled from the scene. It was the battle of Malaga over again.

The foe had also to be met on the old familiar battle-ground of the West Indies. It is impossible to go into details, though the pluck and resource of the British navy were never better illustrated than in the various attacks on French possessions. Suffice it to say that we took the most important island of Martinique, in the attack upon which the father of our present Queen distinguished himself as a young soldier by his gallantry. St. Lucia fell again to us; and for a time we held Guadaloupe as well, but a sudden attack of the enemy in strong force robbed us of this conquest, which we never again regained. *The West Indies, 1794.*

The two following years, 1795 and 1796, added greatly to the number of our foes, but little to our naval reputation. In January 1795 the Dutch declared war against us: in October 1796 the *Dutch declare war, January 1795.*

Spaniards followed their example; and once more we found ourselves matched against the well-known trio. Three so-called victories earned us more contempt than credit; and the only action worthy of our reputation was a masterly retreat. Admiral De Villaret Joyeuse still commanded the Brest fleet. Twice he put to sea to cruise against us; twice he was driven back by furious gales; he took the *Daphne* frigate and many merchantmen, but lost five ships of the line by wreck. The account, therefore, was fairly equal. But on the 16th of June it seemed as if better fortune awaited him. Not far from Brest he sighted a British squadron of five ships of the line (one three-decker and four 74's), his own force numbering twelve ships of the line. Now was his time; he was more than two to one. He chased, the British fled. French ships in those days were ever more speedy than ours, and he began soon to overhaul them. The British *Mars* was overtaken; her rigging was terribly cut to pieces; it seemed as if she must fall into his hands, when Admiral Cornwallis, in the *Royal Sovereign* of 100 guns, fell back to her support and protected her with his powerful battery. Still the odds seemed too great, and the disaster postponed only, not yet averted. But Cornwallis had a card in his hand which he now resolved to play. He sent the *Phaeton*, frigate, with orders to signal to him from a distance, using a code of which he was well aware that the French were in possession. The *Phaeton* made sail as if to escape, and presently her signal flags were seen fluttering in the distance. They were eagerly read by the French; she saw "a sail"—"two"—"three"—"a fleet"—they were "friends"—they were "mostly

Cornwallis escapes by a ruse, 17th June 1795.

ships of the line "—they were "the Channel fleet"! Providentially a few small sails did at that moment appear in her direction. The French were aware that our Channel fleet was at sea; they did not wait for further information, but abandoning the attack on Cornwallis they made off for their own shores. Three days afterwards they sighted the very fleet from the shadow of which they had just retreated. The substance was more formidable than the shadow; they fled again, and this time with greater reason. Our admiral, Lord Bridport, who had relieved Lord Howe, had 14 ships of the line, of which no less than eight were three-deckers; the Frenchman had but one three-decker among his 12. Could we but overtake them a splendid victory was assured to us. For four days we chased them. Early on the fifth day, June 23rd, off the port of Lorient, we began to come up with them. At 6 A.M. we opened fire, and as our ships arrived upon the scene the battle became more general. Two-thirds of each fleet were now engaged; three of the enemy's ships surrendered; the great French flag-ship, *Le Peuple*, was seriously injured. The French officers themselves admitted that they expected their entire fleet to be destroyed; when at 8.15 A.M. Lord Bridport signalled his ships to discontinue the action, took possession of his prizes, and retired. His principal excuse was his nearness to the shore; it was still at least three miles off. He had lost a splendid chance: the weight of responsibility was too much for him; and the greater part of the Brest fleet remained to be a thorn in our side for many a year after. *Bridport's victory off Lorient, 23rd June 1795.*

In the Mediterranean matters were even worse. There Admiral Hotham, in the *Britannia* of 100

Hotham's victory off Genoa, March 1795.

guns, commanded a fleet of 15 sail of the line. The French had by this time got together a fleet of equal number at Toulon and were burning to retake Corsica. With that object the Toulon fleet, under Admiral Martin, sailed on March 3rd. Hotham from Leghorn went in search of it, sighted it on the 10th and gave chase. The *Ça Ira*, 80, losing two top-masts by collision with one of her friends, fell astern. Nelson in the *Agamemnon*, 64, eagerly seized the opportunity. Working "tack and half tack" astern of her at about 100 yards off for two hours, he raked her with alternate broadsides, and might possibly have taken her on that day had he not been recalled by signal; the great *Sans Culottes*, of 120 guns, was coming to the rescue and had already handled the *Illustrious* so severely that she was obliged to make for Genoa. On the following day the *Ça Ira* was seen apart from the others but supported by the *Censeur*, 74. Round these two ships the action grew hot: we strove to take them, the French bore down to their rescue; but it was too late, and a boat from the *Agamemnon* took possession of both.

To Nelson's surprise and indignation Hotham refused to press his advantage further. He himself remonstrated with the admiral; he was complacent but immovable. "We must be contented," he replied; "we have done very well." Nelson was furious; his standard of victory was of a very different order. "Had we taken ten sail and allowed the eleventh to escape when it had been possible to have got at her, I could never have called it well done;" those were his words, and they embody the principle which governed his whole naval career.

A few months later fortune placed a still greater opportunity in Hotham's hands, an opportunity of which he took even less advantage. On July 8th the *Agamemnon*, having been detached for special service at Genoa, hurried back to San Fiorenzo, where the admiral was lying, with the whole French fleet at her heels. Hotham at once put to sea, but Admiral Martin did not exhibit the same eagerness for the encounter as he had in his chase of the solitary *Agamemnon*. He turned back; Hotham followed him, overtook him on the 13th off Hyères, and brought him to action. Though our fleet numbered six more ships of the line than the French, and though we had six three-deckers to their one, our admiral was once more "contented" when we had taken one 74-gun ship, the *Alcide*, and considering, no doubt, that he had again "done very well," he hauled off, alleging, as in the case of Lord Bridport, the danger of proximity to the land, which in this instance was at least eight miles off. Later on in the year his remissness and want of energy caused us the loss of a whole convoy of merchantmen, and of his prize the *Censeur*, which fell into the hands of a French squadron, of whose movements he was fully informed, but against whom he took no precaution until too late.

<small>Hotham's action off Hyères, September 1795.</small>

The spirit of the British navy in the Mediterranean was represented by Nelson. He went everywhere, he did everything, nothing daunted him. Nothing was too great for him to undertake, nothing too small to do well; but as yet he was only a captain, or at best a commodore, and his influence was not over all. In other parts of the world the balance was fairly equal: in the West Indies we lost St. Lucia to the French; in Africa we gained the Cape of Good Hope from the Dutch.

Failure of French invasion of Ireland, 1795.

But again the dream of invasion was beginning to occupy the minds of our foes across the Channel. In the last days of the year 1795 they set afloat a most formidable force to operate against us in Ireland; 17 line-of-battle ships, 13 frigates, 18,000 troops. The expedition sailed from Brest. One ship of the line was lost at starting; only eight ever reached Bantry Bay; the naval and military commanders narrowly escaped capture in a frigate; a gale came on, the whole force was dispersed, not a single soldier landed on our shores. In 1796 Admiral Hotham was replaced by Sir John Jervis, a man of the sternest mould, unsparing alike of himself and of others, but for a while the results of such a change were unnoticeable. The French were gaining ground everywhere on the shores of the Mediterranean; the Spaniards went over to the enemy and added a fleet of 26 ships of the line and 10 frigates to their force at Toulon. We could no longer hold Corsica and Elba; and at length Sir John Jervis found it

British fleet withdrawn from Mediterranean by Sir J. Jervis.

necessary to abandon the Mediterranean altogether. In December 1796 every ship of the line was anchored under the shelter of the guns of Gibraltar. Our greatest triumph in this year was the capture of a Dutch squadron at the Cape, which surrendered without firing a shot.

The year 1797.

The year 1797 was one of the most glorious, and at the same time one of the most disgraceful years in the annals of the British navy. It may be truly said to be without a parallel. We were at war with three great naval powers close to our doors. We had already met the fleets of France with incomplete success; the Dutch were fitting out a powerful fleet in the Texel; the great naval ports of Spain were echoing with the sounds of eager preparation. The safety of England depended entirely upon the efficiency of the navy, her first and only line of defence. We commenced with a brilliant success; then, as if by a sort of paralysis, the whole discipline of our naval service collapsed, not only in the home ports, but all over the world. It was a frightful epidemic, though most mercifully it passed away almost as quickly as it came. Then followed a grievous disaster to our arms, nearly involving the death of Nelson; and finally the year ended with a victory far more complete than that with which it began.

We left Sir John Jervis at anchor under the guns of Gibraltar, but in a short time we find him outside his station altogether, lying in the mouth of the Tagus. The French mind was still busy with the idea of invasion. Ireland was again its object; but more troops were to be employed, and a huge combination of naval forces was to be formed to support them. The fleets of France, Spain, and Holland were to unite at Brest, were to sweep the channel of every British ship, and then——. But the combination never took place. Nelson, returning from Elba in the *Minerve* frigate, peeped into Cartagena to see what was going on. It was empty; the Spanish fleet had already sailed! With all speed he pressed on to warn Jervis. Passing Gibraltar he was chased by two Spanish liners, and narrowly escaped falling into their hands. That night he sailed unobserved through the whole of the great

Spanish fleet, its ships remarkable as ever for their huge size. On February 13th he joined Sir John Jervis off Cape St. Vincent with the news that the Spaniards were close at hand. Their force was known to be much superior to ours, which was but 15 sail of the line;[1] but Jervis declared that he would fight them if they had 50, though two of his force were so damaged by a collision that in ordinary circumstances one at least would have been considered a cripple. On the morning of the 14th the Spanish fleet under Don Josef de Cordova hove in sight; one huge four-decker of 130 guns, six three-deckers of 112 guns, two 80-gun ships, 18 of 74, 27 in all. To this we had to oppose two

[1] COMPARISON OF FORCES AT ST. VINCENT.

	British Fleet.			Spanish Fleet.
100	*Victory*	. Admiral Sir J. Jervis	130	*Santisima Trinidad*
,,	*Britannia*	V.-Ad. Ch. Thompson	112	*Concepcion*
98	*Barfleur*	V.-Ad. Hon. W. Waldegrave	,,	*Conde de Regla*
,,	*Prince George*	R.-Ad. W. Parker	,,	*Mexicano*
,,	*Blenheim*	Captain Frederick	,,	*Principe de Asturias*
90	*Namur*	Captain Whitshed	,,	*Salvador del Mundo*
74	*Captain*	Commodore Nelson	,,	*San Josef*
,,	*Goliath*	Captain Sir C. H. Knowles	80	*Neptuno*
,,	*Excellent*	Captain Collingwood	,,	*San Nicolas*
,,	*Orion*	Captain Sir J. Saumarez	74	*Atalante*
,,	*Colossus*	Captain Murray	,,	*Bahama*
,,	*Egmont*	Captain Sutton	,,	*Conquestador*
,,	*Culloden*	Captain Troubridge	,,	*Firme*
,,	*Irresistible*	Captain Martin	,,	*Glorioso*
64	*Diadem*	Captain Towry	,,	*Oriente*
			,,	*Pelayo*
			,,	*San Antonio*
			,,	*San Domingo*
			,,	*San Firmin*
			,,	*San F^{co} de Paula*
			,,	*San Genaro*
			,,	*San Ildefonso*
			,,	*San J. Nepomuceno*
			,,	*San Pablo*
			,,	*San Isidro*
			,,	*Soberano*
			,,	*Terrible*

of 100 guns (one so slow as to be almost useless), three of 98 guns, one of 90, eight of 74, and one of 64. Counting guns alone, the Spaniards mounted 1054 more than we did!

When seen, the Spanish fleet was making for Cadiz, arranged, whether by accident or design, in two bodies, the smaller one some distance to leeward, the main body sailing in a confused mass with no appearance of regularity. Between these two bodies, Sir John Jervis, in single line ahead, proposed to pass, exerting all his strength upon the larger of the two, while the smaller, being to leeward, would be unable for some time to join in the action. This he did, signalling his ships to tack in succession when each had passed through, in order to follow up the main body. But Nelson, now flying his broad pendant in the *Captain*, 74, the third ship from the rear of the line, seeing better than his chief the evident intention of the Spanish admiral to pass astern of our line and join his lee division, and interpreting the spirit though disregarding the letter of Jervis' signal, turned right round on his keel and threw his ship alone in front of the enemy's leading ships. It was a gallant, a most gallant manœuvre; but it was terribly hazardous. For a while the little *Captain*, one of the smallest 74's in the navy, had to endure totally unsupported the fire of five, or, according to some accounts, of seven of the enemy's largest ships, including the huge *Santisima Trinidad* of 130 guns. Troubridge in the *Culloden*, the ship so seriously injured by collision, followed and supported him, as did in a short while Collingwood in the *Excellent*. By this time the *Captain* was

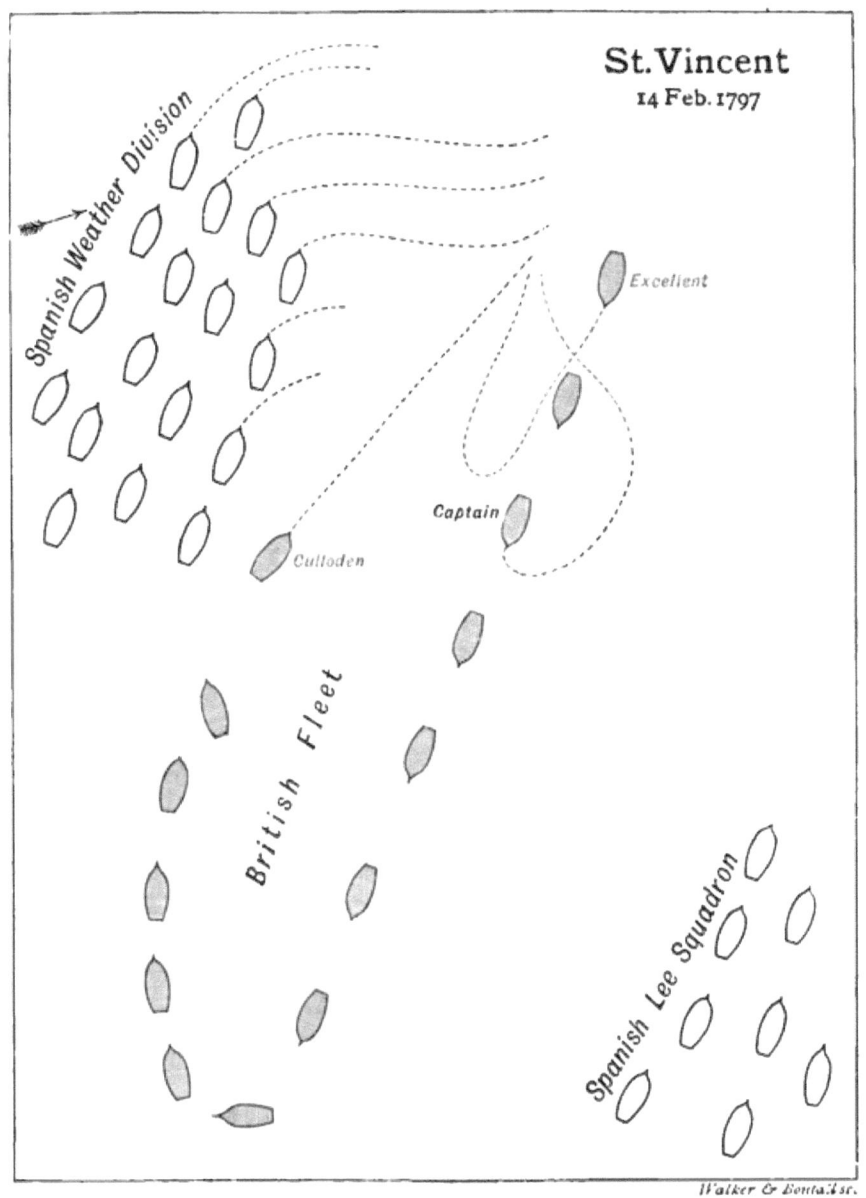

Note.—The position of the *Britannia* cannot be indicated. See pages 177 *end* and 178.

little more than a wreck, her foretopmast gone, her wheel shot away, not a sail, not a shroud, not a rope left. Two great Spanish liners, crippled and helpless under her tremendous fire,—the *San Nicolas*, 80, and the *San Josef*, 112—fell foul of each other, and on to the starboard quarter of the former drove the *Captain* herself, her port cathead hooking in the quarter gallery of the Spaniard. Nelson at once called away his boarders; they broke through the stern windows, forced their way on deck, and hauled down the Spanish flag. No sooner did the *San Josef's* people perceive this than they opened a heavy fire of small arms upon the British boarding-party. Nelson never hesitated. Calling his men once more together, he boarded the great three-decker also, overpowered her resistance, and received on her quarter-deck the swords of all her officers. It was a glorious moment. The *Victory* and every ship of the fleet as she passed gave him three ringing cheers. Two other vessels had also struck to us, the *San Isidro* of 74, and the *Salvador del Mundo* of 112 guns. The *Santisima Trinidad*, disabled by her small antagonist, with only her mainmast standing, is also affirmed to have surrendered, but she made her escape. For more than a month she floundered about helplessly at sea before making Cadiz, pounded viciously by a British frigate to whom she almost fell a prize, and from whom she was only rescued by the timely arrival of a squadron of Spanish 74's. The action closed at 5 P.M. At ten minutes to that hour the *Britannia* had fired her first shot. She was, next to the *Victory*, the finest three-decker in Jervis' fleet: the help of her 100 guns and some 900 men would have been invaluable to us, overmatched as we were; but she was the greatest slug in the whole British navy, and though the battle commenced a little before noon, it was not till five hours later that she could get into action. She had one seaman wounded. What were the feelings of Vice-Admiral Thompson, whose flag she bore, and of the men and officers on board of her, it is impossible to represent. As in previous encounters, there were many who blamed the British admiral for not pressing his advantage farther and taking possession of other ships which might have fallen an easy prey. But the general feeling in England was one of unbounded relief and gratification, which may be the better gauged by the fact that, previous to the announcement of the victory, the Bank of England were thinking of suspending cash payments. Sir John Jervis was raised to the peerage under the title of Lord St. Vincent, and Nelson, the central figure of the fight, the hero of the hour, having just attained his flag, was made a Knight of the Bath; while poor Don Josef de Cordova and most of his officers were smothered with every mark of disgrace and shame which an indignant Government could heap upon them.

But almost ere our shouts of exultation had ceased to echo, all sense of triumph was merged in the calamity which now seized upon our first line of defence. The entire navy broke into open mutiny. There was in truth but too much reason for discontent. The pay was miserably poor, never having been advanced since the reign of Charles II.; the food was equally bad; the men were at the mercy of unscrupulous and grasping pursers; the life was frightfully hard, the discipline harsh and in many cases brutal; and there was no redress. The bluejackets at Portsmouth had already petitioned Lord Howe on the subject. He had referred the petition to presumably responsible officials, who had dismissed the matter as the work of one or two bad characters. But by degrees the suspicions of the Admiralty were aroused, and they ordered Lord Bridport with the Channel fleet to proceed to sea. On April 15th he hoisted the signal to weigh; instead of obeying all the ships manned the rigging and gave three cheers. The blow fell like a bolt out of a clear sky. The men were respectful, but determined. Each ship selected two delegates to lay their complaints before the Admiralty, utterly refusing to resume their duties until their wrongs were redressed. A full inquiry was now made and their statements proved to be only too well founded. Their demands were granted and a general pardon promised. For the moment they were satisfied, but the movements of the law are ever slow. A vexatious delay ensued: the men grew suspicious; and when, on May 7th, the order to weigh was repeated they again refused. This time blood was spilled. A man was shot by a lieutenant of the *London;* the bluejackets seized and would have hanged him on the spot, had not Admiral Colpoys taken the blame upon himself. They contented themselves with disarming their officers and confining them in their cabins. A week later the Act of Parliament was passed: the pardon was proclaimed; the men of Portsmouth and Plymouth returned to their allegiance.

Mutiny at Spithead, 15th April 1797.

But as they did so the fleet at the Nore broke

out. The spirit of disaffection was abroad, and once started it was hard to arrest. The ruling spirit of the eastern port was one Richard Parker, a man of disreputable character. Twice he had served as midshipman, and on each occasion had been dismissed in disgraceful circumstances; he had again obtained a commission as mate, but had been tried by court-martial and been pronounced unfit ever to serve again as an officer. He had fallen lower and lower, and was now on board the *Sandwich*, Admiral Buckner's flag-ship, as a bluejacket. He was well educated, clever, unscrupulous, a fomenter of discontent and disobedience, with a certain dangerous power of organisation and command. On the 13th of May, at his instigation, the men of the *Inflexible* fired into the *San Fiorenzo*, on board which ship a court-martial was sitting. A week later delegates, in imitation of the Spithead fleet, presented a list of demands to the Admiralty, which were not only unreasonable, but foolish. The disease spread quickly. By the end of May eleven of Admiral Duncan's fleet on duty off the Texel hoisted the red flag and joined the mutineers, leaving Duncan with only the *Venerable*, 74, and one other to face the Dutch. Taking a leaf out of Cornwallis' book he amused the Dutch with false signals to an imaginary fleet presumably out of sight of land, and they never stirred. Even his own flag-ship, however, was not free from the infection, and in spite of an affectionate and touching appeal to his men, he was obliged to take the most stringent precautions. Parker now laid his ships across the mouth of the Thames, stopped all traffic and commerce, and made use of violent threats. But his cause was already

Mutiny at the Nore, 13th May 1797.

North Sea fleet mutinies.

falling to pieces. The Government showed the greatest firmness; the Plymouth and Portsmouth men loudly expressed their disapprobation; his own ships began to waver. There was nothing for him to do. If he used violence to an English port the indignation of the entire country would be turned upon him; if he put to sea he was the common enemy of Europe and of his own countrymen. Those who followed him would not dream of permitting him to hand over the fleet to the foe; his stores would soon fail and could only be replenished by force; money he had none. On June 10th two ships left him under fire from the rest, and gave themselves up; each morning as it dawned revealed the defection of others; and on the 14th his own ship hauled down the red flag and allowed Parker to be arrested. He was tried, found guilty, and hanged on the 29th of June. But this was not all. Not even the terror of the stern Jervis, now Lord St. Vincent, nor the memory of his late victory could keep the contamination from the fleet which he commanded off Cadiz. The *St. George* broke out into mutiny; the ringleaders were seized, were instantly tried, and hanged the next day, Sunday, by the hands of their own shipmates, contrary to all use and custom. A similar fate was decreed for other malefactors on board the *Defence*, but their shipmates refused to hang them. The stern old admiral surrounded the ship with launches, each armed with a heavy carronade, and threatened to blow her out of the water at the first sign of disobedience. The signal for execution was given; the men were hanged without a word.

Far away in the South Atlantic the fell disease

Disaffection in Jervis' fleet.

Mutiny in Cape squadron.

again broke out. The squadron at the Cape mutinied; the *Tremendous*, flag-ship of Admiral Pringle, was seized by her crew. The admiral was uncertain how to act, but the governor, Lord Macartney, was a man of different mould. He manned the great battery under which the *Tremendous* lay, made his shot red-hot, loaded his guns, and threatened to destroy her at her anchors, unless the red flag was instantly hauled down. Unprepared for such fierce retaliation the men were taken by surprise; the flag of rebellion came fluttering down, and they returned to their duty.

Mutiny on board Hermione.

One more instance, the worst of all, and the disgraceful history is closed. Captain Hugh Pigot commanded in the West Indies the 32-gun frigate *Hermione*. Possibly he was a man endued with brute courage, at any rate he had lately planned a cutting-out expedition which had been conducted with marked success; but he was the very stamp of officer from whom the British bluejacket most needed to be protected. He was not merely a martinet; he was cruel, brutal, ferocious. His brutality, beyond all reach of restraint, became more frightful every day. At last, while the men were aloft reefing topsails, he threatened to flog the last man off the mizen-topsail-yard. The yardarm men, selected for their smartness, would naturally be the last on deck when piped down from aloft. They knew he would carry out his threat; they made frantic efforts to reach the deck before their comrades, missed their hold, and were dashed to death at his feet. His only remark was an order to "throw the lubbers overboard." From that moment his fate was sealed; and had the vengeance of the men vented itself upon him alone, it would be hard to cast reproach upon them. But in their blind fury they knew no distinction of persons. On the next evening they rose in a body, cut the throat of the first lieutenant, and threw him overboard. They next attacked the captain in his cabin, stabbed him repeatedly, and hurled him, still alive, through the cabin windows. Then, mad with blood, they went round the ship and murdered every officer on board except the master, the gunner, the carpenter, and one midshipman. Finally they carried the *Hermione* into La Guayra, and handed her over to the Spaniards, from whom she was recovered two years later in a marvellously gallant manner by Captain Edward Hamilton of the *Surprise*.

Thus ends the painful story of the mutiny, the most terrible and disgraceful page in the annals of our navy. As it was not without reason that it broke out, so it was not without great benefit to the service when it closed. Since then the condition of the British bluejacket has been an ever-increasing care to the government of the country which he guards, and of which he deserves, and has deserved so well. Well was it for us that at that moment the counsels of the rulers of France were hopelessly divided. Though fully aware of what was going on on our shores, and openly rejoicing at it, they were unable to take advantage of the helpless condition to which our own culpable neglect had reduced us.

The Spanish fleet had fled for shelter to Cadiz. Thither Lord St. Vincent, after refitting at Lagos, had followed them, and there he did all in his power to induce them to come out and fight once more. But they would not stir. Failing to allure them he tried to drive them out. He sent Admiral Nelson

Nelson bombards Cadiz.

in to bombard the fleet from mortar boats; but the only result was to make the Spaniards warp farther in under the shelter of their batteries. It was during this bombardment that Nelson ran almost greater risk of his life, and displayed perhaps greater personal courage than at any other time in his career. His barge with its ordinary crew of 15 was attacked by a large Spanish launch manned by 26 men and the commandante of Cadiz in person; an attack which ended in the slaughter of 18 Spaniards and the capture of the officer and his launch.

Occupied now only with the dreary duty of watching patiently for the sailing of an enemy who never intended to leave the shelter of his fortifications, St. Vincent's mind turned to schemes for annoying the foe in other directions. The Canary Isles were within easy reach of Cadiz. As in the days of Cromwell, Santa Cruz was still the rendezvous of many a rich galleon from the Americas, and such a galleon had been reported as then lying there. Blake had made havoc of a Spanish force there in time past; what should hinder him from doing the same? Nelson eagerly embraced the scheme and undertook the business himself. St. Vincent gave him a squadron, the first separate force which Nelson as an admiral had ever commanded. It consisted of three 74's, one 50, three frigates, and a cutter. Nelson's flag flew on board the *Theseus*, the crew of which ship, in wonderful contrast to the mutinous conduct of the others, had placed a paper on the quarter-deck signed by the ship's company, declaring their devotion to their officers and their willingness to shed every drop of their blood for their admiral and captain. On July 15th Nelson sailed brimful of confidence; on

Nelson sent to attack Santa Cruz.

the 20th he sighted the islands; on the night of the 21st he attempted a surprise with the boats of the squadron, but wind and tide were too strong for them and they returned. On the 24th at 11 P.M. he made his second attempt, but all hope of a surprise was now over. The men were to land at the mole and seize the town. The night was intensely dark, the weather was wild, the sea rough; many of the boats lost their way, and either recoiled from the tremendous surf dashing on the dangerous shore, or attempting to land through it were hurled on to the rocks, staved in and swamped, so that the ammunition was ruined. Nelson himself reached the mole, but at the moment of touching it he fell, shot down by the withering fire of the Spaniards who occupied it in force. Had it not been for his stepson, Josiah Nisbet, he must have died in the boat. He was carried back to his own ship, where his right arm was at once amputated. The attack was a complete and utter failure. Troubridge indeed had managed to collect some 300 men ashore, and, though without ammunition and opposed by 8000 Spaniards, had borne himself so gallantly that the commandante was only too glad to lend him boats to enable him to relieve Santa Cruz of his presence and rejoin his ships. But our loss was very heavy, and no method of reasoning could make it out to be anything but a defeat. The squadron rejoined St. Vincent, and Nelson, who had gone out in such high confidence, returned to England in such terrible suffering that for some time his life was despaired of.

Attack fails. Nelson loses his arm.

Towards the end of the year the gloom and anxiety spread over the nation by the mutiny of the navy and the defeat at Santa Cruz were lightened considerably by a ray of sunlight in the North Sea. The triple combination of fleets at Brest had not yet taken place. The Spaniards had got no farther than St. Vincent when they were driven fiercely back to Cadiz, and dared not sail again; it was now the turn of the Dutch. In the Texel Admiral De Winter had 15 ships of the line and four frigates; but the keen watch kept on him by Duncan had prevented him from venturing out, even during the time of the mutiny at the Nore. But in October Duncan was forced to return to England with his fleet sadly in want of repair from long exposure to the gales of the North Sea, and with his store and provision rooms almost empty. De Winter lost not a moment. He sailed at once for Brest, not, however, unperceived by our look-outs. The *Active*, frigate, sighted him, and with every stitch of canvas set hurried off to Yarmouth to warn the admiral. He at once started in pursuit, and on October 11th off Camperdown on the coast of Holland discovered the fleet which he had watched so long and in such trying circumstances. He was superior in force, his ships being on an average heavier than those of the Dutch and numbering 16 to their 15.[1]

Victory off Camperdown, 11th October 1797.

[1] COMPARISON OF FORCES AT CAMPERDOWN.

British Fleet.

74	*Venerable*	.	.	.	.	Admiral Duncan
,,	*Monarch*	.	.	.	.	Vice-Admiral Onslow
,,	*Russel*	.	.	.	.	Captain Trollope
,,	*Montagu*	.	.	.	.	Captain Knight
,,	*Bedford*	.	.	.	.	Captain Sir T. Byard
,,	*Powerful*	.	.	.	.	Captain Drury
,,	*Triumph*	.	.	.	.	Captain Essington
,,	*Belliqueux*	.	.	.	.	Captain Inglis
,,	*Agincourt*	.	.	.	.	Captain Williamson
,,	*Lancaster*	.	.	.	.	Captain Wells
,,	*Ardent*	.	.	.	.	Captain Burgess

De Winter tried to embarrass him by leading him among the dangerous shoals of that coast, naturally much better known to himself than to Duncan. Our admiral, however, was determined to bring on a general action; he had watched and waited too long to allow himself to be balked of his opportunity when at last it came. He signalled each of his ships to attack as she came up; and himself pressing forward in the *Venerable* made for De Winter's flag-ship, the *Vryheid*, passing under the stern of the *States General* which gallantly endeavoured to interpose and shield her admiral, and raking her with disastrous effect. Then Dutch and English set to work and pounded each other after the fashion so well known to both in the days of Charles II., each pouring his broadsides into the other's hull at close quarters, and endeavouring to crush him by rapidity of fire. Again and again the flag of the *Venerable* was shot away, until nailed to

64	*Veteran*	.	.	.	.	Captain Gregory
,,	*Director*	.	.	.	.	Captain Bligh
,,	*Monmouth*	.	.	.	.	Captain Walker
50	*Isis* .	.	.	.	.	Captain Mitchell
,,	*Adamant*	.	.	.	.	Captain Hotham

Dutch Fleet.

74	*Vryheid*	.	.	.	.	Vice-Admiral De Winter
,,	*Jupiter*	.	.	.	.	Vice-Admiral Reyntjes
,,	*Brutus*	.	.	.	.	Rear-Admiral Bloys
,,	*States General*	.	.	.	.	Rear-Admiral Storey
64	*Cerberus*	.	.	.	.	Captain Jacobson
,,	*Devries*	.	.	.	.	Captain Zegers
,,	*Gelykheid*	.	.	.	.	Captain Ruysen
,,	*Haerlem*	.	.	.	.	Captain Wiggerts
,,	*Hercules*	.	.	.	.	Captain Van Rysoort
,,	*Leyden*	.	.	.	.	Captain Musquetier
,,	*Wassenaer*	.	.	.	.	Captain Holland
50	*Alkmaar*	.	.	.	.	Captain **Kraft**
,,	*Batavier*	.	.	.	.	Captain Souters
,,	*Beschermer*	.	.	.	.	Captain Hinxt
,,	*Delft* .	.	.	.	.	Captain Verdoorn

the mast-head by one of her men; again and again her broadsides tore the *Vryheid* to pieces; until at last totally dismasted, his guns so lumbered up with wreckage that they could not be fired, his few unwounded men frantically working at the pumps, and with three fresh foes upon him, De Winter reluctantly hauled down the flag which he had fought so bravely to defend. His surrender was the signal for the cessation of the fight. Several of the Dutch ships were already in flight; those that remained could hardly be kept afloat. No better or more convincing proof of the fury of this action can be produced than the fact that, of the nine ships of the line and two frigates which surrendered to us on that day, not one could be made serviceable again. The *Delft*, 56, in tow of the *Veteran*, went down during the gale which rose after the action was over, carrying with her all her wounded and her first lieutenant who refused to leave his helpless men, and recalling the fate of the *Hollandia* after Sir Hyde Parker's victory in 1781. Our ships had suffered almost equally. The *Ardent* had 98 round shot in her hull: the pumps were kept hard at it throughout the fleet; and it was with great difficulty that the battered victors brought themselves and their disfigured prizes to the shelter of the Nore. But the effect of the victory was incalculable. The second factor in the great naval combination was crushed well-nigh to death: the credit of Great Britain was immensely strengthened and increased; and we were free once more to face the most formidable of our opponents unhampered by the necessity of guarding our flank. It seems almost unnecessary to mention that Duncan was made a peer, and that rewards and promotions flowed freely from a grateful people. All London was illuminated in token of the national rejoicing; and while Nelson lay dying, as was supposed, of his unhealed wound, a triumphant mob hammered at his door to demand indignantly why his windows were left dark. But when they heard that it **was** Nelson's house, they went silently off down the street pledging themselves that he should suffer no further molestation, so great **was** even then his fame, and so firm his hold upon **the** public heart.

CHAPTER XI

General Humbert lands in Ireland—His surrender—Warren's victory off the west coast of Ireland—Nelson sent to the Mediterranean—French expedition to Egypt—Vanguard dismasted—Pursuit of French fleet—Battle of the Nile—Admiral Bruix's cruise from Brest—Operations on the Italian seaboard—Defence of Acre—Surrender of Dutch fleet to Lord Duncan—Capture of the *Thetis* and *Santa Brigida*—Siege of Malta—Capture of *Généreux* and *Guillaume Tell*—Surrender of Malta—Loss of the *Queen Charlotte* by fire—The *Freya* incident—"Armed Neutrality of the North"—Battle of Copenhagen—Nelson's home command—Attack on Boulogne—Ganteaume's attempt to relieve the army in Egypt—Linois and Saumarez at Algeciras—Treaty of Amiens.

Buonaparte urges invasion.

THE idea of invasion had by no means been abandoned by the French since the fiasco in December 1795. On the contrary, it assumed, as time went on, a more important aspect in their eyes, more especially in those of General Buonaparte, now rapidly becoming the leading spirit of the Republic. In a document dated April 13th, 1798, he urged the completion of the fleets at Brest, Lorient, and Rochefort, the building of hundreds of gun and flat-boats, the concentration of 40,000 troops to cross the Channel and land on our shores. At present, however, he was but a general; in a few years more, as Emperor, he would carry out these schemes on a scale of such vast magnitude as to cause us the greatest apprehension. At this time Ireland seemed the most suitable spot in the British Isles in which to foment rebellion and to land troops. The former was easy, as the terrible outbreak of May 1798 fully testifies; the latter was beset with difficulty and danger. Two expeditions were prepared, at Rochefort and at Brest, intended probably to act simultaneously, but failing in that particular. The one from Rochefort, consisting only of four frigates with a small body of troops under General Humbert, sailed in August, and evading our look-outs, landed its force in Killala Bay. This force was shortly afterwards obliged to surrender to General Lake, while the four frigates narrowly escaped capture at the hands of a superior squadron.

General Humbert lands in Ireland. Surrenders, August 1798.

In the following month the larger and far more threatening expedition sailed from Brest, one ship of the line and eight frigates, carrying 3000 troops. They, too, aimed for the north-west coast of Ireland. But every fathom of their route was dogged by three smart British frigates who divined their purpose, refused to be misled by their change of course, hung incessantly upon their flanks, ran away when chased, returned persistently when the pursuit was abandoned, and finally brought down upon them Sir J. B. Warren with three ships of the line and two more frigates off the coast of Donegal. Ere they could fight, a gale sprang up which gave both squadrons enough to do to ensure their own safety, but on October 12th the French with their ships badly damaged, especially the *Hoche*, 74, found themselves out of their reckoning, and in the midst of Admiral Warren's squadron. There was to be no landing of troops; there could be no retreat. They had to fight; and fight they did, bravely and well as always when

Brest expedition starts for Ireland, September 1798.

there was no help for it; but the fates and the heavy fire of the English were against them. The battle began at 7 A.M. Four hours afterwards the *Hoche*, riddled with shot, with five feet of water in her hold, with 25 guns dismounted and her masts tottering, struck her colours. Her example was followed by three of her frigates; the remaining five, fleeing to the west, attempted in passing to wreak their vengeance on the *Anson*, 34, whose mizen-mast had been carried away, and who was far to leeward without support; but, crippled as she was, she was ready for them, and beat them off one after another until the approach of some of her friends warned them to be off. Only two of the whole squadron ever reached a French port again. The invasion of rebellious Ireland did not prove so easy as it looked.

Brest squadron defeated by Admiral Warren.

But the principal battle-ground of the year 1798 was the Mediterranean, and it was on that quarter that the eyes of Europe were fixed in breathless interest. During the whole of the previous year no British line-of-battle ship and hardly a British frigate had ventured within the Straits of Gibraltar. The triple combination against us had forced us to abandon the Mediterranean entirely to the French and Spaniards; they might build ships, fit out fleets, send out expeditions, unhindered by the interference of any British force or the prying eyes of a frigate. But now it was different; we had dealt a hard blow at the Spaniards, a still harder one at the Dutch. Mischief was undoubtedly being hatched at Toulon; and St. Vincent, who, with an eye ever on Cadiz, had made the Tagus his winter anchorage, was anxious to know what was going on in that busy and dangerous port. On the 29th of April Nelson, now fully recovered of his wound, joined him in the *Vanguard*, 74. Here was the very man for his purpose. Giving him two more 74's and two frigates he sent him into the hornets' nest to find out all that was possible, to take such measures as his small force would permit him against the enemy, and to report to him as speedily as possible. Nelson was delighted. He entered the straits and made direct for Toulon. Close off the port he took a French corvette, made the most searching enquiry among her men, and discovered that 15 ships of the line were ready to sail, that four others were fitting out, and that Buonaparte himself was there busily embarking an army of 36,000 men, the destination of which, however, was unknown.

Nelson sent to watch Toulon.

At once Nelson sent off a small sloop to warn St. Vincent of the danger. He himself hung about in the Gulf of Lions waiting for fresh developments; but on May 20th his squadron was overtaken by so furious a gale that the *Vanguard* was dismasted, and, had it not been for the timely aid of the *Alexander*, must have gone to pieces on the rocky shore of Sardinia. With the help of that ship, however, she reached the shelter of San Pietro on the south-west of the island, and there made in four days such a refit as the resources of the little squadron and the feverish haste of Nelson would permit. With a main-topmast doing duty as a foremast, and with two topgallant-masts in place of topmasts, she sailed once more; and on June 5th Nelson was delighted by the arrival of the *Mutine* brig, with the news that Captain Troubridge with 10 ships of the line and one of 50 guns was hurrying to reinforce him. Two days later Troubridge joined,

Vanguard dismasted in a gale.

Nelson is given a fleet.

O

and Nelson, pronouncing himself "a match for any French force afloat," set out to obey his new instructions, which were to hunt the Toulon fleet wherever it might go, and to "take, burn, sink, or destroy it" when found. The object of the Toulon expedition was an utter mystery. It was variously stated to be Naples, Sicily, Portugal, Ireland ; but Nelson with marvellous intuition at once formed the opinion that its destination was Egypt, and that it was closely connected with a projected attack upon our possessions in India. On June 14th he heard that ten days before it had been sighted off Sicily —13 sail of the line, four frigates, 200 transports, 36,000 troops, nine generals of division and Buonaparte himself. On the 20th he learned at Messina that they had taken Malta, and two days later that they had left that island with a fresh north-west wind. He was more than ever convinced that their destination was Egypt, and with all possible sail he hurried after them. That very night, the night of June 22nd, in thick, dark, foggy weather, he was close to them, unknown to himself or them, and might, had Providence so willed it, have not only defeated the French fleet but destroyed the French army, made a prisoner of Napoleon Buonaparte, and so entirely altered the history of Europe for the next seventeen years. But it was not to be : neither fleet suspected the presence of the other ; and Nelson, pressing on in all haste, steered his eager course for Alexandria, reached it six days later, and found it absolutely empty. It was a bitter disappointment. What should he do next ? He worked back towards Sicily, covering all the area he possibly could lest he might miss the enemy, and discussing with his captains every possible method of attack in all probable circumstances of encounter. He reached Sicily, but learned no fresh news. On July 25th, after filling up with water and fresh provisions at Syracuse, he headed once more for the east. So terribly anxious was he that he even contemplated a return to England should he fail to find what he sought. Near Matapan he learned that four weeks earlier the French fleet had been seen off Candia steering south-east. Though puzzled and perplexed at his ill-success, he was still convinced that they were aiming at Egypt. Once more he headed for Alexandria, and at 3 P.M. on the 1st of August his eyes were gladdened by a signal from the *Zealous*—" Sixteen sail in Aboukir Bay." Just one month before, two days after he had left it in despair, the French had arrived at Alexandria and had landed their general and his army ; but finding the harbour too shallow for his great flag-ship, Admiral Brueys had anchored in the Bay of Aboukir. His ships were drawn right across the bay in single line, forming an obtuse angle at its centre, the curve of the bay representing a bow half drawn, the French line the bowstring, with the flag-ship at the angle. A battery on a small island at the head of his line further strengthened his position, while inside his 13 line-of-battle ships his four frigates found anchorage. Brueys' opinion of the whole situation is interesting, and so utterly mistaken as to be almost amusing. He had reported to his Government that the British fleet, being undoubtedly weaker, was evidently keeping out of his way. He had taken up such a position as, in the words of Commissary Jaubert, "to bid defiance to a force

Battle of the Nile, 1st August 1798.

double our own." Even when the British fleet hove in sight, so strong was his belief in his impregnable position, that he awaited the attack with complacency, convinced that the English would never dream of opening fire so late in the evening. But he did not know Nelson; with him to see his enemy was to go at him, and he at once hoisted his signal for battle.[1] All his plans had been discussed again and again with his captains. They knew exactly what he would do; they knew, before his signal flew, that he would concentrate all his force upon the enemy's centre and van, and leave the helpless rear to wait idly until its turn came. For Nelson saw at once

[1] COMPARISON OF FORCES AT THE NILE.

British Fleet.

74	*Vanguard*	Rear-Admiral Nelson
,,	*Orion*	Captain Sir J. Saumarez
,,	*Culloden*	Captain Troubridge
,,	*Bellerophon*	Captain Darby
,,	*Minotaur*	Captain Louis
,,	*Defence*	Captain Peyton
,,	*Alexander*	Captain Ball
,,	*Zealous*	Captain Hood
,,	*Audacious*	Captain Gould
,,	*Goliath*	Captain Foley
,,	*Majestic*	Captain Westcott
,,	*Swiftsure*	Captain Hallowell
,,	*Theseus*	Captain Miller
50	*Leander*	Captain Thompson

French Fleet.

120	*L'Orient*	Vice-Admiral Brueys
80	*Franklin*	Rear-Admiral Blanquet
,,	*Guillaume Tell*	Rear-Admiral Villeneuve
,,	*Tonnant*	Commodore du Petit-Thouars
74	*Aquilon*	Commodore Thevenard
,,	*Généreux*	Captain Le Joille
,,	*Conquérant*	Captain Dalbarade
,,	*Heureux*	Captain Etienne
,,	*Guerrier*	Captain Trullet
,,	*Mercure*	Captain Cambon
,,	*Peuple-Souverain*	Captain Raccord
,,	*Spartiate*	Captain Emeriau
,,	*Timoléon*	Captain Trullet

that poor Brueys' impregnable position was nothing more or less than a death trap; and signalling his ships to prepare to anchor by the stern, he pressed on to the long-desired encounter. The *Goliath* led the line, followed by the *Zealous*. Seeing that the French were lying at single anchor, it was at once clear that where they had room to swing there must be space to pass between their vanship and the edge of the shoal; moreover, between all the ships of their line there was a gap of 160 yards through which also our ships could pass easily. The *Goliath* held on for the head of the French line. At 6.30 they opened their fire, but disregarding it she rounded their van and anchored opposite their second ship, the *Conquérant*. The *Zealous* following anchored slightly ahead of, but inside the *Guerrier*, the first of their line; the *Orion*, the *Audacious*, and the *Theseus* also passed inside, the first-named sinking the *Serieuse* frigate as she did so. Nelson in the *Vanguard* was the first to take up his position on the outside of the line: others quickly followed his example; and thus the leading ships of the enemy were caught between two fires, while those in the rear could do nothing. The fire of the entire British fleet was concentrated on some seven of the French ships: their destruction was inevitable; while, so confident had the French been in their position and so unprepared for attack on any but their outside, that their port guns were not cleared for action, and were lumbered up with spare gear of every description. So far, all was well; but now a great disaster fell upon us. It was dark; the navigation of Aboukir Bay was imperfectly, if at all known to us. The *Culloden*,

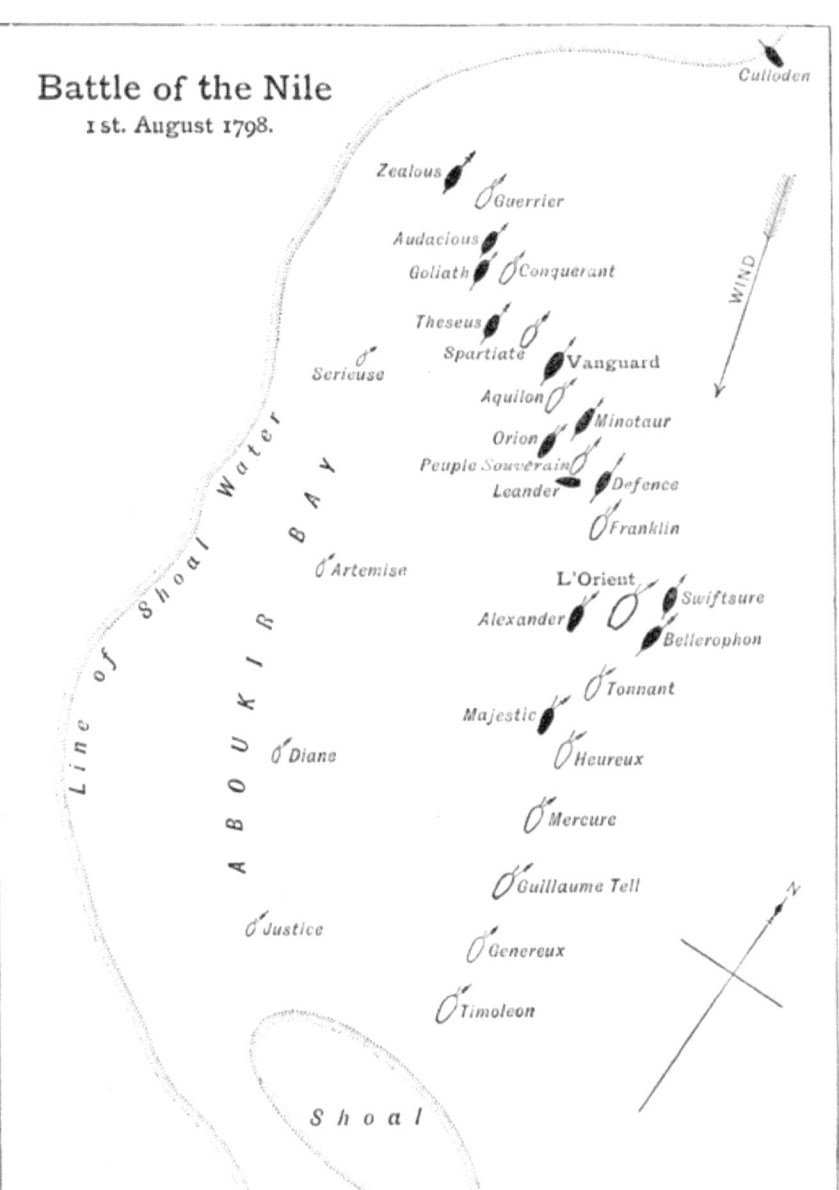

commanded by the gallant Troubridge ran hard and fast upon the edge of the reef far out of range. All the efforts of her men failed to move her. Troubridge, however, in spite of his despair, warned off the *Swiftsure* and *Alexander*, who were following him, and they with the little *Leander*, avoiding the fate which had befallen him, groped their way into action guided by the incessant flashes of the guns. Already the crushing effect of our double fire was beginning to tell. The *Conquérant*, totally dismasted, was the first to strike; the *Guerrier*, with half her topsides torn away, her maindeck ports from bow to waist knocked into one huge rent, and hardly a stump left, followed her example; the *Spartiate* and *Aquilon* also surrendered. But in the meantime Nelson himself, grievously wounded in the head, and for a time entirely blind, was carried below, apparently in a dying state. He refused to allow the surgeons to attend to him to the neglect of others, and though suffering agony, he calmly made arrangements for the command of the fleet in case of his death. When at length his turn came a feeling of intense relief pervaded the ship when it was known that the wound, though terribly severe, was not mortal. Much against his will, Nelson was prevailed upon to remain below. But he did not stay there long. Shortly after nine a huge blaze of light shot up in the very centre of the French line, and the cry went up that the great *L'Orient*, Brueys' flag-ship, was on fire. She had fought hard and well, as by her great size and strength she might have been expected to do, and had forced the *Bellerophon* to withdraw from action disabled; but she herself was totally dismasted, and her ill-fated admiral was already lying dead on her quarter-deck. For an hour she burned fiercely, the huge flames lighting up the bay with the brilliancy of day. All eyes turned upon her, and even Nelson, suffering as he was and more than half-blind, found his way on deck to gaze upon the awful scene. At ten, with a frightful explosion, the effect of which was violently felt throughout both fleets, she blew up, filling the air with flaming brands and dismembered corpses, with shattered beams and masses of iron, and setting fire to the *Franklin* and other vessels which lay in her vicinity. For a period variously estimated at from three to fifteen minutes a great and awful horror fell on all around. Not a gun was fired; but the air resounded with the crash of falling spars and hissing timbers, while above all rose the shrieks of the poor wretches who, hurled into the water scorched and wounded, implored us to save them. Some seventy were thus rescued by our boats. It was a French ship that broke the spell. The *Franklin* fired a gun and recommenced the action, but being set upon at the same time by the *Defence*, *Swiftsure*, and *Orion*, while the *Leander* raked her through her port bow, her main and mizen-masts fell over the side and she shortly afterwards surrendered. When day dawned there were but three ships of the French line whose turn had not yet come—the *Guillaume Tell*, the *Généreux*, and the *Timoléon*. The latter slipping her cable was driven ashore by the *Theseus*, set on fire by her own crew, and abandoned; the others, though chased for some time by the *Zealous*, made sail and escaped with two of the frigates.

It was the most complete victory that had ever

crowned the efforts of the British navy. Of the 13 ships which, the evening before, had formed Brueys' line of battle, nine were taken, one was burned, one blew up. Nelson's orders to "take, burn, sink, or destroy," had been construed by him literally; and he was wont to affirm that had he not been wounded the other two would not have escaped. Even the battery on the island was taken and its guns removed. Nelson's first thought, though racked with the intense pain of his wound and the fever consequent upon it to such an extent that the doctors feared for his life, was to return public thanks to God for so great a victory: his second, to send the news to St. Vincent and to England; and then to refit his battered fleet and those of his prizes which were not altogether ruined. Three of them he was obliged to burn as utterly smashed to pieces, the rest he sent home as the visible pledges of his triumph. The unfortunate *Culloden*, after bumping on the reef all the night of the battle, had been got off next day with incredible exertions, and now lay at anchor with her rudder gone and her bottom so seriously injured that she made seven feet of water an hour. Yet in less than three weeks Nelson took her with his own shattered flag-ship and the *Alexander* to Naples.

It is impossible to describe the exultation in England, in Europe, and in India at the news of the victory. It is from the lips of our foes that we learn how crushing was the blow. Not only, the French complain, was a great fleet destroyed and the command of the Mediterranean wrested from them, but it encouraged Turkey to take up arms; it rekindled the spirit of Germany and brought the

Russians into the Mediterranean; Italy and the Adriatic were as good as lost; India was no longer assailable; Egypt was made an open enemy, and a French army was left to march to and fro there, until there was nothing left for it but surrender. If Nelson was a hero after St. Vincent, he was a demi-god after the Nile. But it is singular how sparing the Government were in their recognition of his magnificent services. Sir John Jervis had been made an earl for the incomplete victory of St. Vincent. Nelson, for the most complete victory in the history of our navy, was only made a baron. Other countries, however, recognised his worth. The East India Company voted him £10,000; the Sultan, the Emperor of Russia, and the King of Sardinia showered splendid gifts upon him; the King of Naples gave him an estate in Sicily worth £3000 a year, with the singularly appropriate title of Duke of Bronte (Thunder). His name was in every one's mouth; he was the one topic of conversation. But for all that he did not for one moment relax his efforts against the French. He took Leghorn, blockaded Malta, saw to the safety of the royal family of Naples, and did everything in his power to paralyse the movements of the enemy in Italy; while towards the end of the year a separate squadron despatched by St. Vincent captured the island of Minorca without the loss of a single man.

Minorca taken, 1798.

The two following years were singularly barren of results in the matter of great naval actions; yet in combats between small squadrons, in actions between single ships, in operations by naval brigades ashore we won success after success. In fact, as Yonge concisely puts it, our entire loss in these two years amounted to a 10-gun brig and a schooner, while our gains included upwards of 30 French and Spanish ships of war, and the entire Dutch fleet in the Texel, which surrendered to us without firing a shot.

The victory of the Nile had brought us plenty of allies full of protestations and promises; but with their absurd and troublesome pretensions they proved far more of a hindrance than a help to us. The movements of the great French and Spanish fleets may be summed up in the old Shakespearian phrase, "alarums and excursions." In April 1799 a magnificent French fleet of 26 sail of the line, of which four were three-deckers of the largest size, with 10 frigates, commanded by six admirals and 13 commodores, with the Minister of Marine at their head, and manned by 24,000 seamen, swept out of Brest, forced our Channel fleet to retire before them, and raised the blockade at Cadiz. Next entering the Mediterranean, it picked up ship after ship, till, with the Spanish force at Cartagena, it amounted to no less than 40 ships of the line and 19 frigates. Then, having spread alarm and apprehension among all our scattered squadrons in the inland sea, it sailed quietly back to Brest and shut itself up there having accomplished nothing. Nelson, still engaged in protecting the kingdom of the two Sicilies, prepared to meet the enemy, if necessary, with but 10 sail of the line. Being reinforced, he thought himself strong enough to bring the royal family back to Naples and to order a series of attacks, conducted by Troubridge in command of a naval brigade ashore, on the garrisons posted by the French in the principal strongholds of the Italian seaboard.

Admiral Bruix's aimless cruise, 1799.

Troubridge's naval brigade ashore, 1799.

They were uniformly successful. St. Elmo fell; Capua, fifteen miles inland with near 3000 officers and men, surrendered; Gaeta and Civita Vecchia followed her example; a detachment of seamen rowed up the Tiber and hoisted the English colours on the walls of Rome. Naples, Rome, and Tuscany were cleared of Frenchmen.

Meanwhile, Buonaparte with the army landed at Alexandria by the ill-fated Nile fleet had marched into Syria, had taken Jaffa by storm, and was advancing on Acre. Commodore Sir W. Sidney Smith in command of a small squadron off Alexandria moved towards Acre to co-operate with the Turks in its defence. It stood sorely in need of assistance. Its fortifications were utterly neglected; its walls were crumbling, its towers ruinous, its batteries without guns. The French army in order to move more quickly marched without its artillery, which was to come round by sea. On March 17th, 1799, Sir Sidney Smith, whose force consisted of the *Tigre*, 80, the *Theseus*, 74, with the *Alliance* frigate, and two gun-vessels, observed the French vanguard advancing along the shore. On the 18th the flotilla conveying Buonaparte's artillery hove in sight and was instantly snapped up by Sir Sidney, the guns being at once landed and mounted on the walls of Acre, with all their much-needed ammunition and appliances. Foiled in his first attempt Buonaparte procured fresh guns overland from Jaffa and commenced the siege. Led by Sir Sidney, and ably backed up by the British officers and seamen, the Turks fought gallantly. For sixty-four days the siege lasted. Nine times the French assaulted the battered walls: nine times they were beaten off with

Defence of Acre by Sir Sidney Smith, 1799.

great slaughter; but, in spite of the efforts of the besieged, they slowly but surely gained ground. On May 7th, the fifty-first day of the siege, a fleet appeared in the offing. The French hailed it as bringing them reinforcements; it was a Turkish squadron with troops for the defence. Buonaparte now made furious efforts to carry the town before the Turks could land. He succeeded so far as to plant the tricolour on the north-east tower of the fortifications. It was a critical moment. Sir Sidney, with every man that could be spared from the ships, hurried to the walls. Buonaparte could be clearly seen standing on Cœur de Lion's mount and eagerly directing the movements of his men. But the Turkish troops had now landed. They did not attempt to hold the breach, but waited silently, sword and dagger in hand, concealed in the shadow. The French came on in massive column. They mounted the breach unopposed; the foremost leaped exultingly down inside, but as they did so their heads were swept off by the Turkish scimitars and piled in a heap at the feet of the Pacha in command "like cabbages." The rest recoiled, appalled at the reception awaiting them, and refused a further attack. Two attempts, made at the instigation of Buonaparte himself, to assassinate Sir Sidney were discovered and foiled: an assault, shamefully delivered while the terms of a truce were being discussed, was beaten off; and on the night of May 20th Buonaparte abandoned his guns and drew off his army, thwarted, set at nought, and defeated by a British naval officer, and eventually, leaving his army to its fate, slipped back to France in a frigate.

We must now leave the Mediterranean and turn to the North Sea. While these stirring events were keeping our squadrons in the south in a constant state of activity, Lord Duncan, off the Texel, was still employed in drearily watching the Dutch fleet of 25 sail which had taken the place of that destroyed at Camperdown. It has been stated that in consequence of the victory of the Nile the hostility of many of the European powers had been roused to activity against France and her allies. Among these was Russia, with whom we now entered into an agreement for a joint attack on Holland by land and sea.

<small>Dutch fleet surrenders without firing a shot, August 1799.</small>

On the 27th of August a large force of some 20,000 men was landed at the Helder, took possession of the fort which commands the entrance to the Texel, and thereby rendered the position of the Dutch fleet no longer secure. Still they might perhaps have made such a fight as they had been wont to do in previous wars, and the Dutch Admiral Story when summoned to surrender indignantly replied that he would defend his ships against double the number of English vessels. But when it came to the point, and when the British fleet stood in fearlessly along a channel which the Dutch themselves never ventured to pass with more than two ships at a time, the Hollanders, whose allegiance was disturbed and undermined by the perplexing state of political affairs in their own country, refused to fight, drew the charges from their guns, heaved the shot overboard, and left Admiral Story no choice but to surrender. Thus, without a shot fired, the whole Dutch naval force passed into our hands; not, however, with so much benefit to us as would appear on the surface, since many of our prizes proved to be so small, so cramped, and so badly built as to be unworthy of a place in our own line of battle.

Towards the end of the year another and a richer prize fell into our hands, reminding one of the capture of the galleon *Hermione* in 1762. Two Spanish frigates, the *Thetis* and the *Santa Brigida*, returning from Vera Cruz loaded with gold and silver, the accumulated wealth of Spanish America for the year, sailed into the jaws of four British frigates just when they had reached unmolested the latitude of Cape Finisterre, and had reasonable hope of winning a Spanish port in safety. Finding themselves chased they separated, endeavoured to save one at the expense of the other, doubled like hunted hares, and actually involved one of their pursuers in such difficulties that she ran on shore. But after a brave and clever running fight, which almost landed them in a friendly harbour, they were at last obliged to surrender with all their glittering cargo. On their arrival in Plymouth, 63 artillery waggons were required to convey the treasure to the citadel, and the four captains who shared in the capture were made richer men by £40,000 a-piece.

The year 1800 was even less productive of great naval events than the preceding one. Of fleet-actions there were none. The Channel was outwardly quiet save for the frigates and privateers which roved up and down in quest of hapless merchantmen or of the cruisers of the enemy; the North Sea was clear of powerful enemies; the Spanish fleets did not venture to leave their strong harbours; the French navy was being reorganised by Buonaparte, who on his return from Egypt had violently turned out the Directory and made himself Chief Consul, the first step towards the Imperial Crown. Whether intended in good faith or not, one of his first acts in his new capacity was a proposal of peace to England, but on such terms as to be utterly inadmissible.

In the Mediterranean the island of Malta was the centre of interest. The French had ever regarded it as a most desirable possession; that alone made us the more eager to take it. It was defended by 5000 troops under General Vaubois, a Frenchman as gallant, as enduring, and as courteous as we ever had to deal with. Ever since the battle of the Nile it had been blockaded by Captain Ball and a sufficient squadron at sea, while a naval brigade of 500 seamen, assisted by a mob of armed peasantry, surrounded the garrison ashore. With such a force any attempt at assault was out of the question. The French were full of confidence, and on hearing of Buonaparte's advancement to be Chief Consul they swore in an outburst of enthusiasm never to surrender the island to the enemies of France. We were obliged to trust to the slow but certain method of starvation. Early in 1800 an attempt was made by the French to relieve it. It was in urgent need of relief. Fever was raging among the troops; the sick were being fed on horse-soup; rats were sold at two shillings a-piece. The *Généreux*, 74, with a frigate and several small craft carrying 3000 fresh troops, sailed from Toulon to make the attempt. On February 18th they were seen by Nelson himself in the *Foudroyant* in company with the *Alexander* and the *Success* frigate, off Sicily. They were unable to make their escape; the *Généreux*, the last but one of Brueys' fleet, surrendered; the attempt was an utter failure. One more effort was made by the

Blockade of Malta by Captain Ball.

The Généreux taken, 18th February 1800.

gallant Vaubois. The *Guillaume Tell*, a magnificent 80-gun ship, the very last of the French line-of-battle at the Nile, was then lying in Valetta harbour. He would despatch her to France to tell the tale of his splendid defence and his sufferings, and, if possible, to procure help; at any rate she might procure her own safety. On the night of the 30th of March, in thick, dark weather and with a strong southerly gale, she put to sea. An hour afterwards she was discovered by the *Penelope* frigate on the watch. The frigate disregarding the odds, made all sail after her, caught her up, luffed under her stern and gave her a broadside, went about on the other tack and gave her the other broadside, and continued to do this until she had brought down her main and mizen-topmasts. The sound of heavy firing now brought the *Lion*, 64, and the *Foudroyant*, 80, successively upon the scene; and the *Guillaume Tell*, whose sole object up to this time had been to get clear away, now gave up all hope of escape in her crippled state, and determined to sell her liberty dearly. Never did a French ship make a more gallant fight against overpowering numbers. Ere she surrendered she had so crippled her two principal opponents that neither of them was in a condition to take possession of her; while she herself, dismasted and unmanageable, with her guns masked by the wreck of her spars, and the water pouring into her lower-deck ports as she rolled heavily and dangerously, fell a victim to the plucky little frigate who had first tackled her. In spite of this second blow General Vaubois still held out for five months longer, hoping against hope; but when at the end of August he found himself with all his food exhausted, his horses eaten, his cisterns empty,

The *Guillaume Tell* taken, 30th March 1800.

his men dying at the rate of over 100 a day, with no possible chance of relief, he recognised that the end had come. The two frigates, *Diane* and *Justice*, slipped out on August 24th and tried to escape. The *Diane* was taken immediately: the *Justice* reached Alexandria in safety, only to be given up next year with the capitulation of the French army; and on September 5th the starving garrison of Malta surrendered and the island was ours.

<small>Malta surrenders, 5th September 1800.</small>

Three months previously Genoa, the last stronghold of the French on the Italian seaboard, had been reduced to submission by the combined efforts of the Austrian army and the fleet under Lord Keith, and for a moment the French power in Italy seemed to be destroyed. But it was only for a moment. While we and our allies were congratulating each other on the fall of Genoa, Buonaparte himself crossed the Alps, entered Milan, won the great battle of Marengo, and recovered his hold upon all Northern Italy at one blow.

The only disaster which befell us this year was the destruction of Lord Keith's flag-ship, the *Queen Charlotte* of 100 guns, by fire off the island of Capraja, while the admiral himself was at Leghorn. She caught fire on the upper deck about half-past six o'clock in the morning of March 17th, and burned so fiercely that all the efforts of her crew were powerless to check the flames. Most of her boats seem to have been burned with her, and those vessels which put out from Leghorn to render her assistance at the order of Lord Keith, who was almost frantic with grief, were deterred from venturing near her, both by the intense heat and by the fact that her guns, being loaded, were going off in

<small>*Queen Charlotte*, 100 guns, burnt off Capraja, 17th March 1800.</small>

all directions. At 11 A.M. she blew up with a frightful explosion, and sank, carrying with her 673 men, including most of her officers.

But though in our dealings with our enemies matters had gone well with us, there was one incident in the summer of this year, 1800, which was pregnant with trouble for us in the immediate future. Acknowledged masters of the sea, we had been in the habit of carrying it with a high hand as regards other nations, and we claimed and exercised a right to search all foreign vessels for any goods belonging to our enemies. It will easily be understood that such a practice was always galling, whenever and wherever put in force; and when in July 1800 the Danish frigate *Freya*, escorting a small convoy, was hove to by a superior British squadron, and ordered to submit to it, it is no matter of wonder that she resisted and fired on the boats which approached for that purpose. An action ensued, and the *Freya* was captured and carried off as a prize; but the indignation caused by this incident, and craftily fanned by Buonaparte himself, produced a confederation against us of the Baltic powers. Denmark, Sweden, Russia, and Prussia, under the name of the Armed Neutrality of the North, bound themselves to resist our asserted right of search; and thus at the beginning of the year 1801 we found ourselves practically at war with three more naval nations, making up the list of our foes at sea to six—France, Spain, Holland, Denmark, Sweden, and Russia. Taught by the hard experience of war, we knew that our only safety lay in prompt and immediate action. A fleet of 20 ships of the line and six frigates, with many small craft, was at once prepared, and, to the

marginalia: The *Freya* incident, July 1800.

marginalia: "Armed Neutrality of the North."

astonishment of every one, placed not under the sole command of Lord Nelson, then at home and unemployed, but under Admiral Sir Hyde Parker, with Nelson as his vice, and Graves as his rear-admiral. On March 12th the fleet sailed from Yarmouth Roads for the Baltic, the commander-in-chief in the *London*, Nelson in the *St. George*, Graves in the *Defiance*. Nelson's idea was to go straight ahead, to make for Copenhagen by the quickest route, and nip the preparations of the Danes in the bud. It was ever his way to urge the boldest measures as the safest. Parker was undecided. He hesitated between the Sound and the Belt as the road to Copenhagen, ultimately selected the Belt and went through the Sound. Next he doubted if the castle of Cronenburg, commanding the entrance to the Sound, would fire on him, wasted a whole day in making the enquiry, and, when answered in the affirmative, hugged the Swedish shore and kept out of range, which he might easily have done without any enquiry. When he got near Copenhagen his indecision increased. Certainly the defences were very formidable. A line of battle-ships, hulks, and floating batteries, some four miles long, was moored close to the shoal water and backed by the fortifications of the town which fired over them; a formidable fort known as the Trekroner stood on a sandbank to the north of the Danish line, and, further, several ships of the line and other powerfully armed vessels co-operated with the Trekroner in protecting the entrance to the harbour. Add to this the notorious difficulties of the channel, the abundant shoals and sandbanks, the baffling currents, and the fact that all buoys and aids to navigation had

Sir Hyde Parker sails for the Baltic, 12th March 1801.

already been removed, and a more decided man than Sir Hyde Parker might be excused for hesitating. Something, however, was done. That night the channel was sounded and fresh buoys were laid down; and next day the admiral resorted to the usual expedient of undecided minds, and called a council of war. Fortunately for us not even the depressing influence of such a meeting could damp Nelson's ardour. He would undertake it all; let the admiral give him 10 ships of the line and all the frigates and it should be done. The admiral gave him 12 ships of the line and all the frigates and sloops; and Nelson, who had now shifted his flag to the *Elephant*, 74, spent the whole of the night of March 30th in an open boat, sounding with his own hands. The Danish line occupied a long narrow channel, three-quarters of a mile wide, between the fortifications of Copenhagen and a dangerous shoal known as the Middle Ground, both channel and shoal running nearly north and south. On the outside of this shoal, towards its south-east end, Nelson anchored his fleet on the 1st of April, hoping for a fair wind on the morrow to carry his ships into the position assigned to each. As at the Nile he ordered his ships to prepare to anchor by the stern. But here was a far harder enterprise than the Nile. The Danish ships were moored close together; there was no passing inside them, there was no doubling on them; on the other side of them were shoal water and heavy batteries. The battle must be fought out ship to ship; and for that very reason Nelson was anxious to get as near the enemy as possible, so that every shot of his might tell, while his own ships would be protected by theirs from the fire of the batteries. While Nelson on the night of the 1st of April lay on the floor of his cabin utterly exhausted, but eagerly giving directions, Captain Hardy of the *London* was silently and patiently sounding with a pole almost alongside the Danish ships to prepare the way for the English fleet. Unfortunately the cowardice and hesitation of the pilots made his energy of no avail. The morning dawned, the wind was in the south-east. All that the ships had to do was to weather the southern end of the Middle Ground, and then with a fair wind turn their heads to the north and proceed up the channel, anchoring by the stern, as at the Nile, when they reached their stations.[1] The frigates were to act against the ships at the mouth of the harbour. At 9.30 A.M. the signal went up, "Weigh in succession." The *Edgar* led; she weathered the end of the shoal and turned up the channel. The *Agamemnon* followed, hugged the shoal too close, anchored to save herself from running aground,

Battle of Copenhagen, 2nd April 1801.

[1] COMPARISON OF FORCES AT COPENHAGEN.

British Force.				Danish Force.	
74	*Elephant*	.	Vice-Admiral Nelson	56	*Provesteen*
,,	*Defiance*	.	Rear-Admiral Graves	48	*Wagner*
,,	*Edgar* .	.	. Captain Murray	20	*Rensburg*
,,	*Monarch*	.	. Captain Mosse	20	*Nyburg*
,,	*Bellona* .	.	. Captain Thompson	48	*Jutland*
,,	*Ganges* .	.	. Captain Fremantle	20	*Suersishen*
,,	*Russel* .	.	. Captain Cuming	22	*Cronburg*
64	*Agamemnon*	.	. Captain Fancourt	20	*Hajen*
,,	*Ardent* .	.	. Captain Bertie	62	*Dannebrog*
,,	*Polyphemus*	.	. Captain Lawford	6	*Elven*
54	*Glatton* .	.	. Captain Bligh	24	*Greniers-float*
50	*Isis* .	.	. Captain Walker	20	*Aggerstans*
38	*Amazon*	.	. Captain Riou	74	*Zealand*
36	*Désirée* .	.	. Captain Inman	26	*Charlotte-Amelia*
,,	*Blanche* .	.	. Captain Hamond	18	*Sohesten*
32	*Alcmène*	.	. Captain Sutton	60	*Holstein*
				64	*Indosforethen*
				20	*Hielpern*

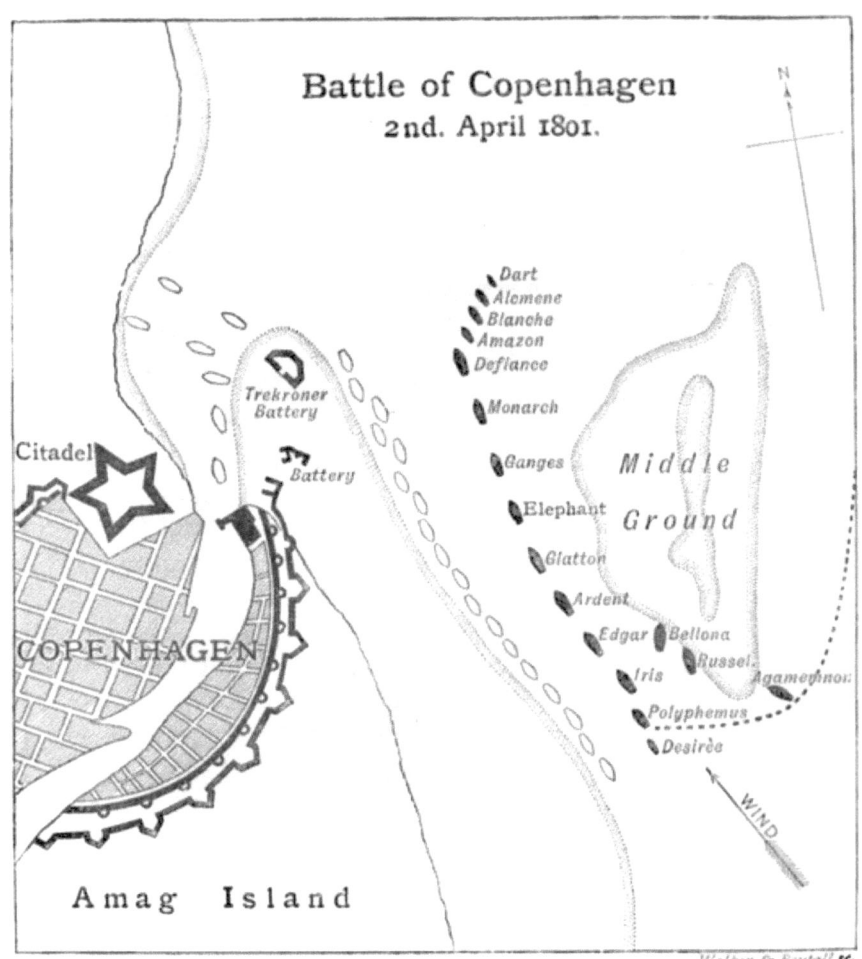

and never afterwards managed to get into action. It was the *Culloden* over again. But worse was to follow. The *Bellona* and the *Russel*, after having rounded the point of the shoal without accident, instead of giving it a wide berth when once they had entered the channel, ran ashore within a yard or two of each other, and remained fixed for the whole of the day, only able to bring a few of their guns to bear on the enemy, and that at too great a distance to be effective. Undismayed by these serious disasters at the very commencement of the combat, and calmly shifting his helm to avoid a like fate himself, Nelson, in the *Elephant*, led the remainder of his fleet along the line, selecting the Danish flag-ship *Dannebrog* as his own opponent. The first gun had been fired about 10 A.M. as the *Edgar* led the way, but the ships were slow in taking up their positions. The wind was light, the current against them, and it was long before the whole British line was under fire. When at length all were engaged it seemed as if the fight must end in the destruction of all concerned. For three hours it went on ceaselessly and furiously, without the slightest symptom of weakening on either side. It was a terrible time for Sir Hyde Parker. Lying under canvas off the north-east end of the shoal he could hear the incessant roar of the guns, could see the dense masses of white smoke which hung over the combatants, but could detect nothing to lead him to suppose that the Danish fire was slackening; while his glasses showed him the *Agamemnon* silent and motionless, with a signal of inability hoisted, and still nearer to the enemy two other British ships, each ashore and each flying a signal of distress. Anticipating disaster, and well knowing Nelson's daring and pertinacity, he determined to share the responsibility if he did not share the danger. He signalled Nelson to discontinue the action. But Nelson at this moment was in his element. He utterly ignored Parker's signal, put his glass to his blind eye and declared he could not see it, acknowledged, but refused to repeat it, and ordered his own signal for "closer battle" to be nailed to the mast. Admiral Graves in the *Defiance* also saw it, and felt bound to repeat though he did not obey it. Riou in command of the frigates saw it, and being far away to the north of the line, almost unsupported and suffering heavily from the terrible fire of the Trekroner, prepared sorrowfully and unwillingly to act upon it. As he did so, he fell dead on the quarter-deck of the *Amazon*, literally cut in two by a round shot. But now the result of the tremendous cannonading was beginning to show. At 1.30 P.M. the fire of the Danes was sensibly slackening: by two the rear of their line was silent; and boats were manned by the British fleet to take possession of the ships which had struck. Here a serious difficulty occurred. The ships which had surrendered were being constantly remanned by a stream of fresh Danes from the shore, who, regardless of the fact that they had struck, opened fire upon the boats as they approached; the forts also did the same, and are even said to have fired into their own ships when they hauled down their colours. It was impossible to man the prizes. Nelson thought for a moment of burning them with fire-ships, but his mind revolted from the awful fate which would befall the crews. He took a most unusual step, a step which he well knew would be misunderstood and misrepresented, but which he took with the same calm determination with which he went into action. He wrote a note to the Crown Prince of Denmark, telling him that he "was authorised to spare Denmark when she ceased to resist, but that if the firing on his boats was continued he must burn his prizes without having the power of saving the brave men who defended them." He would not be hurried or informal. He refused a wafer with which to fasten his letter, and demanded sealing-wax. The man sent for it was killed; still he must have the sealing-wax; it was brought; a candle was fetched from the cock-pit, and in the stern gallery of the *Elephant* he carefully affixed a larger seal than usual to his letter, and sent it ashore under a flag of truce. At this moment, as if to emphasise the purport of his note, the *Dannebrog* burst into flames, and breaking away from her moorings drifted slowly up the Danish line, a piteous spectacle of horror, spreading consternation among her consorts, and driving her men overboard to avoid the awful fate which threatened them. At the end of an hour she blew up. Nelson's flag of truce had been answered by another from the Crown Prince enquiring the object of the British admiral's letter. This led to further conference, and eventually the Danish officer was sent off to communicate with Sir Hyde Parker, then lying at a distance of at least four miles. At three all firing had ceased, and Nelson at once made use of this pause to extricate his ships from their dangerous position, and make ready, if necessary, for a renewal of the combat. The danger was very real. The ships were close to the shoal, far closer than they should have been had the pilots kept their heads, far too close for their maimed and shattered condition. They got under way. The *Monarch* touched the ground, but was literally shoved over the end of the shoal by the *Ganges*; the *Defiance*, the *Elephant*, and the *Désirée* frigate, went ashore, the two flag-ships within range of the Trekroner. There they remained, and Nelson hurried off to the *London* to add the weight of his presence to the conference. It was an anxious time, for though, of the 18 ships of the Danish line, 14 were either taken or destroyed, the Trekroner, and the ships at the mouth of the harbour still remained, and might well have caused us further serious trouble. But our brave foes recognised that they were unequal to the task; the prizes were given up, and an armistice of fourteen weeks was agreed upon. They, however, preferred to regard it as a drawn battle, averring, and rightly, that the request for a cessation of hostilities came from Nelson, and that it was merely a trick on his part to enable him to save his ships. Otherwise, with their wounded masts and spars, their tattered rigging, and their parted cables, they could not have avoided drifting on to the shoal in a huddled mass. It is of course true that Nelson most wisely and properly made use of his opportunity to place as many as possible in safety, but the real retort to the assertion of the Danes lies in pointing to the long line of battered, wrecked, and ruined hulks which that morning had flaunted the Danish flag, and in asking how many of our ships they could claim to counterbalance these. The reply must needs be—none. A week after this the treaty was formally signed. Nelson urged instant action against the Swedes, and, after the usual hesitation, Parker moved off to Carlscrona, leaving him to refit and follow. No sooner was Nelson ready for sea than the wind turned foul and he could not get under way; yet on hearing from Parker that the Swedish fleet was at sea he jumped into a cutter and rowed twenty-four miles out to the island of Bornholm to join his commander-in-chief, declaring that if he had to row to Carlscrona he would do it. But the Swedes took refuge under their defences, and, while Admiral Parker was trying to decide what to do next, news came of the death of the Tzar and a probable change of policy on the part of Russia. Nelson was still trying to induce his chief to go to Revel and assist matters by the visible presence of the British fleet, when a despatch from England superseded Sir Hyde Parker and placed Nelson in his stead. At once the British fleet moved to the Gulf of Finland, but the Russian fleet had left Revel: the death of the Tzar, coupled with the defeat of the Danes, had broken up the Northern Confederacy; and not long after, Nelson, in bad health, resigned his command, and returned home, being rewarded for his services with the rank of viscount.

Nelson supersedes Sir Hyde Parker.

His presence in England was anxiously longed for and eagerly welcomed. For again the nightmare of invasion was spreading apprehension and terror through the land, and this time with more reason than ever before since the days of the Armada. Buonaparte was not the man to do things by halves. All the small ports in the neighbourhood of Calais Strait began to re-echo with the sounds of preparation. A great camp was formed at Boulogne for the reception of the troops; hundreds of heavily armed brigs and flat boats for the conveyance of troops were being built; training and exercising went on incessantly. Nelson, to whom the whole nation was learning to look as its only hope in time of need, was appointed to command a squadron for coast defence which would operate from Orfordness in Suffolk to Beachy Head in Sussex, the part of the coast most liable to attack. He himself did not share the general apprehension, regarding the invasion as "a forlorn undertaking," and "almost impracticable"; but he thought it advisable to obstruct the preparations by an attack upon the crowd of boats lying in readiness at Boulogne. Owing to the shallowness of the water no big ship could operate; it was to be an affair of open boats. On the night of the 15th of August his attack was delivered; but many things were against it and it was a failure. The different divisions of our boats failed to arrive together; some never arrived at all, swept away by the rapid current; the French were ready and alert, the defences far more formidable than we anticipated, and many valuable lives were lost with small benefit to ourselves.

Nelson in command of coast defence.

Failure of attack on Boulogne flotilla, August 1801.

And now the Mediterranean claims our attention again for the time. Though Buonaparte had deserted his Egyptian army and returned to France, he still hoped to rescue it from its position, or at any rate to strengthen and relieve it. With this object, in the first days of the year 1801, he despatched Admiral Ganteaume with a squadron of seven sail of the line, carrying 5000 troops from Brest bound for Alexandria. Hardly avoiding our Channel fleet Admiral Ganteaume put to sea only to be the sport alike of the elements and of the enemy. First fierce gales buffeted him; with difficulty he

Ganteaume sails from Brest for Egypt, January 1801.

arrived in the Mediterranean and made for his destination. Twice Admiral Watson with an inferior force drove him to seek safety in Toulon, where he lay until Buonaparte imperatively ordered him out. At length he reached Alexandria. He had selected a spot for the landing, and was on the point of disembarking his troops when the topgallant-masts of Lord Keith's squadron appeared on the horizon. Immediately he cut his cables and made all haste back to Toulon. Long before this, however, the battle of Alexandria had been fought, Abercrombie had fallen at the moment of victory, and the remains of Buonaparte's Egyptian army had surrendered. Ganteaume's reinforcements, could they have been landed, would have been too late. Balked in his Egyptian design, Buonaparte ordered a portion of the squadron at Toulon to make its way under Admiral Linois to Cadiz, and there pick up six ships of the line which he had bought or hired from Spain to be manned by French crews. Linois sailed with three line-of-battle ships, but learning that Cadiz was blockaded by Sir James Saumarez with a force more than double his own, he put into Algeciras. Sir James heard of it, left his station off Cadiz, and on July 6th arrived off Algeciras with six ships of the line. Linois, shrinking from a contest with such numbers, warped close in under the shelter of the batteries which were many and powerful, so close, indeed, that eventually all his ships were hard and fast aground. Sir James stood in to the attack, but the wind was fluky and baffling: he was at the mercy of the current which ran strong; and he had to anchor in unfavourable positions, slipping his cable when there seemed a

Linois sails from Toulon for Cadiz, 1801.

Saumarez beaten off at Algeciras by Linois, 6th July 1801.

promise of a breeze. The *Hannibal*, in advancing to rake Linois' flag-ship, went aground and could not be got off; and Sir James, baffled by the wind and current, and heavily punished by the batteries, was reluctantly forced to retire to Gibraltar, leaving her in the hands of the enemy. With all haste he set to work to refit. His own flag-ship, the *Cæsar*, was a mere mastless wreck. He proposed to shift his flag and leave her, but his men implored him to remain, vowing to work night and day until she was again fit for sea. He consented; in four days she was masted and ready for action. But in the meantime the Cadiz fleet, relieved from the blockade, had sailed in answer to an urgent summons from Linois—six ships of the line, including two great three-deckers of 112 guns each, the *Real Carlos* and the *San Hermenegildo* —and had anchored at Algeciras. On the 12th of July the rescued and the rescuers got under way, nine ships of the line and some frigates. In all haste Sir James, with but five of the line and one frigate, left Gibraltar in pursuit amidst the cheers of the whole garrison. Shortly before midnight the *Superb*, 74, caught them up, and bringing the *Real Carlos* to action quickly set her on fire. Instantly a panic ensued among the Spanish ships, and they opened a furious and random fire in every direction. Leaving the *Real Carlos* to her fate the *Superb* now engaged the *San Antonio*, which presently surrendered; but in the meantime a terrible tragedy had taken place among our enemies. The fire on board the *Real Carlos* had hardly been extinguished when her huge sister the *San Hermenegildo* fell on board of her. It was pitch dark, panic reigned, each ship mistook the other for an enemy, and a

Saumarez and Linois off Gibraltar, 12th July 1801.

furious cannonade ensued at the closest quarters. The fire in the *Real Carlos* broke out again; it spread with fury, reached the *Hermenegildo*, and at last the two great ships, still pounding each other, blew up with nearly every soul on board. The wind had now freshened to a gale: the *Venerable*, chasing the flag-ship of Linois, ran aground on a reef and was with difficulty got off; and Sir James, having made a terrible requital for the loss of the *Hannibal*, returned to Gibraltar triumphant with his prize.

And now the eyes of both countries were anxiously turning in the direction of peace. England honestly desired the cessation of a war which had been thrust upon her against her will, and which, though it had greatly increased her reputation, had strained her powers to the utmost and weighted her with a heavy load of debt. France had no really peaceful intention; but, in the midst of her ambitious projects she wished for a breathing space in which she might recover from her temporary exhaustion, and, by unrelaxing preparation, make herself more fit to enter again into the struggle. The preliminaries were signed in October 1801 and warlike operations at once ceased, leaving us in a state of considerable suspense and anxiety, which the activity reigning in French, Spanish, and Dutch ports was by no means calculated to dispel. The complete Treaty of Amiens was not signed until March 1802.

Peace of Amiens, March 1802.

CHAPTER XII

Preparations for invasion—War again declared—French ports unceasingly watched—Buonaparte declares himself Emperor—Nelson off Toulon—Admiral Latouche Treville—Spain prepares for war—Capture of Spanish treasure-ships—*Mercedes* blows up—Nelson's weary watch—Buonaparte's plans of invasion—The flotillas—The French fleets—Missiessy is the first to move—Villeneuve slips out of Toulon—Nelson pursues him blindly—Combined fleet escapes to West Indies—Nelson follows—He chases them back to Europe—They encounter Sir R. Calder—Calder tried by court-martial—Combined fleet retires to Cadiz—Nelson is sent there—Battle of Trafalgar.

THE Peace of Amiens was but the sudden lull which presages the fiercer outbreak of the storm. Not for a moment did Buonaparte abandon his schemes or relax his preparations; not for a moment did we remit our watch upon the further borders of the Channel. Buonaparte was at no pains to conceal his hostility. He publicly insulted our minister even before he considered himself sufficiently prepared for a renewal of the war; and though for his own interests he permitted diplomatic relations between the two countries to continue for some time further, nobody on either side of the Channel was deceived by it. Mistrusting his intentions with regard to Malta we refused to give it up; and on the 16th of May 1803 war was again declared. It was remarkable at first for the little tangible result that it produced. On the side of France it took the form of ceaseless

War again declared, 16th May 1803.

preparation for the invasion of England, on our side that of sleepless vigilance. Wherever there was a French fleet in port there was to be found an English force patiently waiting outside, its first object being to draw it from its shelter and destroy it, its second to block it and make it useless. Thus the labour, the burden, and the exposure fell on us, battling incessantly outside against wind and sea, strained, buffeted, and weather-worn, while snug within lay our enemies, safe beneath their batteries, secure from foe and tempest, and as fine as paint could make them. In the meanwhile the countless cruisers of both countries ranged the seas, preyed upon each other's commerce, encountered and fought, almost invariably to our advantage. Wherever along the innumerable creeks and crannies of the French coast a vessel flying the hated tricolour was known to have taken refuge, there a British brig or sloop was certain shortly after to appear, and, no matter how formidable the situation, a determined attempt would be made to cut out the enemy, often with incredible success.

Cornwallis commanded in the Channel, Nelson, poorly furnished with ships, in the Mediterranean; Cornwallis kept a wary watch on Brest, Nelson on Toulon. Both ports were swarming with enemies, and resounding with the noise and bustle of preparation; but it was not the interest of the French to risk an engagement at present and they kept within. All through the year 1803 the situation remained unchanged. The weariness of the duty in the Channel and off Toulon can hardly be imagined or exaggerated. In 1804 Buonaparte's schemes gradually began to unfold themselves and take form and substance. In May he made himself Emperor, removed from the French navy those who still firmly held the Republican principles, of which, till then, he himself had been the champion and apostle, and threw himself more eagerly than ever into the arrangements for invasion. We, on our side, strengthened our existing fleets, and added squadrons of observation at fresh points; the first move must come from the enemy. Toulon, far removed from our base of operations, caused us great anxiety. Nelson's watch was unremitting, but his efforts to entice Admiral Latouche Treville out to fight were all useless. He would come out to chase a solitary ship of the line, or a couple of frigates which were displaying too inquisitive a spirit; but so soon as the main body of Nelson's fleet appeared, he would scuttle back into harbour without firing a shot. This happened more than once. On the 14th of June 1804 he came out with eight sail of the line and found Nelson close in with only five. The English could not come in closer for fear of the French batteries; Treville would not go out farther. After two hours of mutual observation, the French admiral returned to his anchorage, reported that he had chased the whole British fleet, which ran away on seeing him, and was rewarded by Buonaparte with the Grand Cross of the Legion of Honour for his gallantry. He did not enjoy his honours long; a month later he died, and his command was taken by Admiral Villeneuve. The new commander's orders were to seize the first opportunity of escaping, to leave the Mediterranean, and, after ravaging our settlements on the West Coast of Africa, to join Admiral Missiessy in the West Indies, seize all the British possessions,

Nelson watches Toulon.

destroy all British commerce, and then, returning to Europe, raise the blockade of Ferrol and hold himself in readiness to take part in the projected invasion. But though this order was given in the autumn of 1804, it was not until the next year that he found an opportunity of obeying it.

Buonaparte now set to work to involve his old allies in the struggle. Holland was completely dominated by the French, and had no choice but to throw in her lot with them. Spain had at first stood aloof; but now urged by Buonaparte she began again to stir. She consented to pay a huge sum yearly to the French exchequer; she began to equip her navy; she mobilised her army, and received French troops among her battalions. Yet she did not declare war, waiting until the yearly tribute of her American colonies, an even vaster accumulation of wealth than usual, should have arrived. Of all this we were fully informed, and were well aware that the declaration of war was but postponed. We determined to be the first to act. The treasure-ships must never arrive; they must be seized and detained as securities for peace. A squadron of four frigates was told off to watch for them. On the 5th of October they were sighted not far from Cape St. Vincent. They also were four in number, well armed and manned, the *Mercedes*, the *Clara*, the *Fama*, and the *Medea*. A shot was fired across their bows; they were hove to. Their commander was urgently entreated to yield quietly to avoid bloodshed; he was told the detention would probably not be for long. But Spanish pride could brook no such indignity; he would fight. The action began. In less than ten minutes Spaniards and English alike were horrified to see the *Mercedes* blow up; she sank with her crew, with thirteen young Spanish ladies whom she carried as passengers, and with a quarter of a million of treasure. The other three surrendered; they contained, roughly estimated, a million of money. On December 12th Spain, having lost her treasure and having no further object in concealment, declared war. And still Nelson kept his weary watch off Toulon; seldom within sight of the port lest the French should fear to come out; often blown off the land by fierce gales, as often returning to resume his dreary beat; sometimes sheltering between Corsica and Sardinia among the Maddalena Isles; sometimes finding a refuge in the Gulf of Palmas, south of Sardinia; but always leaving a watchful cruiser to note and report every movement of the enemy, and fruitlessly entreating the Admiralty to send him frigates to carry out this duty more efficiently. Twice had spring ripened into summer; twice the long hot summer had faded into autumn; twice had autumn given place to the fierce blasts of winter; and still Nelson was outside Toulon, 1500 miles from home and help. His ships were strained and leaky, rusty and weather-worn, his spars sprung and fished, his rigging rotten and condemned; but his men and officers were as fine a set of seamen as the world ever saw, fit to go anywhere or do anything, with a lordly contempt for the brand-new, smart-coated fleet which never put to sea.

Meanwhile Buonaparte's preparations for invasion were rapidly growing to a head. The shores of France in the neighbourhood of Boulogne were swarming with busy thousands occupied day and night by the insatiable Emperor in perfecting his

The preparations for invasion.

gigantic scheme. The harbour of Boulogne itself had been enormously deepened, enlarged, and fortified to give shelter to the vessels specially built for the crossing of the army of invasion. North and south of Boulogne, at Ostend, at Dunkerque, at Calais, at Vimereux, at Ambleteuse, and at Etaples, the same thing was to be seen on a smaller scale. A vast fleet of 2300 vessels had been specially constructed for the crossing, many with stalls for fifty horses, all heavily armed, all numerously manned. Inland, the country was one huge camp, containing 150,000 troops, who for months were exercised in the evolutions of embarkation and of landing. So perfectly were all the naval arrangements made, so admirably were the soldiers drilled and organised, that at last each division required less than two hours to embark ; only two tides were needed to get clear of the ports into the open channel. Buonaparte reckoned that could he only be master of the sea for six hours, the very existence of England would be ended. But how to obtain that six hours' mastery? His fleets he knew were unable separately to cope with ours : he had had frequent and painful proof of that ; and the Spanish naval power was still less to be depended on than the French. The British fleet must be avoided, not fought ; it must be beguiled, not faced. His plan was to draw away our watchful vessels, if possible, on a wild chase to distant waters, and then, uniting his fleets and those of Spain, to sweep up the Channel with a mighty force of some 60 ships of the line, cover the crossing of the narrow strait, and pour his thousands of troops upon the English shore, as William of Normandy had done more than seven centuries before. As Nelson himself said, it was "a forlorn undertaking"; but none the less the panic in England was widespread. Many attempts had been organised to destroy the flotilla as it lay in its thousands on the other side of the strait, attempts necessarily made in boats owing to the intricacy of the navigation and the danger of the cross currents, but though made with the well-known dash of British seamen, and though furnished with destructive-looking machines then known as catamarans, but which were in reality the clumsy forerunners of the torpedo, they seldom succeeded in doing any serious damage. It was necessary to wait until the French began to move.

At Brest lay Admiral Ganteaume with 21 sail of the line ready for sea, protected by 150 heavy guns ashore, lest we should try to force our way in; for close outside was Cornwallis with a fleet generally superior in numbers. At Ferrol a mixed fleet of French and Spanish ships, numbering 15 of the line, was watched by Cochrane and subsequently by Sir Robert Calder with from eight to ten. At Cadiz lay six ships ready for sea with as many more fitting out; off Cadiz Sir John Orde kept his beat with six. At Cartagena six Spanish ships were ready, at Toulon 11 French ships; over these Nelson kept his watch with a force varying from nine to 11 sail of the line. Other French squadrons lay at Rochefort and at Lorient, and would be dealt with by the British force nearest at hand should they venture out. The tale of the combined fleets was little short of 70 line-of-battle ships. If once these, having decoyed our fleets away, were to unite and gain the Channel they would have little difficulty in overpowering the small force of ships with which Lord

Keith held the Downs and watched the Dutch coast; and then the invasion of England might take place in real and terrible earnest. It is no wonder that it was a time of deep anxiety and apprehension in England. The Spanish Armada with its 30,000 men, convoying Parma with an equal number, was child's play to this mighty armament, whose seamen would fall little short of 50,000, and whose troops numbered at least three times as many more. So strained and pushed to the utmost limit were the resources of that navy upon which alone our safety depended, that the Admiralty found themselves reduced to reinforcing our various fleets with old line-of-battle ships long since condemned. These were now, in their emergency, taken from the moorings at which they had been left to rot, their timbers strengthened with iron knees, their sides patched up with two-inch boards on top of the old planking, and sent once more to sea to face the foe.

In the early days of 1805 the first movements of the French fleets began. On the 11th of January Admiral Missiessy slipped out of Rochefort and made for the West Indies to commence a preconcerted attack on our possessions there. Cochrane off Ferrol heard of it and started in pursuit. Six days after Missiessy's departure, while Nelson was sheltering among the Maddalena Isles, Villeneuve left Toulon. Nelson believing him to be bound for Egypt, bore away thither with the same eager haste which he had shown in 1798, but with the same result; the harbour of Alexandria was empty. Without a moment's delay he hurried back to Malta, where he heard that Villeneuve, whatever his destination, had been driven back to Toulon by a

Missiessy slips out of Rochefort, 11th January 1805.

Villeneuve escapes from Toulon, 17th January 1805.

gale. On the 30th of March Villeneuve again sailed. Five days later Nelson, then in the Gulf of Palmas, heard of it and, still assured that his enemy would make for Egypt, scoured the water between Sicily and Cape Bon to intercept him. But on April 8th Villeneuve was passing Gibraltar, and it was not until eight days afterwards that Nelson learned the truth. Whither was he bound? to the West Indies, South America, Ireland, Brest? All was doubt and almost despair. Instantly Nelson made for Gibraltar; but the wind was now dead foul, and it was not until April 30th that he arrived there. For five more miserable days of uncertainty the wind remained foul. On May 6th it shifted; Nelson fired a gun, hurried his officers on board, and sailed at once. In Lagos Bay he heard his first certain news. Villeneuve had driven away Sir John Orde, had entered Cadiz, had picked up six Spanish sail of the line, and had sailed on April 10th with 17 ships of the line and seven frigates for the West Indies. Thither Nelson on May 11th started in pursuit with 10 sail of the line and three frigates, one month behind him, and with little more than half his force. He had now a fair wind. On June 4th he arrived at Barbadoes; as he did so Villeneuve was leaving Martinique for the northward. Fate for a while protected him. Nelson received false information that he had gone south: an almost impossible accident confirmed the falsehood; and while Villeneuve steered north, Nelson pressed on to the south, convinced that he was on his very heels. Off Trinidad he learned his mistake. He turned northward, but ere he could overtake the French they had learned that he was after them and

Villeneuve passes Gibraltar, 8th April 1805.

Villeneuve sails for West Indies, 10th April.

Nelson starts in pursuit, 11th May.

they were already on their way back to Europe. Despatching small and fast vessels to the Admiralty and to the commanding-officer off Ferrol to warn them that Villeneuve and the combined fleet were on their way home, probably bound for Brest, Nelson stretched after them once more across the wide Atlantic. For more than a month longer did he follow this phantom fleet, no trace of which he ever saw ; save three planks, from the sight of which he derived such poor comfort as he might. On the 19th of July he entered Gibraltar, and next day he went on shore for the first time for two years !

Villeneuve returns with Nelson on his heels.

Nelson arrives at Gibraltar, 19th July.

In the meantime the warning sent by Nelson to the authorities at home had proved of inestimable value. The fleet off Ferrol, now commanded by Sir Robert Calder, was increased by the Admiralty to 15 sail of the line just one week before Villeneuve's combined fleet hove in sight; and though they outnumbered him by five sail of the line, Calder felt himself strong enough to bring them to action. Yet his was a most anxious and perilous position. A hostile fleet of superior force lay in front of him : another hostile fleet of equal force to his own was in Ferrol close under his lee ; while he knew that five more sail of the line had left Rochefort to reinforce Villeneuve. It was not until 4 P.M. on the 22nd of July that the fleets got near enough to open fire, and even then the action was but a partial one. Interrupted and hindered by fog, it never took the form of a close general engagement. Only about two-thirds of our force got into action, and the ships were widely scattered. Yet, when night closed in, two Spanish ships, the *Firme*, 78, and the *San Rafael*, 80, had surrendered : two more of the enemy were greatly

Villeneuve and Calder off Finisterre, 22nd July.

injured; and the advantage was decidedly on our side. Encouraged and stimulated by this success, Calder would have renewed the action the next morning; but when daylight showed him the position of the enemy, they were seen to be seventeen miles to windward, and the choice no longer lay with him. Villeneuve in his turn, thinking that he could detect signs of flight in the British fleet, being still superior in number and observing that at least one of our ships was badly damaged, bore down upon us and would have renewed the combat. But the wind died away and left the two fleets rolling heavily upon an Atlantic swell unable to get within shot of each other, until night again fell upon them. On the morning of the 24th the situation was reversed; the wind had shifted; Villeneuve was to leeward, and Calder could renew the fight if he thought it advisable. But he did not think so. His mind was full of anxiety with regard to the Ferrol and Rochefort fleets,—not without grave reason, for, had he known it, the latter fleet, unseen in the fog, had been almost within hail the day before; and so, securing his prizes and believing himself to have deserved well of his country, he edged away for British waters unhindered by the enemy. Having sent his prizes and his injured ships into port, he returned to Ferrol to resume his watch. For a moment Calder was a hero: the country approved his action and greeted his name with acclamation; but when, on Nelson's arrival in England, they learned that this was the same fleet which had fled before him across the Atlantic though his force numbered little more than half of theirs, the popular enthusiasm died away and they loudly expressed their indignation that Calder had done no more. Times had changed since Hotham, taking two ships from a force of barely equal numbers, had been regarded as a conqueror. Nelson had dazzled the public mind by the overwhelming completeness of his victories, and Sir Robert Calder was presently tried by court-martial and severely reprimanded for not having done his best to renew the action. It seems terribly hard: he had an inferior fleet, he was in the immediate presence of a hopelessly overwhelming force; yet he fought and undoubtedly won a victory. As a French writer on the subject puts it,—" Admiral Calder with an inferior force meets the Franco-Spanish fleet and captures two ships. He is tried and reprimanded. What would they have done with Calder in England had he commanded the superior fleet and lost two ships?"

<small>Calder is tried by court-martial.</small>

Meanwhile Nelson had left Gibraltar and was hastening to the Channel. On August 15th he joined Cornwallis off Ushant, and, leaving most of his fleet with him, proceeded home with the *Victory* and *Superb*. There, while his ship was refitting, he enjoyed a brief period of rest at Merton in Surrey. Villeneuve after his defeat had entered Ferrol and, taking the fleet already there under his command, made up a force of 29 sail of the line, so that when Calder with only nine arrived off the port he found the odds far too heavy for him and fell back on Cornwallis. Villeneuve now came out, but alarmed by the report of a Danish vessel that a British fleet of 25 sail was close to (a tale concocted specially for Villeneuve's benefit by an English 74 who had boarded the Dane), he at once made for Cadiz, drove off Collingwood with his poor little handful of three,

<small>Nelson returns home.</small>

and entered the harbour. Instantly at Collingwood's order the *Euryalus* frigate dashed off to England with the news. Blackwood, her captain, hurried up to town, picked up Nelson at Merton on his way, and the two together went at once to the Admiralty. No time was lost; the gravity of the situation was recognised; everything was placed in Nelson's hands. On the 13th of September he arrived at Portsmouth, bringing with him his coffin, made out of the mainmast of the *L'Orient* and given to him by Captain Hallowell shortly after the Nile. He was cheerful and eager, but at the same time full of a strange prescience of his coming death. The scene on Southsea Beach when he embarked is beyond description. Not only was he the hero of St. Vincent, of the Nile, of Copenhagen, but it was felt that on him, and on him alone, the safety of England depended. In such a place as Portsmouth the vast preparations on the other side of the Channel would lose nothing by the description of the many who had already seen something of them from a distance. The danger to the dwellers on the south coast was terribly real, terribly imminent. Thousands crowded round him; the enthusiasm, the affection which the sight of him inspired are alike marvellous and touching. We are told that many knelt before him blessing him; that they strove to touch his hand, or the skirts of his coat; that his guard was absolutely powerless before the determination of the people, which rose to fury when the officer in command ordered his men to fix bayonets. Nelson was deeply moved; his eyes filled with tears; "I had their huzzas before," he said to Hardy, "I have their hearts now." On Sunday the 15th of September the *Victory* sailed with

Blackwood arrives with news of the combined fleet.

<small>Nelson sails again for Cadiz, 15th September, arrives on the 28th.</small>

the *Euryalus*, and, picking up the *Ajax* and *Thunderer* off Plymouth, Nelson joined Collingwood, who had previously been strongly reinforced, off Cadiz on the 28th. By his own special desire no colours were shown, and no salutes fired; he wished the enemy to be in ignorance of his arrival. Then he began his watch on Cadiz as he had so long and wearily watched Toulon. The combined fleet was vastly superior to him in numbers; moreover, the Spanish fleet in Cartagena was known to be fitting out with the probable intention of still further augmenting Villeneuve's force. Yet with marvellous unselfishness and magnanimity, when the time came for Sir Robert Calder to go home to take his trial, he granted his earnest entreaty that he would send him home in his own ship, and thus deprived himself of the services of a splendid three-decker, in order to spare the feelings of one who had shown undoubted animosity against him in the past. As at Toulon, Nelson kept the main body of his fleet out of sight, communicating by signal with a small inshore squadron who watched every movement of the enemy "as a cat watches a mouse." Thus on the 5th of October Blackwood signalled "Enemy embarking troops": on the 10th, "Enemy all but out of harbour"; and

<small>19th October, "Enemy coming out."</small>

at last on the 19th of October the welcome news, "Enemy coming out." Nelson was fifty miles off at that time, yet in two hours he was aware of it.

Yes, Villeneuve was coming out at last. It was absolutely necessary that he should do something. The difficulty of obtaining supplies at Cadiz was very great; he was in deep disgrace with the Emperor; in fact, he was at that moment actually superseded, and Admiral Rosilly was hurrying down to take his place. He endeavoured to persuade others, though he could not persuade himself, that "a glorious success" awaited him. The British fleet was undermanned, he said; they had fewer motives for fighting well; they had less love of country; they were not more brave than the French. But even in these assurances it is easy to read the despondency in his heart; it is a poor spirit which seeks to raise its own courage by depreciating the enemy.

For some time Villeneuve steered towards the south. Nelson hurried off six fast ships to head him off from the straits, and followed himself in the same direction. On the 21st of October,—the great naval anniversary of the Nelson family commemorating the victory by Captain Suckling and others in the West Indies more than forty years before—the enemy's force was distinctly visible still steering towards the south. But finding his course to the straits blocked by the British fleet, and wishing to keep Cadiz open under his lee, Villeneuve reversed his direction, and at 8.30 A.M. headed towards the north, his fleet formed in an irregular double line ahead, some five miles in length, the centre of the line curving considerably towards the land. His intention seems to have been that the gaps between the ships of his outer or westerly line should be commanded and to a certain extent closed by the ships of the inner line; but the unequal sailing of the ships and the unskilfulness of the seamen prevented the perfect execution of the design. His fleet numbered 33 sail in all, 18 French, 15 Spanish, ships, some of enormous size, commanded by no less than seven admirals and nine commodores. The British force of 27 sail was content

Battle of Trafalgar, 21st October 1805.

with Vice-Admiral Nelson in the *Victory*, Vice-Admiral Collingwood in the *Royal Sovereign*, and Rear-Admiral the Earl of Northesk in the *Britannia*.[1] Nelson's plan of battle had long since been explained in a memorandum to all his captains as well as by constant personal communication, and his confidence both in the simplicity of his scheme, in its efficacy, and in the individual ability of his captains to put it to the test, was unruffled by a single doubt; he declared that "he would give the enemy such a dressing as they had never had before." The idea to which all else was subordinated, and which has since been reduced to an axiom for all time, was to overwhelm a part of the enemy's force with the

---

[1] COMPARISON OF FORCES AT TRAFALGAR.

British Fleet.

100	*Victory*	Vice-Admiral Nelson
,,	*Royal Sovereign*	Vice-Admiral Collingwood
,,	*Britannia*	Rear-Admiral Earl of Northesk
98	*Temeraire*	Captain Harvey
,,	*Prince*	Captain Grindall
,,	*Neptune*	Captain Fremantle
,,	*Dreadnought*	Captain Conn
80	*Tonnant*	Captain Tyler
74	*Belleisle*	Captain Hargood
,,	*Revenge*	Captain Moorsom
,,	*Mars*	Captain Duff
,,	*Spartiate*	Captain Laforey
,,	*Defiance*	Captain Durham
,,	*Conqueror*	Captain Pellew
,,	*Defence*	Captain Hope
,,	*Colossus*	Captain Morris
,,	*Leviathan*	Captain Bayntun
,,	*Achille*	Captain King
,,	*Bellerophon*	Captain Cooke
,,	*Minotaur*	Captain Mansfield
,,	*Orion*	Captain Codrington
,,	*Swiftsure*	Captain Rutherford
,,	*Ajax*	Lieutenant Pilfold
,,	*Thunderer*	Lieutenant Stockham
64	*Polyphemus*	Captain Redmill
,,	*Africa*	Captain Digby
,,	*Agamemnon*	Captain Berry

whole of his own. To this end he formed his fleet also into two columns in line ahead, separated from each other by about a mile, the northern or weather line consisting of twelve ships including, and led by the *Victory*, the southern or lee line of fifteen ships led by Collingwood in the *Royal Sovereign*. In this formation he bore down at right angles to the enemy's line almost dead before the wind which was slightly to the north of west, to hurl his lee line upon the

COMBINED FLEET.

French.

80	*Bucentaure*	. . . .	Vice-Admiral Villeneuve
,,	*Formidable*	. . . .	Rear-Admiral Dumanoir
,,	*Neptune*	. . . .	Commodore Maistral
,,	*Indomptable*	. . . .	Commodore Hubert
74	*Algeciras*	. . . .	Rear-Admiral Magon
,,	*Pluton*	. . . .	Commodore Kerjulien
,,	*Mont-Blanc*	. . . .	Commodore La Villegris
,,	*Intrepide*	. . . .	Commodore Infernet
,,	*Swiftsure*	. . . .	Captain Villemadrin
,,	*Aigle*	. . . .	Captain Gourrège
,,	*Scipion*	. . . .	Captain Berenger
,,	*Duguay-Trouin*	. . . .	Captain Touffet
,,	*Berwick*	. . . .	Captain Filhol-Camas
,,	*Argonaute*	. . . .	Captain Epron
,,	*Achille*	. . . .	Captain Denieport
,,	*Redoutable*	. . . .	Captain Lucas
,,	*Fougueux*	. . . .	Captain Beaudouin
,,	*Héros*	. . . .	Captain Poulain

Spanish.

130	*Santisima Trinidad*	. . .	Rear-Admiral Cisneros
112	*Principe de Asturias*	. . .	Admiral Gravina
,,	*Santa Ana*	. . .	Vice-Admiral De Alava
100	*Rayo*	. . . .	Commodore Macdonel
80	*Neptuno*	. . . .	Commodore Valdes
,,	*Argonauta*	. . . .	Commodore Parejas
74	*Bahama*	. . . .	Captain Galiano
,,	*Montanes*	. . . .	Captain Salzedo
,,	*San Augustin*	. . . .	Captain Cagigal
,,	*San Ildefonso*	. . .	Captain Bargas
,,	*San Juan Nepomuceno*	. .	Captain Churruca
,,	*Monarca*	. . . .	Captain Argumosa
,,	*San Francisco de Asis*	. .	Captain De Flores
,,	*San Justo*	. . .	Captain Gaston
64	*San Leandro*	. . .	Captain Quevedo

R

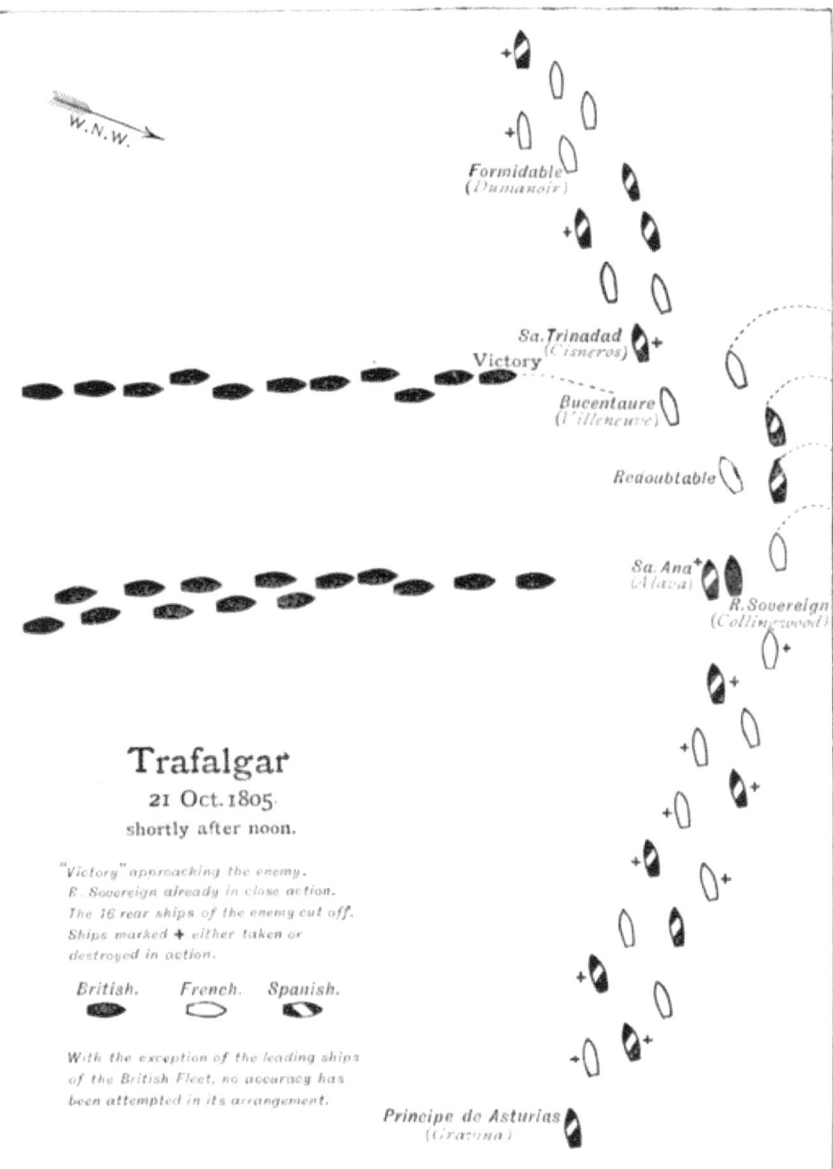

enemy's rear, his weather-line upon the enemy's centre, and overpower them before the ships composing their van could grasp the full meaning of his manœuvre, could retrace their course and come to the aid of their comrades. This was "the Nelson touch." Foreseeing that the circumstances of the coming action would bring him dangerously near the shoals off Cape Trafalgar, when many of his ships must necessarily be crippled, he at this early hour signalled his captains to be prepared to anchor. At 11.40 A.M. his memorable signal, the watchword ever after of the British navy, was hoisted at the *Victory's* mizen-topgallant mast-head, "England expects that every man will do his duty," and greeted with loud cheers by the whole fleet. One more signal, "Engage the enemy more closely," and his commands to his fleet were finished. Each captain knew his duty, and Nelson put small faith in signals when once the battle was begun.

Collingwood, leading the lee line, was far nearer the enemy than Nelson. The *Royal Sovereign*, freshly coppered and the fastest ship of her division, headed straight for the *Santa Ana*, 112, flag-ship of Admiral Alava, passed slowly under her stern, and at ten minutes past noon poured into it at close quarters a tremendous double-shotted broadside, dismounting 14 of her guns, and killing or wounding 400 of her men. Almost at the same moment she poured her other broadside into the *Fougueux*, and then putting her helm hard over engaged the great Spaniard muzzle to muzzle. But her superior speed was somewhat to her disadvantage, and it was quite twenty minutes before the rest of her division could come to her assistance and overpower the rear, now cut off

Collingwood breaks the line.

from the rest and concentrating their fire upon the *Royal Sovereign*.

In the meanwhile Nelson, full of admiration for his well-tried and trusty friend, was gradually in his turn drawing near the enemy's line with every sail that the *Victory* could carry; but the westerly wind was very light and her pace was provokingly slow. When the third shot fired at her was seen to pass over her he dismissed Blackwood to his ship with the prophetic words, "God bless you, Blackwood, I shall never speak to you again;" and in another moment the shot were screaming and hurtling round him in hundreds. He had already known that the enemy would make a dead set at the *Victory*. The first few shot had been mere range-finders: the fifth, passing through her main-topgallant sail, proved that she was well within reach; and at once, as if by signal from the French admiral, every ship of the enemy's van which could bring a gun to bear opened fire upon the *Victory* in the hope of destroying her at the very outset of the fight. It was a vain hope. Slowly and silently she came on, taking no notice of the hurricane of iron crashing into and around her. Firing not a single gun in return, she made steadily and patiently for the enemy's centre, recognising in the towering four-decker over her bowsprit end her antagonist of eight years before, the *Santisima Trinidad*, and shrewdly suspecting that the great 80-gun ship next astern of her was Villeneuve's flag-ship, the *Bucentaure*, though the French admiral hoisted no distinguishing flag. For half an hour the *Victory* endured the fury of the enemy without reply. Already fifty of her men were killed or wounded, her sails were riddled, her foresail almost destroyed, her mizen-topmast had gone over the side, her wheel was knocked to pieces, and yet she fired no gun in answer to the hundreds that roared around her. Suffering but self-reliant she grimly bided her time. At last it came. Drifting slowly under the stern of the *Bucentaure*, and so close that the French ensign almost touched her rigging, she fired her foremost gun, a 68-pounder carronade loaded with one round shot and a keg filled with 500 musket balls, right through the stern windows of the *Bucentaure*, followed in turn by every gun of the remaining 50 upon her broadside, all double, many of them treble shotted. The effect was terrific; 20 of the Frenchman's guns were dismounted, 400 of his men were killed or wounded, and the *Bucentaure* herself was practically reduced to a helpless condition. In the space of a few seconds the *Victory* had done to the French flag-ship with one broadside infinitely more harm than the concentrated fire of the whole French van had done to her in half an hour. A moment or two afterwards, passing clear of the *Bucentaure* and heavily raked herself by the *Neptune*, she fell on board the *Redoutable* and engaged her muzzle to muzzle, gradually supported by the rest of her line as they slowly struggled up and massed themselves upon the enemy's centre.

Victory rakes the Bucentaure.

The *Victory* and the *Redoutable* now lay side by side. The latter closed her lower deck ports at once lest the British should board her through them; but she kept up a most destructive fire upon the upper deck of the *Victory* from small guns and muskets in her tops. In spite of affectionate and anxious remonstrance on the part of his officers, Nelson had insisted on wearing all his orders, weather-worn and tarnished it is true, but still fatally conspicuous; add to this the empty sleeve dangling from his right shoulder, and it would be impossible to mistake him. His ship had been intentionally the target of hundreds of guns; himself was but too likely to be the aim of every musket. About half-past one, as he was pacing the deck with Hardy his captain, he suddenly fell, first on his knees and then on his side, shot through the left epaulet from the mizen-top of the enemy's ship. He knew at once that the wound was mortal, and said so. He was carried below, concealing with his own handkerchief his face and orders lest the knowledge of his fall should reach his men. From the first it was seen that there was no hope; but while he lived he never ceased for one moment to be the commander-in-chief of the fleet. To the last his duty was his chief concern. He constantly enquired as to the number of the enemy's vessels which had surrendered, and expressed himself as content with the 14 or 15 which were reported to him, though, as he said, he had bargained for 20. As his end drew near he anxiously and repeatedly impressed upon Hardy the necessity of anchoring after the battle was over for the safety of the fleet and its prizes. At about half-past four, three hours after the fatal ball was fired, he died, the last broadsides of the battle ringing his death-knell.

In the meantime the *Redoutable*, fouled on her port side by the *Victory*, and now on her starboard side by our *Temeraire*, on whose outer side again lay the *Fougueux*, had hauled down her colours and surrendered after doing to the British navy such mischief as no foreign vessel ever before achieved. The whole resistance of the enemy was already failing.

Of the ships composing their rear 12 were taken; the centre was overpowered by numbers; the great *Santisima Trinidad* and the *Bucentaure* had surrendered; the van, ordered to wear and support their comrades, neglected to act in concert, and, moreover, moved so slowly as to fail in their purpose. Several of these also fell into our hands; one, the ill-fated *Achille*, was set on fire by her own explosives and blew up with most of her men. By five o'clock the fight was over. Admiral Gravina, himself mortally wounded, was making the best of his way with 11 vessels to Cadiz; Admiral Dumanoir with four others was in full flight to the south-west, only to fall a fortnight later a prey to one of our detached squadrons; the remainder were lying battered, mastless, crippled alongside their conquerors, in many cases but little better off than themselves. Then appeared the far-sighted wisdom of Nelson's last charge to Hardy that the fleet should anchor. Already the wind was rising, the dreaded shoals of Trafalgar were barely eight miles off dead to leeward; but the command had now passed to Collingwood, and he declared that to anchor was the last thing he should have thought of. It was not till nine o'clock that he saw the necessity for the step, which to be of service should have been taken at once; and then it was too late. Some three or four of the prizes, however, did anchor and safely weathered the gale which caused the destruction of their fellows; the remainder of the ships strove hard to make to the westward. The wind now rapidly freshened. It became evident that in spite of all exertions many of the prizes must be lost. On the night of the 22nd the *Redoutable* foundered with many of her crew

A gale comes on, many prizes lost.

and a few of our own men; the *Bucentaure* was totally wrecked off Cadiz; the *Fougueux* shared her fate with the loss of nearly all hands; the *Algeciras* in deadly peril was handed over by the prize crew to her own men, who at once overpowered them and succeeded in carrying her into harbour; it was with difficulty that our own shattered ships were saved from destruction. On the 23rd, while the gale still raged, Commodore Kerjulien at Cadiz collected a mixed squadron of five ships of the line and several frigates and dashed out upon our disabled fleet to rob us of our remaining prizes. He would have done more wisely to have remained at anchor. Though the gale still raged with extreme violence, 10 of our best ships cast off their prizes and formed in line of battle to receive him. His experience of the 21st was too fresh in his memory to tempt him to risk an encounter at such odds; but his frigates managed to pick up two of the prizes which we had cast adrift. He was welcome to them: they were so hopelessly knocked about as to be useless both to him and us; and as in returning to Cadiz he lost by shipwreck three out of the five ships of the line with which he had come out to attack us, he can hardly be said to have gained by the transaction. On the night of the 24th the *Monarca* drove ashore and was lost. The continuance of the bad weather now determined Collingwood to destroy all but the most seaworthy of his prizes; among them the great *Santisima Trinidad*, the largest war-ship in the world, and a worthy trophy could she but have been safely brought into port. She was sunk, settling down so fast that it was a matter of doubt whether some of her wounded did not go down with her. It was a work of difficulty in that heavy sea. Some were scuttled, some were burned, the wounded prisoners were sent on shore; and at last of our 17 prizes only four, one French and three Spanish 74's were all that remained as visible proof of our triumph. Seven days after the action the battered hull of the *Victory*, in tow of the *Neptune* and bearing the mortal remains of her Great Admiral, entered Gibraltar Bay; on the 12th of December she arrived off Dover under jury masts. Then with one heart and with one mind the entire nation, losing all trace of exultation at his brilliant victory in the overwhelming sense of sorrow at his tragic death, strove to give expression to the outburst of gratitude, of admiration, and of affection which the remembrance of his great services evoked, in the gorgeous pageant of a national funeral. With the sorrow of the whole nation as his pall, with the love of his fellow-countrymen as flowers round his coffin, they laid his worn and mangled body to rest in the shade of St. Paul's.

But his last great deed had removed entirely the threatening cloud which had for so long hung over England. The vast camp on the other side of the Channel was deserted; the troops were dispersed all over Europe; the thousands of flat boats lay rotting on the shore; the specially constructed harbours were gradually filled up with mud and resumed their normal form; the batteries for their defence crumbled with neglect and disuse. All possibility of the great invasion was utterly destroyed. In spite of the contemptuous indifference with which Buonaparte affected to regard the victory, merely announcing to his Council that "the storm had occasioned the loss of a few ships after a battle imprudently fought"; in spite of the exultation of the Spanish Minister at the death of the British Admiral, followed, as he had the impudence to declare, by the destruction of the whole British fleet, the blow to France and Spain was a final one. Never again, though the war with the former Power lasted for ten years longer, did a French fleet dare to encounter the might and skill of the British Navy; and our command of the sea was now placed so entirely beyond the possibility of denial that for well-nigh a century no one has ever ventured to dispute it.

And since the very existence of Great Britain as a nation depends infinitely more now than it did then upon her First Line of Defence, no effort should be thought too great, no sacrifice too heavy in order to keep the great British Navy in the perfection of strength and efficiency. Thus only can be maintained against all comers that indisputable supremacy, the slowly fashioned and majestic fabric of one thousand years, to the safe-guarding of which every thought and action of Nelson's life was devoted, and on which, in the moment of his death, he placed the crowning stone.

CHRONOLOGICAL TABLE

DATE		PAGE
897	King Alfred builds a navy	2
959	King Edgar protects the coast	3
973	His progress up the Dee	3
979	Ethelred the Unready	3
1016	Edmund Ironside	5
	Canute the Dane	
1066	Norman Invasion	5
1120	Loss of the *Blanche Nef*	7
1189	Richard I.	9
1190	He collects a fleet at Dartmouth	9
1191	He takes Limasol	10
	Fights the Great Dromon	11
1199	John	12
1213	Battle of Damme	12
1216	Henry III.	12
1217	Battle of Sandwich	13
1272	Edward I.	
1293	Sir Robert Tiptoft's victory	18
1327	Edward III.	19
1337	He claims the French Crown	19
1338 to 1339	The French outrage our coast, and take the *Christopher* and *Edward*	20
1340	Battle of Sluys	21
1346	Edward lands in France; battle of Cressy	23
1347	Calais taken	23
1350	"L'Espagnols sur Mer"	24
1360	Decline of navy	28
	Peace of Bretigny	28
1372	Defeat at La Rochelle	29
1375	Outrage by Spanish fleet	30
1377	Richard II.	31
	Decay of navy; coast pillaged	32
1385	France prepares to invade	32
1387	Arundel's victory in the Channel	33

DATE		PAGE
1399	Henry IV.	33
	Mutual reprisals	35
1413	Henry V.	36
	He restores the navy	37
1414	Renews claim to French Crown	37
1415	Takes Harfleur; wins Agincourt	37
1416	Naval battle of Harfleur	38
1417	Huntingdon's victory in the Channel	39
1420	Treaty of Troyes	40
1422	Henry VI.	41
1461	Edward IV.	42
1474	He scours the coast of France	42
1485	Henry of Richmond lands unopposed	42
	Battle of Bosworth	42
	Henry VII. creates a strong navy	42
	Builds the *Great Harry*	42
1492	Columbus discovers America	42
1497	Cabot discovers Newfoundland	43
1509	Henry VIII.	43
1512	*Regent* and *Cordelier* off Brest	44
1520	Henry VIII. embarks at Dover	43
1544	France prepares to invade	44
1545	French at Spithead; loss of the *Mary Rose*	45
1547	Edward VI. } Navy neglected	45
1553	Mary	
1558	Elizabeth	45
1568	Hawkins and Drake at San Juan de Ulloa	46
1576	Frobisher discovers Labrador	46
1577	Drake in the Pacific	48
1583	Sir H. Gilbert lost in the *Squirrel*	46
1585-6	Drake in the West Indies	48
1587	Davis in the Arctic Sea	46
	Drake singes the King of Spain's beard	48
1588	May 30, The Armada sails	49
	July 19, "The Armada is in sight"	51
	July 21, The fight begins	53
	July 29, Attack with fire-ships	56
	July 31, Armada in full flight	57
1589	Drake and Norris on the coast of Spain	60
	Earl of Cumberland takes Fayal	60
1591	Loss of the *Revenge*	60
1596	Howard, Essex, and Raleigh at Cadiz	60
1602	Levison and Monson at Cezimbra	60
1603	James I.	62
1625	Charles I.	62
1649	Cromwell	62
1652	First Dutch War	64
	May 19, Blake and Van Tromp off Dover	64
	August, Ayscough and De Ruyter off Plymouth	64
	September 28, Battle of the Kentish Knock	64
	November 30, Blake defeated by Van Tromp	64

CHRONOLOGICAL TABLE

DATE		PAGE
1653	February 18, Battle of Portland	65
	June 2, Battle off Essex coast	66
	July 31, Battle off Dutch coast; Dutch defeated; Van Tromp killed	67
1654	Peace	68
1656	Cromwell makes war on Spain	68
	Stayner takes a treasure fleet	68
1657	Blake at Santa Cruz	68
1658	Cromwell dies	70
1660	Charles II.	70
1665	Second Dutch War	70
	June 3, Battle off Lowestoft; Opdam killed	70
1666	June 1 to 4, "The Four Days' Fight" off the North Foreland	71
	July 25, "The St. James' Fight"	72
	August 8, "Sir R. Holmes, his bonefire"	73
1667	Dutch fleet in the Thames	73
	Peace of Breda	73
1672	Third Dutch War	75
	May 28, Battle of Solebay	75
1673	Three more drawn battles	79
1674	Peace of London	79
1685	James II.	80
1689	William and Mary	80
	May 1, Battle of Bantry Bay	80
1690	June 30, Battle of Beachy Head	81
1691	France prepares to invade	82
1692	May 19, Battle of La Hogue (or Barfleur)	83
1693	Benbow's fire-ship at St. Malo	84
1697	Peace of Ryswick	86
1702	Anne	86
	War of Spanish Succession	86
	August, Benbow and Du Casse in West Indies	88
	October 12, Rooke at Vigo	87
1703	Great storm; thirteen men-of-war lost; Eddystone lighthouse destroyed	92
1704	July 23, Rooke takes Gibraltar	92
	August 13, Battle of Malaga	94
	October, Leake saves Gibraltar	94
1705	March, Leake saves Gibraltar	94
1707	July 16, Shovel bombards Toulon	95
	October 10, *Cumberland* and consorts taken by Forbin	96
	October 23, Loss of Sir C. Shovel and four ships	95
1708	October 30, Leake takes Minorca	95
1713	Peace of Utrecht	97
1714	George I.	98
1715	First Jacobite Rising	99
1718	Battle off Cape Passaro	100
1726	Wager relieves Gibraltar	100
1727	George II.	100
1729	Peace of Seville	100

DATE		PAGE
1738	Episode of Jenkins's ear	100
1739	War with Spain	101
	November 20, Vernon takes Porto Bello	101
1740	Anson sails for the Pacific	102
1741	War of the Austrian Succession; Vernon fails at Cartagena	101
1743	Anson takes the *Cobadonga*	104
1744	February 11, Matthews and Lestock off Toulon	105
	October 4, Loss of Admiral Balchen in *Victory*	107
1745	Second Jacobite Rising	107
	Lion and *Elizabeth*	107
1747	May 3, Anson's victory off Cape Finisterre	108
	October 14, Hawke's victory off Brest	109
1748	Peace of Aix-la-Chapelle	109
1755	General Braddock's defeat	110
1756	Seven Years' War	110
	May 20, Byng and La Galissoniere off Minorca	112
	June 29, Minorca surrenders	113
1757	March 14, Byng executed	113
1758	April, Hawke at Rochefort	114
	August, Howe destroys Cherbourg	114
	September, Disaster at St. Malo	114
	September 29, Nelson born	114
1759	France prepares to invade	114
	Rodney bombards Havre	115
	August 18, Boscawen and De la Clue off Lagos	116
	November 20, Hawke and Conflans in Quiberon Bay	117
1760	February 28, Elliot and Thurot off Isle of Man	118
	George III.	118
1761	June 7, Belleisle taken	119
1762	January, Spain joins France	119
	May 21, *Hermione*, treasure-ship, taken	120
	August 13, Havana capitulates	122
	October 6, Manila taken	123
	October 31, *Santissima Trinidad*, treasure-ship, taken	123
1763	Peace of Paris	124
1764-6	Byron's voyage of discovery	126
1776-9	Wallis and Carteret's voyage	126
1768	Cook's first voyage	126
1773	Tea-ships attacked at Boston	126
1775	War with American colonies	127
1776	January 1, Sir P. Parker at Norfolk, Virginia	127
	June, Sir P. Parker repulsed at Charleston	127
	July 4, Declaration of Independence	128
	Bushnell tries his torpedo	128
	October 12, Fight on Lake Champlain	129
1777	Surrender of General Burgoyne	129
1778	France joins the Americans	129
	July 27, Keppel and D'Orvilliers off Brest	131
	August 9, Howe and D'Estaing off Rhode Island	130
	December 15, Barrington and D'Estaing at St. Lucia	131
1779	Spain joins France; they plan invasion	134

CHRONOLOGICAL TABLE

DATE			PAGE
1779	July 6,	Byron and D'Estaing off Grenada	134
	August,	French and Spanish fleets off Plymouth	135
	August,	Sir G. Collier at Penobscot	135
1780	January 16,	Rodney and De Langara off Cape St. Vincent	137
		Rodney relieves Gibraltar	138
	March,	Nelson in San Juan River	142
	April 17,	Rodney and De Guichen off Martinique	140
	October,	Great Hurricane in West Indies	**142**
	December,	War with Holland	**143**
1781	February 3,	Rodney takes **St. Eustatius**	**145**
	March,	Darby relieves **Gibraltar**	**144**
	April 29,	Hood and **De Grasse** off Martinique	**146**
	August 9,	Parker and Zoutman off Dogger Bank	145
	September 5,	Graves and **De** Grasse off the Chesapeake	147
		Cornwallis surrenders at Yorktown	147
1782	February 17,	Hughes and Suffren in East Indies ; 1st fight	154
	April 12,	Rodney defeats De Grasse	149
	April 12,	Hughes and Suffren in East Indies ; 2nd fight	154
	July 5,	Hughes and Suffren in East Indies ; 3rd fight	154
	August 29,	Loss of the *Royal George*	157
	September 3,	Hughes and Suffren in East Indies ; 4th fight	154
	September 13,	Grand attack on Gibraltar	153
	October 11,	Howe relieves Gibraltar	154
1783	June 20,	Hughes and Suffren in East Indies ; 5th fight	**154**
		Peace of Versailles	**155**
1789		Mutiny of the *Bounty*	**156**
1790		Vancouver's voyage of discovery	156
1793	February 2,	War with **France**	158
		Hood holds Toulon	158
	December 18,	Toulon evacuated	159
1794	March,	Martinique surrenders	167
	April,	St. Lucia falls	167
	May 22,	Bastia falls	161
	May 28 to June 1,	Howe and De Villaret Joyeuse (glorious first of June)	164
	August 1,	Calvi falls	161
1795	January,	Dutch declare war	167
	March 14,	Hotham's victory in Gulf of Genoa	170
	June 17,	Cornwallis' clever escape	168
	June 23,	Bridport's victory off Lorient	169
	July 13,	Hotham's action off Hyères	171
	December,	French fleet for Ireland dispersed by gale	172
1796	August 17,	Dutch squadron **at** the Cape surrenders	172
	October,	Spain joins France and Holland	172
1797	February 14,	Battle of St. **Vincent**	174
	April **15,**	Mutiny at Spithead	179
	May 13,	Mutiny at the **Nore**	180
		Mutiny in North Sea fleet	180
	..	in fleet off Cadiz	**181**
	..	in fleet at the Cape	**182**
	..	on board *Hermione*	**182**

DATE			PAGE
1797	July,	Nelson bombards Cadiz	184
	July,	Nelson repulsed at Santa Cruz	185
	October 11,	Battle of Camperdown	186
1798	May,	Irish rebellion	191
	August 1,	Battle of the Nile	195
	Humbert invades Ireland		191
	October 12,	Warren's victory off Donegal	192
	November,	Minorca taken	202
1799	April,	Admiral Bruix's aimless cruise	203
	Sir S. Smith at Acre		204
	Ball blockades Malta		208
	Troubridge's naval brigade ashore		203
	August,	Dutch fleet surrenders	206
	October,	*Thetis* and *Santa Brigida*, treasure-ships, taken	207
1800	February 18,	*Généreux* taken by Nelson	208
	March 5,	Loss of the *Queen Charlotte*	210
	March 30,	*Guillaume Tell* taken	209
	July,	The *Freya* incident	211
	September 5,	Malta surrenders	210
	November,	Armed Neutrality of the North	211
1801	January,	Ganteaume sails for Egypt	221
	April 2,	Battle of Copenhagen	214
	July 6,	Saumarez repulsed at Algeciras	222
	July 12,	Saumarez and Linois off Gibraltar	223
	August,	Nelson at Boulogne	221
1802	March,	Peace of Amiens	224
1803	May 16,	War with France	225
1803 to 1805	Cornwallis watches Brest; Nelson watches Toulon		226
1804	October 3,	Spanish treasure-ships taken	228
	December 12,	Spain declares war	229
1805	January 11,	Missiessy leaves Rochefort	232
	January 17,	Villeneuve leaves Toulon	232
	April 10,	Villeneuve leaves Cadiz for West Indies	233
	May 11,	Nelson leaves Lagos in pursuit	233
	July 22,	Calder and Villeneuve off Ferrol	234
	August 19,	Nelson in England	236
	September 15,	Nelson sails from Portsmouth	238
	September 28,	Nelson off Cadiz	238
	October 19,	"Enemy coming out"	238
	October 21,	Battle of Trafalgar	239
	October 22 to 25,	Heavy gale	247
	October 23,	Kerjulien's attack	248
	Collingwood destroys his prizes		248
	December 23,	Nelson's body at Greenwich	248
1806	January 9,	Nelson buried in St. Paul's	249

INDEX

ABERCROMBIE, at Alexandria, 222
Aboukir, battle of, 195
Acre, Richard I. off, 10
    defence of, by Sir S. Smith, 204
Acteon and *Favourite* take *Hermione*, 120
Agincourt, battle of, 37
Aix-la-Chapelle, peace of, 109
Alava, Admiral, at Trafalgar, **243**
Alberoni, Cardinal, 99
Alexandria found empty by Nelson, 194
    battle of, 222
Alfred builds a navy, 2
Algeciras Bay, Spanish fleet in, **154**
    Linois and Saumarez in, 222
Amiens, peace of, 224
Anne, Queen, 86
Anson in the Pacific, 102
    off Cape Finisterre, 108
Armada, the, sails, 49
    puts into Coruña, 50
    sails once more, 51
    in the Channel, 53-55
    off Calais, 56
    flies north, 57
Armed neutrality of the North, 211
    neutrality of the North broken up, 220
Ark Royal, the, 51, 55
Arundel, Earl of, his victory, 33
Ayscough, Sir George, 64

BACCALAOS (or Newfoundland), 43
Balchen, Admiral, lost in *Victory*, **107**

Ball, Captain, blockades Malta, 208
Bantry Bay, battle of, 80
Barbados, Hood and Rodney meet at, 148
Barrington, Admiral, at St. Lucia, 131
Bastia taken by Nelson, 160
Beachy Head, battle of, 81
Bear, the, 50
Beaumont, Admiral, **lost** on Goodwins, 92
Bedford, Duke **of**, at Harfleur, 50
Belleisle, capture of, 119
Benbow, Commodore, his fire-ship, 85
    Admiral, fights Du Casse, 88
Berkeley, Lord, 35
Black Hulk of Flanders, 38
Blackwood, Captain, hurries home from Cadiz, 237
    Nelson's farewell to, 244
Blake, Admiral, 64
    at Santa Cruz, 68
    his death, 69
Blanche Nef, loss of, 7
Bligh, Captain, in the *Bounty*, 156
Boscawen and De la Clue, 116
Boston, Mass., D'Estaing at, 130
    D'Estaing leaves, 131
Boulogne flotilla, attack on, 221
    preparations at, 230
Bounty, mutiny of the, 156
Boys, Commodore, watches Dunkirk, 115
Braddock, General, defeat **of**, **110**
Breda, peace of, 73

S

Brederode, Van Tromp's flag-ship, 65-67
Brest, expedition to Ireland from, 191
  Cornwallis off, 226
  Ganteaume at, 231
Bretigny, peace of, 28
Bridport, Lord, his victory, 169
  his fleet mutinies, 179
Britannia at La Hogue, 84
  at St. Vincent, 177
  at Trafalgar, 240
Brueys, Admiral, at the Nile, 195
Bruix, Admiral, his aimless cruise, 203
Bucentaure at Trafalgar, 245
  lost off Cadiz, 248
Buckner, Admiral, 180
Bucq, Sir John de, 33
Buonaparte at Toulon (evacuation), 159
  sails for Egypt, 194
  attacks Acre, 204
  makes himself Chief Consul, 207
  proposes peace, 208
  wins Marengo, 210
  sends Ganteaume to Egypt, 221
  makes himself Emperor, 227
  prepares for invasion, 230
Burgoyne, General, surrenders, 129
Bushnell's torpedo, 128
Byng, Admiral, off Cape Passaro, 100
  and West at Minorca, 112
  shot, 113
Byron, Admiral, supersedes Lord Howe, 131
  fights D'Estaing, 134

CABOT, John, 43
Cacafuego, the, taken by Anson, 48
Cadiz, Drake attacks, 48
  Howard and Essex at, 60
  De Guichen retires to, 142
  Nelson bombards, 184
  Sir J. Orde off, 231
  Villeneuve retires to, 237
  "Enemy coming out" of, 238
Calais taken, 23
  Calveley sails from, 32
  Armada off, 56
Calder, Sir Robert, off Ferrol, 234

Calder, Sir R., fights Villeneuve, 235
  tried by court-martial, 236
  sent home by Nelson, 238
Calderon, Pedro, 58
Calveley, Sir Hugh, 32
Calvi taken by Nelson, 161
Camperdown, battle of, 187
Canada ceded to us, 124
Cape Breton ceded to us, 124
Cape of Good Hope taken, 172
  mutiny at, 182
Capitana, the, taken by Drake, 53
Capua taken by Troubridge, 204
Carlscrona, Sir H. Parker off, 219
Cartagena (West Indies) attacked by Drake, 48
  Vernon at, 101
Cartagena (Spain), Nelson looks in at, 173
  Spanish ships at, 231
Castaneta, Admiral, off Cape Passaro, 100
Catamarans, early form of torpedo, 231
Catwater, the, 53
Centurion, the, Anson's flag-ship, 102
Cezimbra, 60
Champlain, Lake, fight on, 129
Channel, state of the, 17, 32
Charles II. makes war on the Dutch, 70, 75
Childers, sloop, fired on, 158
Christopher, the, taken, 20
  retaken, 22
Cinque Ports, 15
Civita Vecchia taken by Troubridge, 204
Clarke, Francis, 46
  Sir John, 32
Cochrane, Admiral, off Ferrol, 231
  pursues Missiessy, 232
Cog *Thomas*, the, 24
Collier, Sir G., at Penobscot, 135
Collingwood, Captain, at St. Vincent, 175
  Admiral, at Trafalgar, 240
  breaks the line, 243
  does not anchor till too late, 247
  destroys most of his prizes, 249
Columbus, Bartholomew and Christopher, 42

INDEX

Colpoys, Admiral, 179
Commons, complaints of, 31
Conde, Prince of, 46
Conflans, Admiral, at Brest, 114
   and Hawke, 117
Copenhagen, defences of, 212
   battle of, 216
Cordelier and *Regent*, 44
Cordova, Don Josef de, 174
Cornish, Admiral, at Manila, 123
Cornwallis, Lord, surrenders, 147
   Admiral, his clever ruse, 168
   watches Brest, 226
Corsica, Nelson in, 160
Coruña, Armada at, 50
   Medina Sidonia returns to, 58
   Drake and Norris at, 60
Council of war, Byng's, 112
   Sir H. Parker's, 213
Cromwell, 62
   his war with the Dutch, 64
   makes war on Spain, 68
   death of, 70
Cronenburg, castle of, 212
Cruxenbergh, the, 16
Culloden, the, grounds at the Nile, 199
Cumberland, Earl of, 60
   and consorts defend convoy, 97

DAMME, battle of, 12
Dannebrog, the, blows up, 216
Darby, Admiral, relieves Gibraltar, 144
Dartmouth, Richard I.'s fleet at, 9
   men of, 32
   Du Chatel attacks, 35
Davis, John, 46
Deane, Admiral, killed, 66
Declaration of Independence, 128
De Grasse in West Indies, 146
   off Chesapeake, 147
   defeated by Rodney, 150
De Guichen relieves D'Estaing, 138
De la Clue at Toulon, 114
   and Boscawen, 116
De la Galissoniere at Minorca, 111
De Langara and Rodney, 137
   at Toulon, 159
De l'Etendeur and Hawke, 109
De Ruyter off Plymouth, 64
   in the "four days' fight," 71

De Ruyter in the "St. James' fight," 72
   at Solebay, 77
De St. Croix defends Belleisle, 119
D'Estaing sent to America, 129
   off Rhode Island, 130
   at St. Lucia, 131
D'Estrées, Comte, 75
De Savoisy, Sir Charles, 35
De Suffren and Hughes, 154
De Tourville at Beachy Head, 81
   at La Hogue, 84
De Villaret Joyeuse, 162
De Winter in the Texel, 186
   off Camperdown, 187
D'Orvilliers and Keppel, 131
Douglas, Captain, on Lake Champlain, 129
Dover a cinque port, 15
   burnt, 20
   Armada off, 55
   Van Tromp off, 64
Drake, Sir Francis, 46
   singes King of Spain's beard, 48
   takes the *Capitana*, 53
   attacks Armada off Calais, 56
Du Casse and Benbow, 88
Du Chatel killed at Dartmouth, 35
Duguai Trouin, 96
Dumanoir, Admiral, at Trafalgar, 247
Duncan, Admiral, his fleet mutinies, 180
   at Camperdown, 186
   made a peer, 188
   captures Dutch fleet, 206
Dutch coast, battle off, 67
   defeated at Camperdown, 187
   fleet in the Thames, 73
   fleet surrenders, 206
   war, 1652, 64; 1665, 70; 1672, 75; 1780, 143; 1795, 167; 1804, 228

EDDYSTONE Lighthouse destroyed, 92
Edgar protects the coast, 3
Edmund Ironside, 5
Edward, the, taken, 20
Edward III. claims French crown, 19
   at Sluys, 20

Edward III. at Cressy, 23
"L'Espagnols sur Mer," 24-27
IV. scours French coast, 42
VI., 45
Egypt, Buonaparte sails for, 194
Eight Kings of Edgar's crew, 3
Elephant, Nelson in the, 213
Elizabeth, 45
her parsimony, 51, 53, 59
Elizabeth Jonas, the, 50
Elliot and Thurot off Isle of Man, 118
General, defends Gibraltar, 153
Essex coast, battle off, 66
Ethelred, his wavering policy, 3
Eustace the monk, 12
Evertzen, Admiral, killed, 72

FALKLAND Islands attacked by Spain, 125
Faroe Isles, 57
Fayal, 60
Ferrol watched by Cochrane, 231
Sir R. Calder off, 234
First Jacobite rebellion, 99
Forbin in the Channel, 96
Fort Royal, De Guichen at, 138
Four days' fight, the, 71
Fox, Captain, of *Kent*, tried, 109
French Revolution, 157
Freya incident, the, 211
Frobisher, Martin, 46

GAETA, taken by Troubridge, 204
Ganteaume, Admiral, sails for Egypt, 221
retires to Toulon, 222
at Brest, 231
Gaunt, John of, 24
Généreux, the, escapes from the Nile, 200
taken by Nelson, 208
Genoa taken, 210
Genoese caracks, 39
George I., 98
George II., 100
George III., 118
Gervays Alard, 16
Gibraltar, taken by Rooke, 93
Spanish attempts on, 94, 100, 134
relieved first time, 138
relieved second time, 144

Gibraltar, great attack on, 153
relieved third time, 154
Saumarez and Linois off, 223
Gilbert, Sir Humphrey lost, 46
Glorious first of June, 165
Graves, Admiral, at Sandy Hook, 147
and De Grasse off Chesapeake, 147
sails under Sir H. Parker, 212
Gravina, Admiral, at Trafalgar, 247
Gravesend burnt, 32
Great Harry, the, 42
Grenada, Byron and D'Estaing off, 134
Grenvile, Sir Richard, in *Revenge*, 60
Groyne, the, Armada at, 50
Guillaume Tell, the, taken, 209

HAMILTON, Captain, retakes *Hermione*, 183
Hannekin, in *La Salle du Roi*, 27
Hardy, Captain, sounds Danish Channel, 214
Captain of *Victory*, at Trafalgar, 246
Sir Charles, 136
Hardyng at Harfleur, 39
Harfleur taken, 38
Harland, Admiral, 132
Harvey, Captain John, 166
Hastings, a cinque port, 15
burnt, 20
burnt again, 32
Hauley, John, of Dartmouth, 35
Havana, the, taken, 122
Havre, French fleet at, 44
Hawke, Admiral, his victory off Brest, 108
in Quiberon Bay, 117
Hawkins, Sir John, 46
his care of the navy, 50
his ill-treatment, 59
Helder, the, seized, 206
Henry IV., 33
entrusts defence of coast to merchants, 36
Henry V. restores navy, 36
sails in the *Trinity Royal*, 37
Henry VI., 41
Henry VII. builds *Great Harry*, 42

Henry VIII., 43
Herbert, Admiral (Lord Torrington) 80
Hermione, the treasure-ship, 120
  mutiny on board, 182
Hoche, the, **taken** by Admiral Warren, **192**
Hollandia, the, founders, 145
Holmes, Sir Robert, his bonefire, 73
Hood, Sir Samuel, and De Grasse, 146
  at Sandy Hook, 147
  outwits De Grasse, 148
  Lord, holds Toulon, 159
Hotham, Admiral, off Genoa, **170**
  off Hyères, **171**
Howard, Sir **Edward**, 43
  of Effingham, 51
  Sir Thomas, 55
Howe, Lord, at Sandy Hook, 128
  off Rhode island, 130
  relieves Gibraltar, 154
  commands channel fleet, 158
  glorious first of June, 165
Hubert de Burgh, 12
Hughes, Sir E. and De Suffren, 154
Humbert, General, surrenders, 191
Huntingdon, Earl of, his victory, 39
Hurricane in West Indies, **142**
Hyder Ali, 155
Hythe, a cinque port, 15

INFLEXIBLE, the, on Lake Champlain, 129
Insubordination in Rodney's fleet, 140
Invasion, how to meet, 1
  by the Romans, 2
  by the Anglo-Saxons, 2
  by the Danes, 3
  by the Normans, 5
  by Eustace the monk, 12
  threatened, 1385, 32; 1545, 45; 1588, 49; 1759, 115; 1779, 136
  of Ireland 1689, 80
  of Ireland by Thurot, 118
  of Ireland fails, 1795, 172
  again intended, 1797, 173
  Buonaparte urges, 190
  of Ireland, Humbert's, 191
  of Ireland from Brest, 191
  French preparations for, 230

Ireland, fight in Bantry Bay, 80
  Thurot at Carrickfergus, 118
  expedition against, fails, 172
  Humbert's expedition to, 191
  Brest squadron off, 191

JACOBITE Rebellion, first, 99; second, 107
Jamaica taken by Penn, 68
  threatened by Spain, 142
James I., 51
James, Duke of York, commands off Lowestoft, 70
  at Solebay, 75
Jenkins, his ear, 100
Jersey, attack on, 135
Jervis, Sir John, supersedes Hotham, 172
  abandons Mediterranean, 172
  at St. Vincent, 175
  made Lord St. Vincent, 178
  quells mutiny, 181
John, King, battle of Damme, 12

KEITH, Lord, his flag-ship burnt, 210
  drives Ganteaume from Alexandria, 222
  holds the Downs, 232
Kempenfeldt, Admiral, in *Royal George*, 151
Kentish Knock, battle of the, 64
Keppel and D'Orvilliers, 131
  tried by court-martial, 133
  introduces copper sheathing, 134
Kerjulien, Commodore, after Trafalgar, 248
Killala Bay, Humbert lands in, 191
King of the sea, Edward III. as, 28
Kirby, Captain, shot for mutiny, 91

LABRADOR, 46
Lake, General, forces Humbert to surrender, 191
Lawson, Admiral, 66
Leake, Sir John, protects Gibraltar, 94
  takes Minorca, 95
Leghorn, taken by Nelson, 202
Lestock, Admiral, his conduct off Toulon, 106
Levison, Sir R., attacks Cezimbra, 60

Linois and Saumarez at Algeciras, 222
  off Gibraltar, 223
Lisbon, Drake attacks, 48
  Armada sails from, 49
London, peace of, 79
L'Orient, Brueys' flag-ship, blows up, 200
Lorient Port, French squadron at, 231
Louis XIV. makes alliance with Charles II., 57
  proclaims James III., 86
Lowestoft, battle off, 70

MACARTNEY, Lord, quells mutiny at the Cape, 182
Maddalena isles, 229
Magna Charta, 12
Malaga, Rooke's victory off, 94
Malta, taken by French, 194
  blockaded by Ball, 208
  surrenders, 210
Manila, capture of, 123
Marengo, battle of, 210
Mary of England, 45
Mary Rose, loss of the, 45
Martinique, taken by us, 120, 167
Matthews and Lestock off Toulon, 105
Medina Sidonia, Duke of, 49
Mercedes, treasure-ship, blows up, 228
Middle ground shoal, 213
Minorca, taken by Leake, 95
  surrenders to the French, 113
  exchanged for Belleisle, 124
  given up by us, 155
  taken again, 202
Missiessy, slips out of Rochefort, 232
Monçada, Hugo de, 49
Monk defeats the Dutch, 66
  off North Foreland, 71
Monson, Sir W., at Cezimbra, 60
Montague, Admiral, 162
Mother of All, the, 38
Mull, isle of, 57
Mutiny, the, at Spithead, 179
  at the Nore, 180
  in St. Vincent's fleet, 181
  at the Cape, 182
  on board the *Hermione*, 182

NARRAGANSETT, Howe and D'Estaing off, 130
Nelson, born, 114
  at San Juan, 142
  in Corsica, 160
  in Agamemnon, 170
  at St. Vincent, 175
  knighted, 178
  bombards Cadiz, 184
  attacks Santa Cruz, 185
  disturbed by mob, 189
  sent to watch Toulon, 193
  pursues Buonaparte to Egypt, 194
  at the Nile, 195
  made a baron, 202
  takes the *Généreux*, 208
  sails for the Baltic, 212
  at Copenhagen, 213
  sends flag of truce, 218
  rows to Bornholm, 220
  supersedes Sir H. Parker, 220
  made a viscount, 220
  attacks Boulogne flotilla, 221
  watching Toulon, 227-229
  pursues Villeneuve, 232
  returns to Gibraltar, 234
  goes home, 236
  embarks at Southsea, 237
  arrives off Cadiz, 238
  at Trafalgar, 240
  his great signal, 243
  "The Nelson touch," 243
  mortally wounded, 246
  buried in St. Paul's, 249
Nicholas of the Tower, the, 37
Nielly, Admiral, 164
Nile, battle of the, 195
Nisbet, Josiah, 185
Norman invasion, 5
Northesk, Earl of, at Trafalgar, 240
North Foreland, battle of the, 71
Norwich, Bishop of, 32
Nova Scotia ceded to us, 124
Nuestra Señora de Cobadonga, the, 104

OPDAM, Admiral, killed off Lowestoft, 70
Oquendo, Miguel de, 49
  his ship taken, 53
  his death, 59

INDEX

Orde, Sir John, off Cadiz, 231
  driven away, 233
Orkney Islands, 57
Orwell, port of, 16

PALLISER, Sir Hugh, 132
Palmas, Gulf **of**, 229
  Nelson in, 233
Panic on South Coast, 136
Paris, peace of, 124
Parker, Sir Hyde, supersedes Byron, 135
  blockaded at St. Lucia, 138
  off Dogger Bank, 145
  sails for the Baltic, 212
  his indecision, 212
  signal to Nelson, 216
  superseded, 220
Parker, Sir Peter, at Charleston, 127
Parker, Richard, mutiny at the Nore, 180
Parma, Duke of, 49, 55
Partition treaty, 86
Passaro, Cape, battle off, 100
Paternoster, the, 16
Pay, Harry, of Poole, 35
Pearl Rock, Rodney and De Guichen off, 140
Pedro Niño, 35
Pembroke, Earl of, 29
Penobscot, Sir G. Collier at, 135
Penn, Admiral, 65
  takes Jamaica, 68
Peter Bert of Sandwich, 16
Philip II. of Spain, 45, 47, 49, 60
Philip V. of Spain attacks Sicily, 99
Pigot, Captain, in *Hermione*, 182
Plymouth burnt, 20, 32, 35
  armada off, 51
  huge fleet off, 135
Poole, Harry Pay of, 35
  attacked, 36
Portland attacked, 35, 36
  Armada off, **55**
  battle of, 65
Porto Bello taken by Vernon, 101
Portsmouth burnt, 28
  men of, 32
Preparations for invasion, 230
Pringle, Admiral, at the Cape, 182
Privateers, the, 46
Puerto Rico pillaged, 60

QUEEN CHARLOTTE, the, burnt at sea, 210

RACE of St. Matthew, 35
Recalde, Martinez de, 49
  his death, 59
Redoutable, the, Nelson shot from, 246
  founders, 247
Regent and *Cordelier*, 44
Revenge, loss of, 60
Richard I. collects a fleet, 9
  at Limasol, 10
  fights the Great Dromon, 10
Richard II., decline of navy, 31
Robert Cleves, 16
Robert de Battayle, 16
Robert de Courtenay, 12
Robert de Namur, 24
Rochelle, La, battle of, 29
Rochefort, General Humbert sails from, 191
  French squadron at, 231
Rodney, **bombards Havre**, **115**
  at Martinique, **120**
  sails for Gibraltar, **137**
  and De Langara, 137
  and De Guichen, 140
  and De Grasse, 149
Rome, British flag hoisted at, 204
Romney, a cinque port, 15
Rooke, Sir George, at La Hogue, 84
  at Vigo, 87
  takes Gibraltar, 93
  victory off Malaga, 94
  removed from command, 95
Roses, wars of the, 42
Rossan Point, 57
Rowley, Admiral, guards Jamaica, 142
Royal George, loss of the, 151
Royal Sovereign, the, at Trafalgar, 240
Rupert, Prince, **70**, 71
Russel, Admiral, at La Hogue, 82
Rye, a cinque port, 15
  burnt, 20, 32
Ryswick, treaty **of, 86**

ST. ELMO taken by Troubridge, 204
St. Eustatius, Rodney seizes, 145

St. Helen's Roads, 45
"St. James' Fight," the, 72
St. Lucia, Barrington and D'Estaing at, 131
  Rodney at, 139, 142
  lost, 172
St. Malo, Benbow attacks, 85
  French troops at, 135
St. Vincent, battle of, 175
  Lord, quells mutiny, 181
Salle du Roi, the, 24, 26
Sandwich, battle of, 13
  a cinque port, 15
  burnt, 20
  sacked, 41
Sandwich, Earl of, off Lowestoft, 70
  killed at Solebay, 77
Sandy Hook, Lord Howe at, 130
  Graves and Hood at, 147
San Domingo attacked, 48
  Spanish fleet at, 148
San Felipe, the, wrecked at Nieuport, 56
  sunk by Grenvile, 60
San Fiorenzo, Corsica, 160
San Josef, the, Nelson takes, 177
San Juan, Nelson at, 142
San Juan de Ulloa, 46
San Lorenzo, the, lost at Calais, 56
San Mateo, the, lost off Sluys, 56
San Nicolas, the, Nelson takes, 177
San Pietro, Sardinia, 193
Santa Ana of the Armada, lost, 51
  at Trafalgar, 243
Santa Cruz, Blake at, 68
  Nelson at, 185
Santiago de Cuba, Vernon at, 102
Santisima Trinidad, treasure-ship, 123
  at St. Vincent, 177
  at Trafalgar, 244
  scuttled, 248
Saumarez and Linois at Algeciras, 222
  off Gibraltar, 223
Scarborough attacked, 32
Secret treaty of Dover, 75
Seine, battle of the, 17
Seven Years' War, 110
Shovel, Sir C., at La Hogue, 84
  lost at sea, 95

Sluys, battle of, 20
Smith, Sir S., at Acre, 204
Society Isles, 156
Southampton attacked, 20
Spanish succession, war of, 86
Spain throws in her lot with France, 119
  attacks Falkland Isles, 125
  declares war, 134
  claims Vancouver Island, 157
  joins France, 172
  prepares for war, 228
Spragge, Sir Edward, 73
  killed, 79
Stamp Act, 126
Stayner, Captain, takes treasure-ships, 68
Stirling Castle, the, disobeys orders, 140
Story, Admiral (Dutch), surrenders, 206
Squirrel, the, loss of, 46

TAGUS, the, Sir J. Jervis off, 173
Teaships at Boston, 126
Texel, Duncan off the, 180
  De Winter sails from the, 186
  Dutch fleet surrenders at the, 206
Thetis and *Santa Brigida*, treasure-ships, 207
Thomas of Lancaster, 35
Thompson, Vice-Admiral, at St. Vincent, 178
Thurot, M., at Dunkirk, 115
  takes Carrickfergus, 118
  defeated and killed, 118
Tiptoft, Sir Robert, his victory, 18
Tonga Islands, 156
Torpedo, Bushnell's, 128
  early form of, 231
Torrington, Lord, at Beachy Head, 81
Toulon, evacuation of, 159
  expedition for Egypt at, 193
  Nelson off, 227
Trafalgar, battle of, 239-247
Treasure-ships, *Cacafuego*, 48
  Cobadonga, 104
  Hermione, 120
  Mercedes and consorts, 228
  Santisima Trinidad, 123

INDEX

Treasure-ships, *Thetis* and *Santa Brigida*, **207**
  taken by Stayner, 68
Trekroner, Copenhagen, 212
Trench-the-Mer, the, 10
Treville, Admiral Latouche, 227
Trincomalee, Hughes and Suffren off, 155
Triple Alliance, the, 73
Triumph, the (Elizabeth), 50
  Blake's flag-ship, 64, 67
Troubridge, Captain, at St. Vincent, 175
  at Santa Cruz, 185
  joins Nelson with a fleet, 193
  runs *Culloden* aground, 199
  his naval brigade ashore, 203
Troyes, treaty of, 40

UTRECHT, peace of, 97

VALDEZ, Pedro de, 49
  taken by Drake, 53
Valentia Bay, 57
Vancouver, Captain, 156
Vanguard, the, dismasted, 193
  at the Nile, 197
Van Tromp, Martin, 64
  his broom, 65
  killed off Dutch coast, 67
  Cornelius, off Lowestoft, 70
  defeated, 79
Vaubois, General, defends Malta, 208
  surrenders, 210
Vengeur, sinking of the, 165
Vernon, Admiral, takes Porto Bello, 101
Versailles, treaty of, 155
Victory, the (Elizabeth), 50
  lost with all hands, 107

Victory, Keppel's flag-ship, 132
  Jervis' flag-ship, 177
  Nelson's flag-ship, 236
  at Trafalgar, 240
  rakes *Bucentaure*, 245
  carries Nelson's body **to Dover**, 249
Vienne, John **de, 32**
Vigo, Drake **at, 48**
  Drake **and Norris at, 60**
  Rooke **at, 87**
Ville de Paris, De Grasse's flag-ship, 150
Villeneuve, Admiral, his orders, 227
  escapes from Toulon, 232
  sails to West Indies, 233
  returns to Europe, 234
  fights Calder off Finisterre, 234
  retires to Cadiz, 236
  sails for the last time, 238

WADE, Captain, shot for mutiny, **91**
Warren, Admiral, and French squadron **off** Donegal, 191
Watson, **Admiral, drives back** Ganteaume, **221**
West, Admiral, at **Minorca, 112**
Weymouth, 55
Wight, Isle of, attacked, 32, 35
William of Orange, 80
  his death, 86
Winchelsea, a cinque port, 15
  burnt, 20, 28
  Edward III. and Spaniards off, 24
  twice burnt, 32

YARMOUTH, burnt, 32
  roads, Baltic fleet in, 212

ZOUTMAN and Parker off Dogger Bank, 144

"BRITANNIA" SCIENCE SERIES.

STEAM AND STEAM MACHINERY.

J. LANGMAID, STAFF-ENGINEER, R.N., and
H. GAISFORD, ENGINEER, R.N.

6s. net.

PHYSICS NOTE BOOK.

Descriptions and Laws in Letterpress, with space for Students' Drawings of Experiments.

A. E. GIBSON M.A., and REV. J. C. P. ALDOUS.

5s. net.

PHYSICS FOR SCHOOL USE.

F. R. BARRETT, B.Sc., A. E. GIBSON, J. C. P. ALDOUS, AND OTHERS.

Revised by an eminent scientific man.

TRIGONOMETRY FOR PRACTICAL MEN.

W. W. LANE, M.A., R.N.

GEOMETRICAL DRAWING, PERSPECTIVE, MECHANICAL DRAWING.

Designed to meet the requirements of Examinations.

BY J. H. SPANTON, H.M.S. "BRITANNIA."

MACMILLAN AND CO., LONDON.

www.ingramcontent.com/pod-product-compliance
Lightning Source LLC
Chambersburg PA
CBHW032108230426
43672CB00009B/1677